Statehood in Times of Climate Change

Europäische Hochschulschriften

European University Studies

Publications Universitaires Européennes

Reihe II **Rechtswissenschaft**

Series II Law

Série II Droit

Band/Volume **5690**

Frederik von Paepcke

Statehood in Times of Climate Change

Impacts of Sea Level Rise on the Concept of States

PL ACADEMIC RESEARCH

Bibliografische Information der Deutschen Nationalbibliothek
Die Deutsche Nationalbibliothek verzeichnet diese Publikation in der Deutschen Nationalbibliografie; detaillierte bibliografische Daten sind im Internet über http://dnb.d-nb.de abrufbar.

Zugl.: Kiel, Univ., Diss., 2014

Gedruckt auf alterungsbeständigem,
säurefreiem Papier.

D 8
ISSN 0531-7312
ISBN 978-3-631-65900-7 (Print)
E-ISBN 978-3-653-05274-9 (E-Book)
DOI 10.3726/978-3-653-05274-9

PL Academic Research ist ein Imprint der Peter Lang GmbH.
Peter Lang – Frankfurt am Main · Bern · Bruxelles · New York · Oxford · Warszawa · Wien

Diese Publikation wurde begutachtet.

www.peterlang.com

Acknowledgement

Composing a dissertation is much easier with parents like mine. Hence my heartfelt thanks to them for three decades of support, encouragement, money, upbringing, advice and above all the freedom to decide for myself what I want to do.

Next I want to thank my supervisor, Professor Florian Becker, for a diligent supervision that has been precise and detailed, sufficiently strict and always fair and transparent. I had the freedom to stick to my opinion in case of different viewpoints – and there were some few occasions. Beyond, I am sure my supervisor is record holder in terms of quick (and helpful) answers.

Dr. Carmen v. Schöning, as well as her excellent ladies, deserve lifelong gratitude for the tremendous support to professionally transform my sometimes helpless phrasing into language I do not have to be embarrassed to publish. The same is true for Richard Delaney for his valuable last-minute help.

I furthermore would never have come up with this somewhat exotic topic if it had not been for two institutions. First, the Mission of Tuvalu to the United Nations, i.e. Ambassador Pita and his wife Lita: Thank you for an extraordinary experience which enabled me to deepen my view into the world of diplomacy and also to gain an understanding of the complexity not only of legal and political problems in the context of climate change. The experience to watch international negotiations from the perspective of a small island state was unique and also disillusioning.

Second, I want to thank Mark Jariabka and his NGO "Islands First" for making this working experience possible.

A third institution deserves appreciation: The Stiftung der Deutschen Wirtschaft (German Economy Foundation) not only supplied me with financial scholarship that enabled me to focus on my thesis without worrying about money. They also provided ideational support that was both educating and fun, amidst a group of divers, open-minded fellows.

My aunt Burgi and my uncle Roger hosted me twice in D.C., enabling me to work much more efficient than before (and afterwards). Thank you for your great hospitality and generosity, the delicious food, the evening drinks, the discussions about the topic of this thesis (and many others!) and overall a most unique time!

My last and final thank you goes to my uncle Michael – the incarnated advice, who came up with the idea to write about this topic.

Contents

List of Abbreviations

ARS	Articles on Responsibility of States for Internationally Wrongful Acts
AOSIS	Alliance of Small Island States
CERDS	Charter of Economic Rights and Duties of States
COP	Conference of the Parties
GHG	Greenhouse Gas(es)
HRC	Human Rights Council
ICJ	International Court of Justice
ICCPR	International Covenant on Civil and Political Rights
ICESCR	International Covenant on Economic, Social and Cultural Rights
IPCC	International Panel on Climate Change
ITLOS	International Tribunal for the Law of the Sea
MCRDS	Montevideo Convention on Rights and Duties of the States
OHCHR	Office of the U.N. High Commissioner for Human Rights
SIDS	Small Island Developing States
UN	United Nations
UN Friendly Relations Declaration	Declaration on Principles of International Law concerning Friendly Relations and Co-operation amongst States in Accordance with the Charter of the United Nations
UNCED	United Nations Conference on Environment and Development
UNCLOS	United Nations Convention on the Law of the Sea
UNDHR	Universal Declaration of Human Rights
UNEP	United Nations Environmental Programme
UNFCCC	United Nations Framework Convention on Climate Change
UNGA	United Nations General Assembly
Vienna Convention 1985	1985 Vienna Convention for the Protection of the Ozone Layer
WTO	World Trade Organisation

§ 1. Introduction

"Hot War about Climate,"[1] "Mania of Starry-Eyed Idealists,"[2] "Breaking Global Warming Taboos: 'I Feel Duped on Climate Change,'"[3] "Let's Not Braise the Planet,"[4], "Climate Change Will Shake the Earth,"[5] "Obama's Global-Warming Folly."[6]. These selected headlines of articles published within the last few years give an idea about the pathos and the emotionalism that has found its way into debates in the complex field of climate change.

The emotionalisation of the social debate about global warming bears the risk of opinion-forming that is based rather on one's political affiliation than on the available facts. This trend seems particularly prevalent perceivable in the USA. Whereas, for example, 47% of the Republican voters and 46% of the Democratic ones said in 1998 that the effects of global warming had already begun, this percentage shifted constantly until 2008, when this opinion was shared by 41% of the Republican voters and 76% of the Democratic voters.[7]

1 The original German headline reads "Heißer Krieg ums Klima." See Axel Bojanowski, "Heißer Krieg ums Klima," Spiegel Online Wissenschaft, 3 May 2010, available at http://www.spiegel.de/wissenschaft/natur/forscherskandal-heisser-krieg-ums-klima-a-688175.html, last accessed 29 April 2014.

2 The quoted part of the original German headline reads "Wahn der Weltverbesserer." See Axel Bojanowski, "Vorwürfe gegen Klimaforscher: Wahn der Weltverbesserer," Spiegel Online Wissenschaft, 13 March 2013, available at http://www.spiegel.de/wissenschaft/natur/klimafalle-von-storch-und-krauss-ueber-politik-und-klimaforschung-a-885364.html, last accessed 29 April 2014.

3 See interview with Fritz Vahrenholt, "I Feel Duped on Climate Change," Spiegel Online International, 8 February 2013, available at http://www.spiegel.de/international/world/breaking-global-warming-taboos-i-feel-duped-on-climate-change-a-813814.html, last accessed 29 April 2014.

4 See Mark Bittman, "Let's Not Braise the Planet," The New York Times, 1 July 2013, available at http://opinionator.blogs.nytimes.com/2013/07/01/lets-not-braise-the-planet/?ref=globalwarming, last accessed 29 April 2014.

5 See Bill McGuire, "Climate Change Will Shake the Earth," The Guardian, 26 February 2012, available at http://www.guardian.co.uk/environment/2012/feb/26/why-climate-change-shake-earth?INTCMP=SRCH, last accessed 29 April 2014.

6 See Charles Krauthammer, "Obama's Global-Warming Folly," The Washington Post, 4 July 2013, available at http://articles.washingtonpost.com/2013-07-04/opinions/40369711_1_warming-climate-change-global-temperatures, last accessed 29 April 2014.

7 See Riley E. Dunlap, "Climate-Change Views: Republican-Democratic Gaps Expand," Gallup, 29 May 2008, available at http://www.gallup.com/poll/107569/

In 2011, 78% of those voting Democrat, 53% of those voting Republican, and 34% of Tea Party sympathizers affirmed this point of view.[8] This increasing opinion gap stands in surprising and stark contrast to the increase in scientific knowledge about the world's climate achieved in the course of the last two decades.

Climate change, which, according to *Ban Ki-moon,* is "the defining issue of our time,"[9] is not only complex in terms of its scientific approach. It also entails multitudinous political, social, economical, and of course legal issues. It is, for example, expected that the end of this century will see up to 250 million climate refugees.[10] Where shall they move? What rights do they have?[11] Does the rise in the sea level lead to a general liability in international law?[12] How to mitigate climate change, how to adapt to it?[13] These challenges amount to the statement that "climate change has introduced the potential for a seismic shift in the way we have organized human systems on the planet", leading to a "postclimate era in law and human society."[14]

Amid this myriad of international challenges evolving from climate change, some Small Islands Developing States[15] are facing troubles of existential proportions: Their homeland is very likely to become uninhabitable due to sea level rise[16]. However, as unique as these concerns may be – compared with the overall dimension of issues arising in this field thus far, they are of only minor importance for the international community.

---

climatechange-views-republicandemocratic-gaps-expand.aspx, last accessed 29 April 2014.

8 See *Leiserowitz et al.*, p. 4.

9 Protocol of the 6.587th meeting of the Security Council, 20 July 2011, U.N Doc. S/PV.6587, p. 3.

10 See Human Tide: The Real Migration Crisis – A Christian Aid Report, May 2007, p. 6. Available at http://www.christianaid.org.uk/images/human-tide.pdf, last accessed 29 April 2014. The study will hereinafter be referred to as Human Tide.

11 *Markard et al.*, ZAR 2009, 27 (27 et seqq.), e.g., summarize this discussion with regard to new migration laws for Europe.

12 *Kehrer* discusses this topic in her doctoral thesis.

13 The main strategies pursued in addressing climate change, namely mitigation, adaption and (since recently) loss and damage will be briefly discussed further below, see § 2. E.

14 *Burkett* in: Gerrard/Wannier, 89 (120).

15 Hereinafter, Small Islands Developing States will be referred to as SIDS.

16 See U.N. Doc. E/CN.4/Sub.2/AC.4/2004/CRP.1, p. 2 para. 3; *Gordon*, 78 U. Colo. L. Rev. 2007, 1559 (1561).

This scenario leads to a conundrum for international law.[17] Out of the various consequential legal questions, this thesis addresses one: What happens to a state when its territory becomes permanently uninhabitable due to sea level rise? The statehood of these states will be the core object of this study.

To allow a legal assessment to be conducted, the current level of scientific knowledge of climate change first will be outlined, with a focus on the challenges global warming imposes on SIDS (see § 2). Subsequently, current statehood criteria will be elucidated against the backdrop of their history. Also, the ongoing discussion in this regard will be addressed. Additionally, the implications of these criteria for SIDS' future statehood, based on the current understanding will be assessed (see § 3). § 4 will be guided by the notion that an option could be established for statehood not to cease but to continue, if and insofar as SIDS have a claim to new state territory based on the no harm rule in conjunction with other principles and aspects of international law. At first glance, this idea sounds far-fetched,[18] but – as will be illustrated in that chapter – various aspects of international law argue in favour of such a claim. Recent negotiation efforts to implement binding compensation for climate change damages were undertaken exceptionally fierce[19] and indicate the rising relevance of this topic.

Ultimately, the findings of §§ 3 and 4 will form the basis for a comprehensive assessment of what will happen to SIDS statehood when their territory is inundated due to sea level rise (see § 5).

For any legal assessment in the field of climate change, it is especially important to not give too much consideration to the often sharp repartee between political and other interest groups, and instead to focus on international law. Nevertheless, the political and juridical dimensions of the problem are at times closely interlinked. Therefore, brief political considerations will be entertained where appropriate to both contribute to an overall understanding of this thesis' topic and to better assess which legal results have a reasonable chance at practical implementation.

---

17 See *Burkett* in: Gerrard/Wannier, 89 (89).

18 See *Powers/Stucko* in: Gerrard/Wannier, 123 (123).

19 See Markus Becker, "Entwicklungsländer fordern Entschädigung für künftige Katastrophen," Spiegel Online Wissenschaft, 20 November 2013, available at http://www.spiegel.de/wissenschaft/natur/klimakonferenz-in-warschau-streit-um-loss-and-damage-a-934652.html, last accessed 29 April 2014.

§ 2. Impact of Climate Change on Small Island Developing States

A. Introduction

Before any legal assessment can be made, it is necessary to consider the actual state of affairs: To what extent has the global climate changed already? What are the forecasts for its further development? (Both of these questions will be addressed in Part C.) Which uncertainties, difficulties and peculiarities arise in this complex and controversial field of climate science and climate politics – and what exactly is climate change? (See Part B.) What are the particular impacts on SIDS (see Part D.) and what measures have been taken so far to address climate change, especially from the SIDS's perspective? (See Part F.)

In addition to providing a detailed overview of the current scientific level of knowledge, the answers to these questions will also outline the overall dimension of climate change, especially with regard to its political implications.

Due to the corporate nature of international law, its quality depends on the behaviour of the parties governed by it towards each other.[20] State practice is one of the pillars upon which international law is based.[21] Therefore it is important to also address those aspects of climate politics – including contradicting interests – that set certain limits to what is possible politically. This, in turn, is a necessary prerequisite in order to assess what is legally permissible.

B. Global Warming: Difficulties and Peculiarities

This chapter will briefly outline some of the peculiarities of clime change, with most of the remarks being aimed at contributing to an understanding of why the international community continues to balk at taking the kind of decisive action that would halt global warming.[22]

1. Defining Climate Change

Problems in the field of global warming begin with the definition of 'climate change.' There are significant differences even among UN bodies on how this

---

20 See *Kunig*, Jura 1998, 160 (163).

21 See Art. 38 (1) lit. b., c. ICJ Statute.

22 See *Gordon*, 78 U. Colo. L. Rev. 2007, 1559 (1560).

term should be understood. The International Panel on Climate Change[23] refers to this term as

> *"a change in the state of the climate that can be identified (e.g. using statistical tests) by changes in the mean and/or the variability of its properties, and that persists for an extended period, typically decades or longer. It refers to any change in climate over time, whether due to natural variability or as a result of human activity."*[24]

The United Nations Framework Convention on Climate Change,[25] in contrast, provides the following definition in its Art. 1 No. 2:

> *"'Climate change' means a change of climate which is attributed directly or indirectly to human activity that alters the composition of the global atmosphere and which is in addition to natural climate variability observed over comparable time periods."*

Within this thesis, the IPCC understanding of the term will be applied. This definition does not presuppose an anthropogenic cause. The causal link between human greenhouse gas[26] emissions and global warming, which would be a prerequisite for any liability to be triggered, is still a matter of scientific debate.[27] The definition provided within the UNFCCC anticipates human responsibility and therefore is not adequate for a strictly legal examination of liability in the context of climate change.

2. Climate Change Research – a 'Post-Normal Science'

In some ways, climate change research differs from the work done in other scientific fields. In the early 1990s, *Funtovicz/Ravetz* coined the term of "post-normal science," which is intended to describe a scenario where "systems uncertainties" or "decision stakes" (or both) are high.[28] They defined systems uncertainties as "the idea that the problem is concerned not with the discovery of a particular fact (as in traditional research), but with the comprehension or management of a reality that has irreducible complexities and uncertainties."[29] Decision stakes are

---

23 Hereinafter, the International Panel on Climate Change will be referred to as IPCC.

24 4th IPCC-Report (2007), p. 30, available at http://www.ipcc.ch/publications_and_data/ar4/syr/en/contents.html, last accessed 29 April 2014.

25 Hereinafter: UNFCCC, available at http://unfccc.int/key_documents/the_convention/items/2853.php, last accessed 29 April 2014.

26 Hereinafter, greenhouse gas(es) will be referred to as GHG.

27 This discussion will be addressed further below, see § 4. B. 4. d. aa. (1).

28 See *Funtowicz/Ravetz*, 13 Environ. Toxicol. Chem. 1994, 1881 (1884).

29 *Funtowicz/Ravetz*, 13 Environ. Toxicol. Chem. 1994, 1881 (1882).

defined as a reference "to all the various costs, benefits, and value commitments that are involved in the issue through the various stakeholders."[30]

Global environmental risk, described as perhaps the greatest collective task now facing humanity, leads to the emergence of new scientific approaches in problem-solving strategies.[31] The rationality of basic scientific research is an ideal that is no longer universally appropriate with regard to the extent, complexity, pervasiveness and (in the 1990s) novelty of this environmental issue.[32]

The quality of scientific input to the policy process is known to be problematic.[33] Climate scientists face the dilemma that there is little chance of providing precise advice – and politicians will have to learn that there is no simple truth.[34] Two decades after *Funtowicz/Ravetz* published their essay, there seems to have been insufficient progress in that regard.

3. Political Hurdles

Pillorying politicians for their failure to effectively address and avert climate change is not the solution to the problem. Perhaps an explanation might first be sought for why tackling this problem in international politics is so difficult, despite the fairly broad consensus among all nations about the threats posed by climate change.

There is little incentive to take the serious – and painful – steps needed to address climate change – and this holds especially true for politicians of the wealthier nations. Excessive costs impend.[35] To assess the economics of moving to a low-carbon global economy, the UK Chancellor of the Exchequer in 2005 announced the 'Stern Review on the Economics of Climate Change,' which was published in 2006.[36] According to this study, the costs of effective action can be

30 *Funtowicz/Ravetz*, 13 Environ. Toxicol. Chem. 1994, 1881 (1882).

31 See *Funtowicz/Ravetz*, 13 Environ. Toxicol. Chem. 1994, 1881 (1881).

32 See *Funtowicz/Ravetz*, 13 Environ. Toxicol. Chem. 1994, 1881 (1885).

33 See *Funtowicz/Ravetz*, 13 Environ. Toxicol. Chem. 1994, 1881 (1881).

34 See Axel Bojanowski, "Heißer Krieg ums Klima," Spiegel Online Wissenschaft, 3 May 2010, available at http://www.spiegel.de/wissenschaft/natur/forscherskandal-heisser-krieg-ums-klima-a-688175.html, last accessed 29 April 2014.

35 See *Sands*, p. 701.

36 Hereinafter: Stern Review, available at: http://web.archive.org/web/20061114045919/http://www.hm-treasury.gov.uk/independent_reviews/stern_review_economics_climate_change/stern_review_report.cfm, last accessed 29 April 2014, Preface, p. i.

limited to around 1% of the global GDP each year.[37] These potential expenses imply delicate cost risks especially for developed states.[38]

Political leaders, furthermore, are generally elected for a few years only, while the effects of both efficient or non-efficient climate policies will take decades to become apparent. Creating the right conditions for effective policies would require policy design to be strong enough to resist the volatility of electoral cycles.[39] This requirement cannot be considered as being fulfilled by contemporary political frameworks.

What is more, the last decades of international negotiations have shown that it is quite impossible to achieve a consensus within the international community on the concrete measures to be taken, and in fact on a determination of which measures are effective. So far, calls for an effective international response, based on a shared vision of long-term goals,[40] remain without a satisfying answer. One of many reasons for this certainly is the Herculean task to find (mandatory) consent within a group of almost 200 state.

The individual alternative – moving forward unilaterally – is rather unappealing. Depending on the respective state, unilateral action would lead to only small advancements globally, while costs would have to be borne domestically. After the 4th IPCC-Report from 2007 had been the first to assess that most of the observed increase in global average temperatures since the mid-20th century is 'very likely' (i.e. a probability greater than 90%)[41] due to the observed increase in anthropogenic GHG concentrations,[42] the US-Secretary of Energy, *Samuel Bodman*, declared: "We are a small contributor to the overall, when you look at the rest of the world, so it's really got to be a global solution."[43] At that point, the United States, where about 5% of the world's population live, were responsible for about a quarter of worldwide GHG emissions.[44]

---

37 See *Stern Review*, Summary of Conclusions, p. vi.

38 This counts especially with a view to the so-called principle of common but differentiated responsibilities, see below § 4. C. 2. b.

39 See "The Emission Gap Report 2012 – A UNEP Synthesis Report," p. 44, available at http://www.unep.org/pdf/2012gapreport.pdf, last accessed 29 April 2014.

40 See *Stern Review*, Summary of Conclusions, p. vi; similarly: *Tomuschat* in: Hestermeyer et al., 3 (3 et seq.).

41 See 4th IPCC-Report (2007), p. 27.

42 See 4th IPCC-Report (2007), p. 39.

43 The New York Times: "Science Panel Says Global Warming Is Unequivocal" (3 February 2007), p. A.1.

44 See The New York Times: "Science Panel Says Global Warming Is Unequivocal" (3 February 2007), p. A.1.

Regardless of whether the steps to be taken are designed as a multilateral or as unilateral measure, they are hard to implement – at least where the matter of significant and sufficient measures is concerned. This is unlikely to change as long as the severest consequences of climate change remain future scenarios which neither policy makers nor voters experience or suffer from in the here and now.

4. Lobbyism

Obviously, addressing climate change – i.e. reducing the emission of GHG – is not in every single stakeholder's (short-term) interest. To a certain extent, the discussion about climate change has degenerated into a sort of "trench warfare" on multiple fronts between scientists, the media, environmental associations, and politicians.[45] Powerful economic lobbyists are accused of trivialising the dangers emerging from global warming, or of being supported by American right wing politics, not only by conspiracy theorists, but also by scientists.[46] In the 1990s and early 2000s especially, major stakeholders in the GHG industry have conducted massive public relations and lobbying campaigns.[47] It has been said that in order to cast doubt on climate change science and to undermine calls for regulation, the fossil fuel industry has organised its special interests in a campaign having the semblance of a grassroots movement, as, for example, via the organisation called 'The Advancement of Sound Science Coalition.'[48]

Dubats chose a prominent example to illustrate how easily politics can manipulate the public discourse on scientific issues.[49] In 2003, a study[50] by retired mining executive *Steven McIntyre* and economist *Ross McKitrick* discussed a fatal error in the way proxy data was handled, suggesting that this erroneously lead to the hockey-stick shape of a graph that visualized global warming.[51]

45 See Axel Bojanowski, "Heißer Krieg ums Klima," Spiegel Online Wissenschaft, 3 May 2010, available at http://www.spiegel.de/wissenschaft/natur/forscherskandal-heisser-krieg-ums-klima-a-688175.html, last accessed 29 April 2014.

46 See Axel Bojanowski, "Heißer Krieg ums Klima," Spiegel Online Wissenschaft, 3 May 2010, available at http://www.spiegel.de/wissenschaft/natur/forscherskandal-heisser-krieg-ums-klima-a-688175.html, last accessed 29 April 2014.

47 See *Dubats*, 7 Nw.J. L. & Soc. Pol'y 2012, 511 (512).

48 See *Dubats*, 7 Nw.J. L. & Soc. Pol'y 2012, 511 (518).

49 See *Dubats*, 7 Nw.J. L. & Soc. Pol'y 2012, 511 (520).

50 See *McIntyre/McKitrick*, 14 Energ. Environ. 2003, 751 (751 et seqq.).

51 See *Dubats*, 7 Nw.J. L. & Soc. Pol'y 2012, 511 (519 et seq.).

This study triggered a Senate hearing,[52] at which *James M. Inhofe*, the Republican Senator from Oklahoma, who is also the chairman of the Environment and Public Works Committee, asked "With all of the hysteria, all of the fear, all of the phony science, could it be that man-made global warming is the greatest hoax ever perpetrated on the American people? It sure sounds like it."[53] In the meantime, however, the U.S. National Academy of Science had affirmed the result of the scrutinised original study.[54] *Dubats* refers to this episode as an industry campaign against climate change science that, tactically clever, created a perceived distance between the source of the information and its dissemination.[55] Although described by the German publication 'Zeit Online' as "one of the dustiest shelf warmers available to the PR line of false discreditation," this myth continues to be excavated by the media in spite of the falsification of the accusations.[56]

The 'Information Council of the Environment' is another example of this kind of questionable lobbyism: In 1991, an intern strategic paper for its lobbying efforts proposed to address people with little or no education in a campaign that made global warming appear unrealistic.[57]

In this context, it bears noting that there are also interest groups who benefit from climate change – e.g. the industry of renewable energies. They may very well enter the fray one day with "counter-lobbyism" efforts of their own. However, when the broad consensus within the scientific community is compared with the considerable scepticism harboured in politics and society (especially in the US), the lobbyism casting climate change into doubt currently seems to be the more effective one.

---

52 See *Dubats*, 7 Nw.J. L. & Soc. Pol'y 2012, 511 (520).

53 Andrew C. Revkin, "Politics Reasserts Itself in the Debate Over Climate Change and Its Hazards," The New York Times, 5 August 2003, available at http://www.nytimes.com/2003/08/05/science/politics-reasserts-itself-in-the-debate-over-climate-change-and-its-hazards.html, last accessed 29 April 2014.

54 See *Dubats*, 7 Nw.J. L. & Soc. Pol'y 2012, 511 (520), referring to: *Brumfiel*, Geoff: "Academy Affirms Hockey-Stick graph," in: 441 Nature, 2006, p. 1032 et seq.

55 See *Dubats*, 7 Nw.J. L. & Soc. Pol'y 2012, 511 (520).

56 See Joachim Schellnhuber et al., "Zwei Grad und nicht mehr," Zeit Online, 15 April 2010, available at http://www.zeit.de/2010/16/Klimaschutz, last accessed 29 April 2014. The original German quoted part reads: "eine[r] der staubigsten Ladenhüter im Diskreditierungsgeschäft."

57 See Axel Bojanowski, "Heißer Krieg ums Klima," Spiegel Online Wissenschaft, 3 May 2010, available at http://www.spiegel.de/wissenschaft/natur/forscherskandal-heisser-krieg-ums-klima-a-688175.html, last accessed 29 April 2014.

This all makes it more difficult for policy makers to rationally address climate change based on the current scientific level of knowledge.

5. Credibility Issues

As the result of special interests in the economy and at the political level as well as the aim of scientists to achieve unambiguous results, the scientific discourse on climate change has partly developed into a war of opinions.[58] The debate had its climax in the so-called 'Climategate-Affair.'[59] This term describes the unauthorised release of hundreds of e-mails from a major climate research centre in England, revealing that an IPCC report contained a handful of errors.[60] The information leaked has been used to attempt to undermine the UN process through the IPCC, a panel that won the Nobel Peace Price in 2007[61] yet nevertheless is considered to be "under more hostile scrutiny" than any other scientific body.[62]

In the aftermath, various scientists tried to regain the public's confidence by putting in place procedures to ensure greater transparency.[63] Additionally, 255 members of the 'US National Academy of Sciences' published an open letter in defence of the theory of climate change, claiming to be "deeply disturbed by the recent escalation of political assaults on scientists in general and on climate scientists in particular."[64] They reiterated the "compelling, comprehensive, and consistent objective evidence that humans are changing the climate

---

58 See Axel Bojanowski, "Heißer Krieg ums Klima," Spiegel Online Wissenschaft, 3 May 2010, available at http://www.spiegel.de/wissenschaft/natur/forscherskandal-heisser-krieg-ums-klima-a-688175.html, last accessed 29 April 2014. spiegel.de/wissenschaft/natur/forscherskandal-heisser-krieg-ums-klima-a-688175.html, last accessed 29 April 2014.

59 See Axel Bojanowski, "Heißer Krieg ums Klima," Spiegel Online Wissenschaft, 3 May 2010, available at http://www.spiegel.de/wissenschaft/natur/forscherskandal-heisser-krieg-ums-klima-a-688175.html, last accessed 29 April 2014.

60 See *Feng/Buhi*, 18 Buff Envtl. L.J. 2010-2011, 1 (69), Fn. 306.

61 See http://www.nobelprize.org/nobel_prizes/peace/laureates/2007/ipcc-facts.html, last accessed 29 April 2014.

62 *Feng/Buhi*, 18 Buff Envtl. L.J. 2010-2011, 1 (69), Fn. 306.

63 See John M. Broder, "Scientists Taking Steps to Defend Work on Climate," New York Times, 2 March 2010, available at http://www.nytimes.com/2010/03/03/science/earth/03climate.html, last accessed 29 April 2014.

64 Letter available at http://www.guardian.co.uk/environment/2010/may/06/climate-science-open-letter, last accessed 29 April 2014.

in ways that threaten our societies and the ecosystems on which we depend."[65] Nevertheless, the damage wrought by the Climategate-Affair is generally held to be irreparable, as a loss of credibility is the central communication risk of science.[66]

This is not the only example which lead to a credibility loss. In early 2012 it was revealed that *Peter Gleick*, president of the 'Pacific Institute' and also the launch chairman of the 'new task force on scientific ethics and integrity,' had obtained data from the 'Heartland Institute,' an association of climate change sceptics, under an assumed name.[67] The documents subsequently published by the Pacific Institute included a paper detailing a strategy of how to spread sceptical theses with regard to climate change. However, this document did not originate from the Heartland Institute.[68] While its initial source remains unclear, *Gleick* has said he regrets having used these methods, saying he was blinded by his frustration over climate change sceptics attacking science.[69]

These examples of credibility troubles elucidate why, in facing a seemingly uncertain future regarding global warming, it is easier to facilitate short-term and more convenient political decisions which demand fewer sacrifices here and now.

---

65 Letter available at http://www.guardian.co.uk/environment/2010/may/06/climate-science-open-letter, last accessed 29 April 2014.

66 See Axel Bojanowski, "Heißer Krieg ums Klima," Spiegel Online Wissenschaft, 3 May 2010, available at http://www.spiegel.de/wissenschaft/natur/forscherskandal-heisser-krieg-ums-klima-a-688175.html, last accessed 29 April 2014.

67 See Axel Bojanowski, "Wissenschaftlerskandal: Klimaforscher entwendet Geheimpapiere von Lobbygruppe," Spiegel Online Wissenschaft, 23 February 2012, available at http://www.spiegel.de/wissenschaft/natur/wissenschaftlerskandal-klimaforscher-entwendet-geheimpapiere-von-lobbygruppe-a-816964.html, last accessed 29 April 2014.

68 See Axel Bojanowski, "Wissenschaftlerskandal: Klimaforscher entwendet Geheimpapiere von Lobbygruppe," Spiegel Online Wissenschaft, 23 February 2012, available at http://www.spiegel.de/wissenschaft/natur/wissenschaftlerskandal-klimaforscher-entwendet-geheimpapiere-von-lobbygruppe-a-816964.html, last accessed 29 April 2014.

69 See Axel Bojanowski, "Wissenschaftlerskandal: Klimaforscher entwendet Geheimpapiere von Lobbygruppe," Spiegel Online Wissenschaft, 23 February 2012, available at http://www.spiegel.de/wissenschaft/natur/wissenschaftlerskandal-klimaforscher-entwendet-geheimpapiere-von-lobbygruppe-a-816964.html, last accessed 29 April 2014.

6. Assessing Climate Change from a Legal Perspective

The hurdles to science-based politics provide an explanation for the unsatisfactory progress in the field of addressing climate change.

The present thesis considers the legal future of SIDS' statehood and cannot assess the quality or reliability of the different opinions within the fields of science, lobbyism, politics, and conspiracy theory evolving around the topic of scientific evidence for climate change. Accordingly, it will focus on the findings of the Working Group I contribution to the fifth and most recent Assessment Report Climate Change on behalf of the Intergovernmental Panel on Climate Change, published online in unedited form in September 2013.[70] 209 lead authors, 50 review editors, and more than 600 contributing authors have worked on this comprehensive study.[71]

The IPCC has been criticised for aligning its reports with the political pressure brought to bear on it. Especially the Summary for Policymakers, which has the greatest practical implications, political influence has diluted the paper's scientific accuracy: While China downplayed the human responsibility for climate change, the USA and Japan successfully rephrased a suggested linkage between hurricanes and climate change, most likely in order to avoid undesired results in their respective countries.[72]

Notwithstanding these modifications, the IPCC Reports are recognised as summarising the best scientific knowledge available at the time of their respective publication.[73] Despite the climate change scepticism, international lawyers – being, by profession, legal and not climate science experts – commonly assess climate change liability based on the assumption that the IPCC-Report is founded in fact.[74] Hence, this study will also be the major scientific reference point for the present thesis.

---

70 Available at http://www.ipcc.ch/report/ar5/wg1/#.UkwQuyTTY38, last accessed 29 April 2014. This report will hereinafter be referred to as 5th IPCC-Report (2013), draft.

71 See http://www.ipcc.ch/, last accessed 2 October 2013.

72 See Bernhard Pötter, "IPCC-Report: Wie die Politik den Klimabericht beeinflusst hat," Spiegel Online Wissenschaft, 2 February 2007, available at http://www.spiegel.de/wissenschaft/natur/ipcc-report-wie-die-politik-den-klimabericht-beeinflusst-hat-a-464048.html, last accessed 29 April 2014.

73 See *Voigt*, 77 Nordic J. of Int. L. 2008, 1 (12).

74 See E.g. *Brunnée et al.*, in Lord et al., 3 (5 et seq.) para. 1.10; *Voigt*, 77 Nordic J. of Int. L. 2008, 1 (12); examining liability for sea level rise: *Kehrer*, e.g. p. 4, footnote 10.

C. Climate Change – Present and Future Developments

While the causation between anthropogenic GHG emissions and global warming will be examined at a later point[75], the present subchapter will address selected facts concerning the current status of global climate change as well as the forecast made in its regard.

To begin with, "[i]t is certain that Global Mean Surface Temperature [...] has increased since the late 19th century [...]. Each of the past three decades has been warmer than all the previous decades in the instrumental record, and the decade of the 2000's has been the warmest. The global combined land and ocean temperature data show an increase of about 0.89°C (0.69°C–1.08°C) over the period 1901-2012 and about 0.72°C (0.49°C–0.89°C) over the period 1951-2012 when described by a linear trend."[76]

Between 1901 and 2010, the global mean sea level has risen by 0.19 (0.17 to 0.21) meters.[77] It is *very likely* (i.e. 90–100% probability)[78] that the mean rate of sea level rise was 1.7 (1.5 to 1.9) mm per year between 1901 and 2010.[79] Between 1993 and 2010, the rate was *very likely* higher at 3.2 (2.8 to 3.6) mm per year.[80]

This sea level rise is primarily caused by the expansion of the ocean water as it warms, as well as the transfer to the ocean of water currently stored on land (particularly from glaciers and ice sheets).[81] Both of these causal factors are attributable to an increase in temperature.

The following illustration visualises and summarizes the key findings for the climate development from about 1850 until today:

75 See below § 4. B. 4. d.
76 5th IPCC-Report (2013), draft, p. TS-5.
77 See 5th IPCC-Report (2013), draft, p. TS-12.
78 5th IPCC-Report (2013), draft, p. TS-4; original emphasis.
79 See 5th IPCC-Report (2013), draft, p. TS-12.
80 See 5th IPCC-Report (2013), draft, p. TS-12.
81 See 5th IPCC-Report (2013), draft, p. TS-12.

Figure 1: Multiple complementary indicators of a changing global climate.[82]

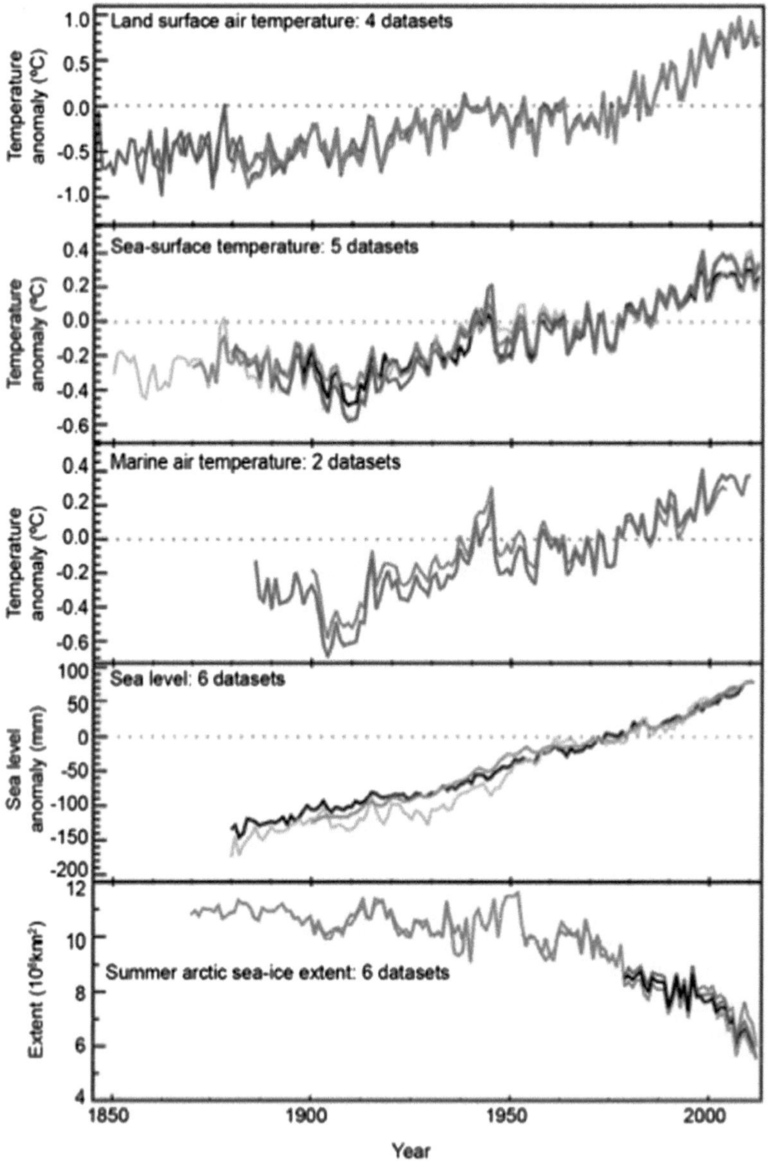

82 Source: 5th IPCC-Report (2013), draft, p. TS-81.

The forecast is even worse. The different projections regarding the expected sea level rise until the end of this century, as compared with the average sea level between 1986 and 2005, range from 0.26 m to 0.97 m.[83] This projection is considerably increased compared to the 4th IPCC-Report from 2007, which projected 0.18 m to 0.59 m sea level rise (relative to 1980-1999).[84] The average global temperature is *likely* (i.e. 66–100% probability)[85] to increase between 1.5°C and 4.5°C relative to 1986-2005.[86]

Once this development reaches so-called tipping points, it will pose a major threat.[87] This term refers to changes in the Earth's climate that are irreversible, for example the collapse of the Atlantic thermohaline circulation and the acceleration of climate change due to carbon-cycle feedbacks (such as weakening carbon absorption and higher methane releases).[88] In a UN Security Council Debate on the impact of climate change on maintaining international peace and security held in July 2011, *Achim Steiner*, UN Under-Secretary-General and Executive Director of the United Nations Environmental Programme[89] in this context warned, *inter alia,* of the dangers posed by melting permafrost in the arctic which, in the course of this century still, are liable to trigger the release of close to 100 billion tonnes of ancient, stored carbon with a warming effect equivalent to 270 years of carbon dioxide emissions at current levels.[90] According to the 4th IPCC-Report, climate change is *likely* (i.e. >66% probability)[91] to lead to some irreversible impacts.[92] Whereas, according to the 5th IPCC-Report, "[a]nthropogenic warming will *very likely* [i.e. 90–100% probability] lead to enhanced methane emissions from both terrestrial and oceanic clathrates,"[93] studies that examine the threat of permafrost-related processes do not yield consistent results, beyond the fact that,

---

83 See 5th IPCC-Report (2013), draft, p. TS-63.

84 See 4th IPCC-Report (2007), p. 45, table 3.1. The answer to the question of why this expected sea level rise could lead to the annihilation of states will be addressed further below, see § 2. D.

85 5th IPCC-Report (2013), draft, p. TS-4; original emphasis.

86 See 5th IPCC-Report (2013), draft, p. TS-45.

87 See Stern Review, p. 293.

88 See Stern Review, p. 293.

89 Hereinafter, the United Nations Environmental Programme will be referred to as UNEP.

90 See "UNEP Chief Addresses UN Security Council Debate on Climate Change and Security" (20 July 2011), available at http://www.unep.org/newscentre/Default.aspx?DocumentID=2646&ArticleID=8817, last accessed 29 April 2014.

91 4th IPCC-Report (2007), p. 27.

92 See 4th IPCC-Report (2007), p. 54.

93 5th IPCC-Report (2013), draft, p. TS-36; original emphasis. For the numerical equivalent to a "very likely" probability, see p. TS-4 of the draft 5th IPCC-Report (2013).

under plausible future warming scenarios, present-day permafrost will become a net emitter of carbon during the 21st century.[94]

In this context, it is important to consider how likely these developments are to occur also beyond the end of the current century. Even if GHG concentrations were to be stabilised, anthropogenic warming and sea level rise would continue for centuries to come.[95]

D. Impacts on Small Island Developing States

As early as in 1994, the UN Global Conference for the Sustainable Development of Small Island Developing States noted that

> *"[w]hile small island developing States are among those that contribute least to global climate change and sealevel rise, they are among those that would suffer most from the adverse effects of such phenomena and could in some cases become uninhabitable."*[96]

In the Human Development Report 2007-2008, *Steiner* pointed out the dangers of increased droughts, extreme weather events, tropical storms, and sea level rises, *inter alia*, for SIDS within our lifetimes, warning of apocalyptic consequences.[97]

There are currently 51 SIDS listed by the UN.[98] The 4th IPCC-Report lists several impacts that especially will affect SIDS and other small islands:

1. The threats they are already suffering from, e.g. inundation, storm surge, erosion and other coastal hazards, are expected to be exacerbated by sea level rise. Thus vital infrastructure, settlements and facilities that support the livelihood of island communities are threatened.
2. Erosion of beaches and coral bleaching is expected to lead to deterioration in costal conditions and thus to affect local resources.
3. Many small islands are expected to suffer from reduced water resources by mid-century to the point where they become insufficient to meet demand during low-rainfall periods.
4. An increased invasion by non-native species is expected to occur due to higher temperatures, especially on mid- and high-latitude islands.[99]

---

94 See 5th IPCC-Report (2013), draft, p. TS-36.
95 See 4th IPCC-Report (2007), p. 46.
96 U.N. Doc. A/CONF.167/9, Annex I, Part One, section III, para. 2.
97 See UNDP, Human Development Report 2007-2008, p. v.
98 See "SIDS Members," available at http://sustainabledevelopment.un.org/index.php?menu=1520, last accessed 29 April 2014.
99 For these examples, see 4th IPCC-Report (2007), p. 52.

These impacts aggravate the effects that global warming will have particularly for SIDS. In summary, their great exposure, their high sensitiveness to climate change as well as their insufficient adaptive capacity lead to the particular vulnerability of SIDS.[100]

The most severe threat some SIDS are facing, however, is their annihilation by sea level rise.[101] Both sea level rise and extreme weather events related to climate change are threatening the habitability and, in the longer term, the territorial existence of a number of SIDS.[102] Certain SIDS thus will become uninhabitable, requiring their populations to abandon their homelands and to relocate elsewhere.[103] The government of Tuvalu, for example, has warned that it may need to evacuate the islands within the coming decades.[104] This scenario is unprecedented.[105] Furthermore, while the eventual need for the population to move is inevitable, there is no reliable time frame within which decisions have to be taken.[106]

Hereinafter, these SIDS that might become uninhabitable will be referred to as "endangered states"[107]. The following five states have been identified to be the ones most likely affected:

> "*Tuvalu: highest point 5 ms; population 11,468*
> *Nauru: highest point 61 ms; population 12,809*
> *Kiribati: highest point 81 ms; population 100,798*
> *The Maldive Islands: highest point 2.4 ms; population 339,330*
> *The Bahamas: highest point 63 ms; population 299,697.*[108]"

In the context of the different scenarios of the 5th IPCC-Report regarding sea level rise (between 0.26 m and 0.97 m),[109] it must be asked, in light of the elevations of the respective states (highest point between 2.4 m and 81 m) how areas exhibiting such topographic differences can all be assessed as becoming uninhabitable. There are four reasons that explain this seeming inconsistency.

---

100 *Millar et al.* in: Gerrard/Wannier, 433 (436).
101 See *Gordon*, 78 U. Colo. L. Rev. 2007, 1559 (1561); E/CN.4/Sub.2/AC.4/2004/CRP.1, p. 2 para. 3; *Grote Stoutenburg* in: Gerrard/Wannier, 57 (57).
102 See U.N. Doc. A/HRC/10/61 (2009), p. 14 et seq. para. 40; *Zerger*, ZAR 2009, 85 (85).
103 See *Jarvis*, 9 Seattle J. Soc. Just. 4477 2010-2011, 447 (449).
104 See U.N. Doc. E/CN.4/Sub.2/AC.4/2004/CRP.1, p. 8 para. 22.
105 See U.N. Doc. A/HRC/10/61 (2009), p. 14 et seq., para. 41.
106 See U.N. Doc. E/CN.4/Sub.2/2005/28, p. 3 para. 5.
107 See *Burkett* in: Gerrard/Wannier, 89 (93).
108 U.N. Doc. E/CN.4/Sub.2/AC.4/2004/CRP.1, p. 7 para. 16.
109 See 5th IPCC-Report (2013), draft, p. TS-63.

To begin with, the data on which the IPCC-Report is based are insufficient. Despite "substantial progress" having been made since the 4th IPCC-Report, "the published literature as yet provides only a partially sufficient basis for making projections related to particular scenarios."[110] The complete elimination of the Greenland ice sheet would, for example, result in a contribution to the sea level rise of an additional 7 meters.[111] Even based on a global temperature rise of 8°C, it would take approximately 2,000 years for the Greenland glacier to have thawed completely, however.[112] Nevertheless, when it comes to the uncertainties regarding the ice sheet flows, the potential damage that a melting Greenland ice sheet may wreak should not be underestimated.

Secondly, the sea level does not rise consistently all over the world: The thawing of the Greenland glacier, for example, will cause a loss of gravitational force in that region, leading to comparatively higher rises in tropical and subtropical regions.[113] This effect might even intensify in some regions, e.g. by the weather phenomenon El Niño, which causes the sea level to rise at triple the speed at which it rises elsewhere (i.e. about 1 cm/year between 1993 and 2012) along the coasts of The Philippines.[114]

Thirdly, the results could turn out worse than projected by the IPCC-Report. The *Copenhagen Diagnosis* from 2009 compiling the major policy-relevant climate science published since the close-off of material for the 4th IPCC-Report has presented alarming findings.[115] According to this publication, satellite measurements show that the sea level is rising about 80% faster than the estimated in the 3rd IPCC-Report for the period since 1993.[116] Second, accounting for loss in

---

110 5th IPCC-Report (2013), draft, p. TS-64.

111 See 4th IPCC-Report (2007), p. 47.

112 See *Robinson et al.*, 2 Nature Clim. Change 2012, 429 (431), Fig. 3b.

113 See Axel Bojanowski, "Ozeanbeulen bedrohen Küstenstädte," Spiegel Online Wissenschaft, 27 September 2012, available at http://www.spiegel.de/wissenschaft/natur/ozeane-karte-zeigt-unterschiedlichen-meeresspiegel-a-857812.html, last accessed 29 April 2014.

114 See Axel Bojanowski, "Ozeanbeulen bedrohen Küstenstädte," Spiegel Online Wissenschaft, 27 September 2012, available at http://www.spiegel.de/wissenschaft/natur/ozeane-karte-zeigt-unterschiedlichen-meeresspiegel-a-857812.html, last accessed 29 April 2014.

115 See Copenhagen Diagnosis, p. 5. It aims at both evaluating the evolving science midway through an IPCC cycle while serving as an update that supplements the IPCC-Report from 2007. Available at http://www.copenhagendiagnosis.com, last accessed 29 April 2014.

116 See Copenhagen Diagnosis, p. 37.

ice-sheet mass, the sea level rise until 2100 is likely to be at least twice as high as that presented in the 4th IPCC-Report, with an upper limit of approximately two meters based on new ice-sheet understanding.[117]

This correction is also part of the criticism that the 5th IPCC-Report faced from some climatologists: Its upper limit for sea level rise does not include "credible peer-reviewed scientific work," according to which nearly twice the amount (ca. 2m) of sea level rise is to be expected within this century.[118] Other authors, however, have criticised that the 5th IPCC-Report camouflages uncertainties over how to explain the decelerating rate of warming that took place in the course of the last 15 years.[119] In other words, there is also the chance that matters could turn out better than projected. This uncertainty cannot be overcome at the present time.

Fourth, the necessity to relocate endangered states' citizens arises not only in the event of a total inundation of the respective country. Kiribati is a vivid example in this context. Despite its highest point being 81m above sea level, it consists of "mostly low-lying coral atolls."[120] Accordingly, a large part of its habitable area could already be inundated while some of its elevations would still be above sea level. A territory containing high ground thus does not guarantee that it will be capable of sustaining its population, especially if it loses what is at present a coastal area in which the population lives.[121] Moreover, sea level rise leads to the mingling of saltwater with fresh water aquifers and thereby contributes to the uninhabitability of certain regions.[122]

---

117 See Copenhagen Diagnosis, p. 37.

118 See Mann, Michael, "The New IPCC Climate Change Report Makes Deniers Overheat," The Guardian 28 September 2013, available at http://www.theguardian.com/commentisfree/2013/sep/28/ipcc-climate-change-deniers, last accessed 29 April 2014. The study on the upper limit for sea level rise referred to by the author of the Guardian Article was published by skepticalscience.com and is available at http://www.skepticalscience.com/rahmstorf-foster-cazenave-2012.html, last accessed 29 April 2014.

119 See e.g. *Pielke*, Roger, Jr.: "Five Points on the IPCC Report (Wonky, Long)" available at http://rogerpielkejr.blogspot.de/2013/09/five-points-on-ipcc-report-wonky-long.html, last accessed 29 April 2014.

120 CIA Wold Factbook, available at https://www.cia.gov/library/publications/the-world-factbook/geos/kr.html, last accessed 29 April 2014.

121 See U.N. Doc. E/CN.4/Sub.2/AC.4/2004/CRP.1, p. 6 para. 14.

122 See U.N. Doc. E/CN.4/Sub.2/AC.4/2004/CRP.1, p. 6 para. 14.

Overall, it is therefore likely that entire state territories will become uninhabitable[123] – this likelihood being so high that some governments have already taken measures to relocate their entire populace in the long run.[124] The legal assessment of this thesis is thus based on the assumption that one or more endangered state will become uninhabitable.

In 2007, *Apisai Ielemia*, then Prime Minister of Tuvalu, described his state's perspective on climate change: Freshwater resources are decreasing, "beaches have disappeared, small islets have been washed away, coral reefs are starting to die, and crops are dying from salt-water intrusion."[125] While the causes for these developments emerge "from countries many thousands of kilometres away [his nation is] at the mercy of the international community."[126] *Ielemia* therefore concluded: "If there is one issue that strikes at the heart of my nation, Tuvalu, it is climate change."[127]

E. Addressing Climate Change

1. Introduction

The international community in general and endangered states in particular are approaching the potential threats of climate change from different vantage points. Apart from the legal action that endangered states are considering to take, or once considered in the past,[128] the measures addressing climate change can be differentiated into mitigation on the one hand, and adaption on the other. Additionally, the fairly recent concept of 'loss and damage' will be discussed.

---

123 The legal requirements based on which a (former) state territory is to be referred to as 'uninhabitable' will be outlined further below, see § 3. B. 3. b. bb.

124 Examples of relocation measures will be provided further below, see § 2. E. 3.

125 *Apisai Ielemia*: "A Threat to our Human Rights: Tuvalu's Perspective on Climate Change," published 1 June 2007, available at: http://unchronicle.un.org/article/threat-our-human-rights-tuvalu-s-perspective-climate-change/, last accessed 29 April 2014.

126 *Apisai Ielemia*: "A Threat to our Human Rights: Tuvalu's Perspective on Climate Change," published 1 June 2007, available at: http://unchronicle.un.org/article/threat-our-human-rights-tuvalu-s-perspective-climate-change/, last accessed 29 April 2014.

127 *Apisai Ielemia*: "A Threat to our Human Rights: Tuvalu's Perspective on Climate Change," published 1 June 2007, available at: http://unchronicle.un.org/article/threat-our-human-rights-tuvalu-s-perspective-climate-change/, last accessed 29 April 2014.

128 Those legal measures will be addressed at a later point, see below § 4. F. 5.

2. Mitigation

Mitigation measures aim at diminishing or removing the anthropogenic causes for global warming and the consequences thereof, primarily by reducing the emission of GHG.[129] A prominent example for mitigation is codified in Art. 2 UNFCCC. According to this provision,

> *"[t]he ultimate objective of this Convention [...] is to achieve [...] stabilisation of greenhouse gas concentrations in the atmosphere at a level that would prevent dangerous anthropogenic interference with the climate system."*

The UNFCCC does not contain a concretisation of a specific level of GHG concentrations. This determination has been agreed upon indirectly in 2010 in Cancún where the Conference of the Parties[130] recognised, *inter alia*

> *"that deep cuts in global greenhouse gas emissions are required according to science [...] so as to hold the increase in global average temperature below 2°C above pre-industrial levels [...] [and furthermore recognised] the need to consider [...] strengthening the long-term global goal on the basis of the best available scientific knowledge, including in relation to a global average temperature rise of 1.5°C."*[131]

These mitigation aims are of great significance for endangered states, since a rise in temperature will cause the sea level to rise. However, there are doubts as to the international community successfully achieving this target. In early 2013, for example, a study was released according to which the development of GHG emission currently is on a track that would lead to a temperature increase of 4.2-5.0°C.[132] The study concludes that a quick implementation of large and concerted mitigation efforts across the globe would be necessary to accomplish the goal of ensuring the temperature increase remains below 2°C.[133] As a second commitment period of the Kyoto Protocol will not be implemented before 2020, the 2°C-target has become less significant in mitigation negotiations.[134] Countries like endangered states simply "do not have the political leverage to halt the global

129 See *Stehr/von Storch*, GAIA 2008, 270 (270).

130 Hereinafter, the Conference of the Parties will be referred to as COP.

131 U.N. Doc. FCCC/CP/2010/7/Add.1, p. 3 para. 4.

132 See *Peters et al.*, Nat. Clim. Chang. 2013, 4 (5).

133 See *Peters et al.*, Nat. Clim. Chang. 2013, 4 (6).

134 See Christoph Seidler, "Fünf Grad plus: Erde droht dramatische Erwärmung," Spiegel Online Wissenschaft, 2 December 2012, available at http://www.spiegel.de/wissenschaft/natur/erderwaermung-forscher-warnen-vor-5-grad-temperatur-plus-a-870282.html, last accessed 29 April 2014.

warming that threatens them."[135] Economic concerns of developed countries traditionally supersede the environmental concerns of less developed countries.[136]

Given the way the negotiations are proceeding, it is very likely that the international community will not reach the goal it has set for itself.[137] A team of climate change experts launched a website providing a climate action tracker[138] which shows "the global-mean temperature increase above pre-industrial by 2100" – based on the current progress in terms of mitigating climate change.[139] Currently, a temperature rise of 3.7°C [3.0°C–4.6°C] is expected.[140]

This means that the likelihood of further and significant sea level rise is growing. Mitigation strategies hence are of little relevance for the question of how to legally address a future scenario in which the climate will have changed.

3. Adaption

Adaption measures aim to enable society to deal with the threats climate change poses now and in the future.[141] Also, adaption aims to alleviate those damages that have already occurred.[142]

The loss of a state territory constitutes a damage that cannot be addressed by mitigation, but only by adaption measures. Some endangered states are already pursuing pragmatic rather than legal efforts in preparing for the likely inundation of their homeland. Tuvalu, for example, tried to claim asylum for its citizens in New Zealand and Australia.[143] While Australia was not willing to comply with this request, New Zealand has decided to admit 75 Tuvaluans annually.[144]

---

135 *Cooper*, 6 N.Y.U. Envtl. L.J. 1998, 480 (525).

136 See *Cooper*, 6 N.Y.U. Envtl. L.J. 1998, 480 (525).

137 See *Gillespie*, 22 UCLA J. Envtl. L. & Pol'y 2003-2004, 107 (129).

138 For the climate action tracker, see http://www.climateactiontracker.org, last accessed 29 April 2014.

139 http://www.climateactiontracker.org, last accessed 29 April 2014.

140 See http://www.climateactiontracker.org, last accessed 29 April 2014.

141 See *Stehr/von Storch*, GAIA 2008, 270 (270).

142 See *Stehr/von Storch*, GAIA 2008, 270 (270).

143 See Gerhard Fischer/Urs Wälterlin, "Angst vor dem Untergang," Süddeutsche Zeitung, 19 May 2010, available at http://www.sueddeutsche.de/wissen/klimawandel-angst-vor-dem-untergang-1.913230, last accessed 29 April 2014.

144 See *Culley*, 8 Ocean & Coastal L.J. 2002, 91 (104); E/CN.4/Sub.2/AC.4/2004/CRP.1, p. 8 para. 22; Gerhard Fischer/Urs Wälterlin, "Angst vor dem Untergang," Süddeutsche Zeitung, 19 May 2010, available at http://www.sueddeutsche.de/wissen/klimawandel-angst-vor-dem-untergang-1.913230, last accessed 29 April 2014.

Additionally, funds were raised to create a new settlement for Tuvaluans on the Fijian Island of Kioa.[145]

In 2008, the Maldives announced that it was putting in place measures enabling their citizens to move elsewhere when their current homeland will have become uninhabitable.[146] Sri Lanka and India were asked to be partners in these efforts, due to these nations' similar cultures, cuisines, and climates.[147] Australia was likewise contacted in light of the amount of unoccupied land it has available.[148] *Mohamed Nasheed*, then president of the Maldives, put his objective in concise terms: "We do not want to leave the Maldives, but we also do not want to be climate refugees living in tents for decades."[149] Subsequent political instability, however, led to the early termination of *President Nasheed's* tenure, thus interrupting his efforts at preparing the nation for global warming.[150]

Kiribati implemented a similar strategy in 2012 by negotiating with Fiji to buy up to 5,000 acres of freehold land on Vanua Levu, Fiji's second largest island, where citizens of Kiribati could be housed.[151] *Anote Tong*, president of Kiribati, also suggested the possibility of constructing man-made islands resembling giant oil rigs (at an estimated total cost of around US$ 2 billion) that were to serve as residential

---

145 See The Age: "Tuvalu's Tides Divide Scientists" (25 August 2004), available at http://www.theage.com.au/articles/2004/08/24/1093246516150.html, last accessed 29 April 2014.

146 See Randeep Ramesh, "Paradise Almost Lost: Maldives Seek to Buy a New Homeland," The Guardian, 10 November 2008, available at http://www.guardian.co.uk/environment/2008/nov/10/maldives-climate-change, last accessed 29 April 2014.

147 See Randeep Ramesh, "Paradise Almost Lost: Maldives Seek to Buy a New Homeland," The Guardian, 10 November 2008, available at http://www.guardian.co.uk/environment/2008/nov/10/maldives-climate-change, last accessed 29 April 2014.

148 See Randeep Ramesh, "Paradise Almost Lost: Maldives Seek to Buy a New Homeland," The Guardian, 10 November 2008, available at http://www.guardian.co.uk/environment/2008/nov/10/maldives-climate-change, last accessed 29 April 2014.

149 Randeep Ramesh, "Paradise Almost Lost: Maldives Seek to Buy a New Homeland," The Guardian, 10 November 2008, available at http://www.guardian.co.uk/environment/2008/nov/10/maldives-climate-change, last accessed 29 April 2014.

150 See New York Times: "A Mission for Climate Is Interrupted by a Coup" (10 April 2013).

151 See Paul Chapman, "Entire Nation of Kiribati to Be Relocated Over Rising Sea Level Threat," The Telegraph, 7 March 2012, available at http://www.telegraph.co.uk/news/worldnews/australiaandthepacific/kiribati/9127576/Entire-nation-of-Kiribati-to-be-relocated-over-rising-sea level-threat.html, last accessed 29 April 2014.

areas.[152] Additionally, the government launched an "Education for Migration" programme with the purpose of qualifying the people of Kiribati "to make them more attractive as migrants."[153] The youth of Kiribati are being prepared "to leave behind their culture, their way of life, and lifestyle."[154] Additionally, the concept of building a series of sea walls (at an estimated total cost of around US$ 1 billion) has also been discussed, with calls for funding by the international community.[155]

Various endangered states hence have developed strategies for enabling their citizens to migrate to other states. As yet, none of these strategies involve a relocation strategy under which the respective state itself would or could be relocated.

According to a working paper of the Commission on Human Rights from 2004, nothing is being done on a multilateral level to address the problem of states completely disappearing from the face of the earth for environmental reasons.[156] Generally, adaption measures play a minor part in international environmental law as compared to mitigation strategies.[157] Endangered states, however, should focus more on adaption strategies. As sea level rises inevitably, "the best approach for SIDS is to prepare for the inevitable rather than taking the lead at forcing mitigation."[158] SIDS may thus have to craft solutions on their own as the international community is unwilling or unable to help.[159]

---

152 See Kathy Marks, "Sinking Pacific Island Kiribati Considers Moving to a Man-Made Alternative," The Independent, 8 September 2011, available at http://www.independent.co.uk/environment/climate-change/sinking-pacific-island-kiribati-considers-moving-to-a-manmade-alternative-2350964.html, last accessed 29 April 2014.

153 Paul Chapman, "Entire Nation of Kiribati to Be Relocated Over Rising Sea Level Threat," The Telegraph, 7 March 2012, available at http://www.telegraph.co.uk/news/worldnews/australiaandthepacific/kiribati/9127576/Entire-nation-of-Kiribati-to-be-relocated-over-rising-sea level-threat.html, last accessed 29 April 2014.

154 Paul Chapman, "Entire Nation of Kiribati to Be Relocated Over Rising Sea Level Threat," The Telegraph, 7 March 2012, available at http://www.telegraph.co.uk/news/worldnews/australiaandthepacific/kiribati/9127576/Entire-nation-of-Kiribati-to-be-relocated-over-rising-sea level-threat.html, last accessed 29 April 2014.

155 See Kathy Marks, "Sinking Pacific Island Kiribati Considers Moving to a Man-Made Alternative," The Independent, 8 September 2011, available at http://www.independent.co.uk/environment/climate-change/sinking-pacific-island-kiribati-considers-moving-to-a-manmade-alternative-2350964.html, last accessed 29 April 2014.

156 See U.N. Doc. E/CN.4/Sub.2/AC.4/2004/CRP.1, p. 7 et seq. para. 19-24.

157 See *Verheyen*, p. 138.

158 *Gillespie*, 22 UCLA J. Envtl. L. & Pol'y 2003-2004, 107 (129).

159 See *Jarvis*, 9 Seattle J. Soc. Just. 2010-2011, 447 (460).

The present thesis will discuss the adaption strategies pursued in view of prospective damage caused by global warming. Mitigation will only play an indirect role: The failure to stipulate or successfully implement sufficient mitigation strategies that would prevent the permanent inundation of state territories could, for example, be used as an argument to trigger liability.[160]

4. Recent Development: Loss and Damage

As of recently, 'loss and damage' is being discussed as an alternative strategy to address the effects of climate change. Thus far, no universally accepted definition of this term exists, but broadly speaking, it can be taken to refer to "a range of harms incurred in developing countries from the impact of climate change, which cannot be avoided either through mitigation or adaptation."[161]

The present and future threats posed by climate change combined with social vulnerability make it necessary to explore new avenues both theoretically and practically.[162] Discussions about loss and damage therefore have emerged under the UNFCCC as a distinct thematic area since the Cancún Agreements in 2010,[163] where the COP recognised "the need to strengthen international cooperation and expertise in order to understand and reduce loss and damage associated with the adverse effects of climate change."[164] Furthermore, it decided to establish a work programme in order to consider approaches addressing loss and damage associated with climate change impacts in developing countries that are particularly vulnerable to the adverse effects of climate change.[165]

At their subsequent meeting in Durban in 2011, the COP agreed "to engage a large and diverse representation of experts, in particular from developing countries, including the least developed countries and small island developing States"[166] in order to implement a "work programme on loss and damage".[167] The topic 'loss and damage' was divided into three thematic areas:

---

160 This thought will be examined in detail further below, see § 4. B. 4. e. aa.

161 IRIN: "Climate Change: When the Damage Is Done" (23 November 2012), available at http://www.irinnews.org/report/96867/climate-change-when-the-damage-is-done, last accessed 29 April 2014.

162 See *Warner et al.*, UNU-EHS 2012, p. 10.

163 See *Warner et al.*, UNU-EHS 2012, p. 13.

164 U.N. Doc. FCCC/CP/2010/7/Add.1, p. 6 para. 25.

165 See U.N. Doc. FCCC/CP/2010/7/Add.1, p. 6 para. 26.

166 U.N. Doc. FCCC/CP/2011/9/Add.2, p. 6 para. 4.

167 U.N. Doc. FCCC/CP/2011/9/Add.2, p. 5 et seqq.

1. "Assessing the risk of loss and damage associated with the adverse effects of climate change and the current knowledge on the same,"[168]
2. "[a] range of approaches to address loss and damage associated with the adverse effects of climate change, including impacts related to extreme weather events and slow-onset events, taking into consideration experience at all levels,"[169] and
3. "[t]he role of the Convention in enhancing the implementation of approaches to address loss and damage associated with the adverse effects of climate change."[170]

The topic has been further enlarged upon in Doha, where the COP discussed "[a]pproaches to address loss and damage associated with climate change impacts in developing countries that are particularly vulnerable to the adverse effects of climate change to enhance adaptive capacity"[171].

Loss and damage has been discussed controversially, as the term might also be construed to imply an entitlement to compensation on the part of SIDS and a legal obligation to provide it on the part of developed countries.[172] SIDS (led by the Alliance of Small Island States[173]) "have been [the] strongest and most persistent advocates for the need to address loss and damage, rallying their position around the fact that their ability to adapt to climate change will be limited when their land is being drowned by rising sea levels."[174]

For endangered states, this topic could become particularly relevant. A briefing paper for an expert meeting on loss and damages established that "[r]isk reduction, like adaptation, becomes impossible after a certain point, for example, when a territory becomes uninhabitable. Migration and planned relocation are only coping mechanisms in that situation."[175] The paper considers loss and

---

168 U.N. Doc. FCCC/CP/2011/9/Add.2, p. 6.

169 U.N. Doc. FCCC/CP/2011/9/Add.2, p. 6 et seq.

170 U.N. Doc. FCCC/CP/2011/9/Add.2, p. 7.

171 U.N. Doc. FCCC/CP/2012/8/Add.1, p. 21.

172 See IRIN: "Climate Change: When the Damage Is Done" (23 November 2012), available at http://www.irinnews.org/report/96867/climate-change-when-the-damage-is-done, last accessed 29 April 2014.

173 Hereinafter, the Alliance of Small Islands States will be referred to as AOSIS.

174 IRIN: "Climate Change: When the Damage Is Done" (23 November 2012), available at http://www.irinnews.org/report/96867/climate-change-when-the-damage-is-done, last accessed 29 April 2014.

175 *Hoffmaister/Stabinsky*, Briefing Paper 2012, p. 2, II. 2.

damage in the context of lost opportunities to achieve sustainable development.[176] "The continuing accumulation of greenhouse gases in the atmosphere, the denial of historical responsibility by developed countries, and the limited support that has been forthcoming for adaptation, limit how much developing countries can do."[177] Furthermore, it has been pointed out that this topic is an issue of equity, as "[t]he countries most vulnerable to loss and damage are not responsible for the climate change that is destroying lives and livelihoods."[178]

As already pointed out, one main issue is the lack of clarity about the term 'loss and damage.'[179] "The topic of Loss and Damage is still a very new one, and also very important one, as it opens up a major new strategy to respond to climate change beyond mitigation and adaptation. The discussions around this topic are still in their infancy but will undoubtedly grow in importance over time."[180]

At the present time, the topic 'loss and damage' is not developed enough to draw legal conclusions for endangered states. This might, however, change in the near future, as most recent developments indicate: At the latest COP in Warsaw in November 2013, developing countries stronger than ever before argued for compensation for climate change damages based on loss and damage. Their delegates e.g. left the negotiation table frustrated due to the blocking of industrial nations to negotiate a loss and damage fund that collects money in cases of climate change related damages.[181] Their protest has been supported by environmental associations (Oxfam, Greenpeace, WWF, Nabu, BUND, Friends of the Earth and others) who left climate negotiations, complaining about the 'cynicism' of industrial nations (*inter alia* Germany, Poland, Australia, Japan, the EU as a whole, the USA) as well as developing countries (e.g. China, India and Brazil) to assure concern about climate change but to ultimately pursue interests

176 See *Hoffmaister/Stabinsky*, Briefing Paper 2012, p. 4, III. 1.

177 *Hoffmaister/Stabinsky*, Briefing Paper 2012, p. 2, II. 1.

178 *Hoffmaister/Stabinsky*, Briefing Paper 2012, p. 3, II. 4.

179 See Saleemul Huq, "Politics Of Climate Change – COP18 in Doha: Loss and Damage," The Daily Star, 22 November 2012, available at http://archive.thedailystar.net/newDesign/news-details.php?nid=258380, last accessed 29 April 2014.

180 Saleemul Huq, "Politics Of Climate Change – COP18 in Doha: Loss and Damage," The Daily Star, 22 November 2012, available at http://archive.thedailystar.net/newDesign/news-details.php?nid=258380, last accessed 29 April 2014.

181 See Markus Becker, "Entwicklungsländer fordern Entschädigung für künftige Katastrophen," Spiegel Online Wissenschaft, 20 November 2013, available at http://www.spiegel.de/wissenschaft/natur/klimakonferenz-in-warschau-streit-um-loss-and-damage-a-934652.html, last accessed 29 April 2014.

of the fossil fuel industry.[182] This form of resistance is unprecedented in the 20 years of COP negotiations.[183]

This COP is the first time that loss and damage is at the centre of developing countries' concern, as they seem to give up their hope for effective mitigation after 20 years of negotiations.[184] The third era of climate change is being proclaimed.[185] Representatives of LDC therefore talked of "a red line", claiming that "it's all or nothing" as "[industrial countries] have consistently delayed helping developing countries adapt to climate change and have not reduced emissions, as agreed."[186]

Industrial nations however fear tremendous costs if they agreed upon a liability.[187] Between 1980 and 2012, costs of close to 4 trillion USD have been caused by disasters whereas there is a strong upwards trend of this expense.[188] For the future, adaption costs for Africa alone are expected to rise up to 700 billion USD per year according to a recent UNEP report.[189] The construction of a shoreline

---

182 See Axel Bojanowski, "Uno-Tagung in Warschau: Umweltverbände verlassen Klimakonferenz," Spiegel Online Wissenschaft, 21 November 2013, available at http://www.spiegel.de/wissenschaft/mensch/ngos-verlassen-uno-klimakonferenz-warschau-cop19-a-934883.html, last accessed 29 April 2014.

183 See Markus Becker, "Konferenz in Polen: Industriestaaten düpieren arme Länder bei Klimagipfel," Spiegel Online Wissenschaft, 21 November 2013, available at http://www.spiegel.de/wissenschaft/natur/klimakonferenz-kein-kompromiss-bei-loss-and-damage-in-sicht-a-934894.html, last accessed 29 April 2014.

184 See Markus Becker, "Entwicklungsländer fordern Entschädigung für künftige Katastrophen," Spiegel Online, Wissenschaft 20 November 2013, available at http://www.spiegel.de/wissenschaft/natur/klimakonferenz-in-warschau-streit-um-loss-and-damage-a-934652.html, last accessed 29 April 2014.

185 See Markus Becker, "Entwicklungsländer fordern Entschädigung für künftige Katastrophen," Spiegel Online, Wissenschaft 20 November 2013, available at http://www.spiegel.de/wissenschaft/natur/klimakonferenz-in-warschau-streit-um-loss-and-damage-a-934652.html, last accessed 29 April 2014.

186 John Vidal, "Climate Talks: Wealthy Countries Urged to Foot Bill for Weather-Related Disasters," The Guardian, 19 November 2013, available at http://www.theguardian.com/global-development/2013/nov/19/climate-talks-wealthy-countries-bill-weather-disasters-un-warsaw, last accessed 29 April 2014.

187 See Markus Becker, "Entwicklungsländer fordern Entschädigung für künftige Katastrophen," Spiegel Online, Wissenschaft 20 November 2013, available at http://www.spiegel.de/wissenschaft/natur/klimakonferenz-in-warschau-streit-um-loss-and-damage-a-934652.html, last accessed 29 April 2014.

188 See *Gitay et al.*, World Bank Report 2013, Executive Summary, p. vii.

189 See UNEP News Centre: "Africa Climate Adaptation Costs Could Soar to USD $350 Billion Annually by 2070 if Warming Hits 3.5-4°C," UN Report (19 November

protection for Caribbean SIDS only against future sea-level rise would cost about 1.1 billion USD.[190] In light of these risks, the US delegate pragmatically pointed out the need to look at the world as it is, especially the fiscal situation in the USA and other states, which does not give room for such compensation.[191]

Summarized, whereas industrial nations strongly oppose the idea of any obligation to compensate climate change damages, developing countries stand in unprecedented and surprising unison to pursue their interests.[192]

Considering this current negotiation gridlock, it is unclear to which extent loss and damage might develop into a concept with binding consequences. Yet the paradigm shift in the negotiation strategy of developing countries, including endangered states, is proof for the rising relevance of compensation for climate change damages out of which the loss of a state territory would be the most severe one for a state.

2013), available at http://www.unep.org/newscentre/Default.aspx?DocumentID=2755&ArticleID=9705, last accessed 29 April 2014.

190 See *Ashe*, 23 Nat. Res. Forum 1999, 187 (191).

191 See Markus Becker, "Entwicklungsländer fordern Entschädigung für künftige Katastrophen," Spiegel Online, Wissenschaft 20 November 2013, available at http://www.spiegel.de/wissenschaft/natur/klimakonferenz-in-warschau-streit-um-loss-and-damage-a-934652.html, last accessed 29 April 2014.

192 See Markus Becker, "Konferenz in Polen: Industriestaaten düpieren arme Länder bei Klimagipfel," Spiegel Online Wissenschaft, 21 November 2013, available at http://www.spiegel.de/wissenschaft/natur/klimakonferenz-kein-kompromiss-bei-loss-and-damage-in-sicht-a-934894.html, last accessed 29 April 2014.

§ 3. The Contemporary Concept of States

A. Introduction

Current international law does not provide a generally accepted definition of the notion 'state'. Nevertheless, the international community has to decide on whether an entity – according to international law – is a state or not.[193] This issue will become crucial to endangered states.

Although the international community has experienced a proliferation of non-state actors, states have remained the sole comprehensive subjects of international law thus far.[194] For example, it is only states who can be (full) members in the United Nations, file a suit with the International Court of Justice[195] or, according to Art. 35 No. 2 UN-Charter, invoke the Security Council or the General Assembly concerning a dispute in which they are involved.

This chapter will outline, in broad strokes, the contemporary concept of a state (B.), focusing on the minimum requirements that a state's territory must meet, which is a primary concern of endangered states. Brief summaries of the ongoing discussion on the criteria for statehood (C.) and the historical development of the notion of a state (D.) will illustrate how the concept has adapted to various circumstances and exigencies over time, albeit never to the benefit of its accuracy.

B. Content

Despite the lack of a binding definition of the notion of state,[196] a consuetudinary and broadly accepted understanding of the elements of a state is "a sovereign legal community on a territorial basis."[197] The constitutive elements are

---

193 See *Doehring*, para. 2, marginal no. 42.

194 See *Kunig*, Jura 1986, 344 (346), *Grant*, 37 Colum. J. Transnat'l L. 1998-1999, 403 (404). Examples for non-state actors are the UN and the International Labour Organisation, *Shearer*, p. 543.

195 See *Doehring*, para. 2, marginal no. 44. The International Court of Justice will hereinafter be referred to as ICJ.

196 See *Grant*, 37 Colum. J. Transnat'l L. 1998-1999, 403 (404).

197 *Geiger*, para. 51. On the broadly accepted understanding of the elements of a state, see *Isensee* in: HStR, para. 15 No. 49, see also *Grant*, 37 Colum. J. Transnat'l L. 1998-1999, 403 (409) with further references. Rejecting: *Smend*, p. 129 et seqq., who defines the state as a more fluid system of interaction.

therefore people, state territory, and sovereignty.[198] This understanding is also referred to as the "doctrine of three elements" by *Jellinek*.[199] It is a reflection of humankind's efforts, throughout history, to organise and divide itself into regional structures.[200]

1. People

The constitutive element of "people" is not a very difficult pre-condition for a state to meet. A people is understood to be a permanent union of human beings living in a certain area, without there being any requirement as to minimum number.[201] The Pacific island territory of Pitcairn, for example (which had been offered independence by the UN),[202] is home to a permanent population of only approximately 50 people.[203]

The question of the existence of a people will be of no major relevance for the present study. Yet it should be stressed that this is the one element that the other elements – state sovereignty and state territory – are meant to serve.[204]

2. Sovereignty

Sovereignty is differentiated as internal and external sovereignty.[205] Internal sovereignty comprises the abilities to constitute the state as such and to amend its constitution.[206] It is also a category of power: Only the modern state has the monopoly on the legitimate use of force.[207]

External sovereignty involves legal independence, i.e. the state does not acknowledge any other legal authority besides itself except for international law.[208] In this thesis, external sovereignty will be of primary interest as it is a characteristic under international law[209]. It is the foundation of the principle of sovereign equality set out in Art. 2 No. 1 UN-Charter, upon which modern international

198 Concerning the discussion with regard to additional criteria, see below § 3. C.
199 See *Jellinek*, p. 180 et seq.
200 See *Geiger*, para. 51.
201 See *Isensee* in: HStR, para. 15, marginal no. 52.
202 See e.g. UNGA Res. 2869 (20 December 1971).
203 See *Grote Stoutenburg* in: Gerrard/Wannier, 57 (61).
204 See *Isensee* in: HStR, para. 15, marginal no. 54.
205 See *Epping* in: Ipsen, para. 5, marginal no. 7.
206 See *Epping* in: Ipsen, para. 5, marginal no. 8.
207 See *Isensee* in: HStR, para. 15, marginal no. 53.
208 See *Isensee* in: HStR, para. 15, marginal no. 53.
209 See *Isensee* in: HStR, para. 15, marginal no. 53.

law is based. While this principle of equality is not always reflected in global political reality, the sovereign state remains the determining factor in international law.[210]

3. State Territory

a) General Requirements

A state territory is not only formed by a certain terrain on the surface of the earth – it also comprises the airspace above as well as the terra underneath,[211] i.e. a conic section starting at the centre of the Earth. It is predominantly considered a constitutive criterion of the state.[212] Yet this point of view is not without opposition: It has been argued as early as in 1907 that a state without a territory is "perfectly possible".[213] However, the territory of a state principally is indeed a necessary pre-requisite for effectively exercising governmental functions like prosecution, jurisdiction, and administration.[214] These are barely exercisable without a corresponding geographic zone.

According to the United Nations Convention on the Law of the Sea[215], water is considered to be part of a state's territory only if it is an inland body of water, or if the respective State has enforced its right to establish the width of its territorial sea up to, but not exceeding, 12 nautical miles measured from baselines, Art. 2 Nr. 1, 3 UNCLOS.[216] The baselines, defined in Art. 5 UNCLOS, always depend on the corresponding land. Hence, the territory of a sovereign state cannot exist without at least a small area of land.

b) Inhabitable Territory as State Territory

None of the above-mentioned states[217] facing the threat of uninhabitability are expected to disappear completely below the surface of the sea. Amongst the

---

210 See *Isensee* in: HStR, para. 15, marginal no. 54.

211 See *Brownlie*, p. 115; *Darsow*, p. 22 et seqq.

212 See *Darsow*, p. 23.

213 See *Salmond*, p. 99.

214 See *Salmond*, p. 99.

215 The United Nations Convention on the Law of the Sea will hereinafter be referred to as UNCLOS, available at http://www.un.org/Depts/los/convention_agreements/texts/unclos/closindx.htm, last accessed 29 April 2014.

216 For a more detailed overview of the different zones of sovereignty see *Häußler*, JA 2002, pp. 817 et seqq.

217 See above § 2. D. (Tuvalu, Kiribati, The Bahamas, The Maldive Islands, Nauru).

states most likely to be affected, the Maldives, with their highest point at only 2.4 m,[218] are followed by Tuvalu with its highest point at 5 m.[219] A sea level rise of at least 2.4 m is very unlikely to happen within this century.[220] Yet all of the states mentioned above are expected to become uninhabitable at some point.

The question needing to be addressed here thus is: Can an island, or a group of islands, retain its character as a state territory once the whole of this territory becomes uninhabitable, or does the loss of its state territory mean that it is lacking one of the constitutive criteria for statehood? This scenario has not yet occurred in the history of states or international law, making the question a new one, and one urgently requiring an answer.[221]

The question of what happens once the whole of a state's territory becomes uninhabitable must be distinguished explicitly from the leading question as to the consequences for future statehood of endangered states.[222]

aa. The Relationship between State and Territory

Addressing the matter of the height (according to current international law) to which the sea level must rise until a territory threatened by inundation loses its qualification as state territory requires an analysis of the existing theories on the character of state territory and its relation to the state itself.

(1) Preliminary Remarks

Before states existed in the understanding we have of them today, societies were primarily formed based on personal allegiance rather than territorial considerations.[223] From the post-Roman era until the fourteenth century, in particular, personal commitment to a sovereign and to the Church determined people's affiliations.[224] The Peace of Westphalia in 1648 is commonly identified as the crucial point towards the creation of modern international law, as it is based on defined territorial units that enjoy territorial sovereignty.[225] Yet according to

---

218 See the CIA World Factbook, available at https://www.cia.gov/library/publications/the-world-factbook/geos/mv.html, last accessed 29 April 2014.

219 See U.N. Doc. E/CN.4/Sub.2/2005/28 No. 25.

220 See above § 2. C.

221 See U.N. Doc. E/CN.4/Sub.2/2005/28 No. 13.

222 This question will be addressed below, see § 5. B.

223 See *Zippelius*, p. 78 et seq.; *Shaw*, NYIL 13, 61 (62); *Mayer*, p. 14; *Gottmann*, p. 16 et seq.

224 See Mayer, p. 15; *Shaw*, 61 (62).

225 See *Weiss* in: Vig/Axelrod, 98 (98); *Shaw*, NYIL 13, 61 (62).

Mayer, it was *Klüber*[226] who, in the year 1817, was the first to define the state as a civic society existing within a certain district.[227] Today, territorial sovereignty is the determining factor in international law: All states of the world are territorial states.[228] The 1970 Declaration of Principles of International Law contains the following terms: "All States enjoy sovereign equality. [...] In particular, sovereign equality includes the following elements: [...] (d) The territorial integrity and political independence of the States are inviolable."[229]

Based on this understanding of state territory – and the related territorial sovereignty – differing opinions have been expressed with regard to the relation between states and their respective territories.

(2) Patrimonial Theory

The oldest amongst these opinions is the so-called patrimonial theory. It reflects a feudal understanding, regarded "outdated"[230] today, of a state's superior property with regard to its territory (*dominum directum*), with the possessing citizen being equipped with only subordinate property (*dominum utile*).[231] This theory rightly has been criticised as obsolete, and has been by-passed by contemporary legal principles, according to which the law is divided into civil and public law, or *dominum* and *imperium*, respectively, with the latter (and not the first) term describing the relation of a state to its territory.[232]

(3) Object Theory, or Property Theory

The patrimonial theory evolved into the so-called object theory, or property theory, according to which the state does not possess its territory by civil law (*dominum*), yet the territory remains the object of state power (*imperium*).[233] This state power over its territory is to be considered constitutional property law – yet without analogy to private property law.[234] Besides being the object of

---

226 See *Klüber*, § 1, S. 1.

227 See *Mayer*, p. 18 et seq.

228 See *Kriele*, p. 95.

229 Declaration of Principles of International Law Concerning Friendly Relations and Co-operation Among States in Accordance with the Charter of the United Nations, available at http://www.unhcr.org/refworld/topic,459d17822,459d17a82,3dda1f104,0.html, last accessed 29 April 2014.

230 *Graf Vitzthum* in: HStR § 16 marginal no. 6.

231 See *Schade* in: Kraus, p. 2.

232 See *Zippelius*, p. 81; *Schade* in: Kraus, p. 2.

233 See *Schade* in: Kraus, p. 3 with further references.

234 See *Gerber*, p. 66.

state power, the territory is the most characteristic attribute of the corresponding state.[235] In other words, the territory shapes the corporeal qualification of a state.[236] This understanding of a state as being identified by its territory leads to the persuasion that a state territory is as indivisible as the state personality itself.[237] Consequently to this corporeal approach, a division of a state's territory, or a cession of a sub-territory, is considered self-destruction, or at the very least self-mutilation or amputation.[238] An exception is made in this theory, however, with regard to minuscule cessions for the purposes of boundary adjustments, as long as they are compensated.[239]

This theory has been criticised in many respects: Above all, the analogy to the human body is incongruous as any loss of territory simultaneously constitutes an increment for another state's territory – a situation entirely different from an amputation or loss of limb.[240] Additionally, the analogy to civil property rights cannot explain the legal situation in federal states.[241]

(4) Space Theory, or Quality Theory

Fricker shaped the so-called space theory, or quality theory, and opposed the idea that the state territory is on the one hand object of the state, on the other hand a *momentum* of the legal subject "state".[242] Only the latter applies: The state territory is nothing but the denotation of a *momentum* of the state.[243] The state therefore is not a ruler *over* the territory, but a ruler *within* a territory.[244] According to *Fricker*, the term "state territory" is used to designate the state in its spatial outlines.[245] Hence, any modification of a state's territory will also entail a change of the state itself.[246]

This last conclusion has been found untenable.[247] When *Fricker* subsequently resorted to comparing the state with the human body, in the manner of the

235 See *Gerber*, p. 67.
236 See *Gerber*, p. 67.
237 See *Gerber*, p. 68.
238 See *Gerber*, p. 68.
239 See *Gerber*, p. 68.
240 See *Radnitzky*, 20 AöR 1906, 313 (322).
241 See *Shaw*, NYIL 13, 61 (76).
242 See *Fricker*, p. 23.
243 See *Fricker*, p. 17.
244 See *Fricker*, p. 26.
245 See *Fricker*, p. 27.
246 See *Smend*, p. 170; *Fricker*, p. 27.
247 See *Schade* in: Kraus, p. 5; *Radnitzky*, 20 AöR 1906, 313 (315).

object theory outlined above, this was likewise subjected to severe criticism.[248] Furthermore, this theory cannot explain conventional cessions of territory.[249]

(5) Objectivist Theory, or Competence Theory

Radnitzky finally developed the so-called objectivist theory, or competence theory, according to which territorial sovereignty describes nothing but the reach of a state's regional competence.[250] By virtue of this competence, the state can be cedent or cessionary when state territory is given up.[251] The understanding of territory as the sphere of the state's competence does not collide with the rules applicable to private property, nor does the existence of federal states create a problem: Both states are competent in the same region, but their competences differ in terms of their substance.[252] Besides its regional and contentual competence, the state also has jurisdiction over its citizens; to a significant extent, this overlaps with its regional competence.[253] In keeping with this line of thought, the notion of territory thus has been minimised to become a mere limiting factor for the exercise of state power.[254]

Over the course of the past decades, this opinion has come to be the prevailing one in legal scientific literature as it provides the most convincing explanations specifically in those areas in which the other theories remain silent.[255]

(6) Interim Result

The above summary demonstrates the continuously evolving understanding of the relationship between a state and its territory.

None of the authors of these concepts, however, ever considered that state territory – and thereby territorial sovereignty – may be lost in any other than the 'conventional' ways of occupation, annexation, cession, adjuration or usucaption, and instead by sea level rise.

bb. Interim Conclusions: Sinking State Territories

Firstly, the following fact shall be stressed: When the territory of a state has been submerged entirely by the sea, it cannot be considered a state territory any

248 See *Radnitzky*, 20 AöR 1906, 313 (336).
249 See *Radnitzky*, 20 AöR 1906, 313 (338).
250 See *Radnitzky*, 20 AöR 1906, 313 (340).
251 See *Radnitzky*, 20 AöR 1906, 313 (341).
252 See *Radnitzky*, 20 AöR 1906, 313 (342).
253 See *Radnitzky*, 20 AöR 1906, 313 (347).
254 See *Shaw*, p. 76.
255 See *Graf Vitzthum* in: HStR § 16 marginal no. 6.

longer.[256] The word 'territory,' which derives from the Latin *terra,* designates soil that is not covered by water.[257] This does not, however, entirely answer the question as to the precise moment at which the ground in question ceases to be a state territory. *Hampson*, outlining the legal problems emerging from this scenario that endangered states might face in the near future, asks, "when does a State count as having disappeared: At the point when the population can only survive by leaving, even if parts of the territory remain above water, or only when the entire territory is submerged?"[258]

This question will be examined in greater detail within this subchapter by interpreting the term 'state territory' with a view to the competence theory just outlined.

According to one opinion, as long as the land is not entirely inundated, "the territorial effectiveness criterion would *per se* remain fulfilled" as not only uninhabitable islands, but even rocks (Art. 121 (3) UNCLOS) qualify as land.[259] However, this does not necessarily imply that this land still can be considered state territory.[260] If land is uninhabitable, it most likely does not qualify as state territory.[261]

This raises the question as to the definition of uninhabitability.

An interpretation of the wording 'state territory' does not provide a satisfying answer. One could argue, for example, that a territory must merely belong to a state in order to qualify as state territory – an argument suitable for the property theory. This means that the possibility of living there (i.e. inhabitability) would not be an obligatory pre-requisite. If any such part of the earth's surface can be assigned to a certain state, it would qualify as 'state territory.'

Yet this reasoning is not convincing – rather, it would seem a better fit for the term 'state's territory'. The term 'state territory,' however, according to competence theory, is not meant to indicate the ownership structure of a certain property. On the contrary, the territory of any specific state may be owned not only by the state itself but also by any legal entity or natural person – regardless of their nationality – and even by another state. The wording thus gives no indication whether an uninhabitable area is still to be considered state territory.

---

256 Similar: see *Grote Stoutenburg* in: Gerrard/Wannier, 57 (60).
257 See VG Köln, verdict from 3 May 1978, 9 K 2565/77, DVBl. 510 (511).
258 U.N. Doc. E/CN.4/Sub.2/AC.4/2004/CRP.1, p. 3 para. 8.
259 *Grote Stoutenburg* in: Gerrard/Wannier, 57 (60).
260 See *Grote Stoutenburg* in: Gerrard/Wannier, 57 (61).
261 See *Grote Stoutenburg* in: Gerrard/Wannier, 57 (61).

A systematic approach to the interpretation of the term would require defining an internationally binding legal regime. The treaty most widely recognised thus far for addressing state criteria is the Montevideo Convention on Rights and Duties of the States dated 26 December 1933.[262] It was signed by the representatives of 19 pan-American states, out of which only 5 ratified it[263] and thus cannot count as an internationally binding legal regime. Beyond that, Art. 1 b. of MCRDS only mentions a defined territory as a prerequisite, without providing any further indication as to minimum requirements in this respect. Therefore, the interpretation of the term cannot be approached systematically.

The same applies to the attempt at historical deduction[264]: The situation is without precedent. What is more, there has not been a comparable case thus far that would open up the possibility for an analogous approach.

Accordingly, only a teleological explanation will serve to answer the present question.[265] For this purpose, a look at two of the definitions already stated is expedient: First of all, a state is "a sovereign legal community on a territorial basis."[266] The word *on* indicates the requirement that the community is – predominantly or at least partly – located on its territory. Otherwise it could be referred to as being a community *with* a territorial basis. Secondly, a people is defined as "a permanent union of human beings living on a certain territory."[267] The state territory thus is "the physical basis that ensures that people can live together as organized communities. Only land that hosts a permanent population can serve its function to delimit societies and their national legal spheres from each other and from the global common."[268] This understanding of the people is further evidence for the understanding of a state territory as an environment where it is possible to live.

---

262 Hereinafter, the Montevideo Convention on Rights and Duties of the States will be referred to as MCRDS. For more detail on the historical context see below § 3. D. 3.

263 See *Grant*, 37 Colum. J. Transnat'l L. 1998-1999, 403 (456). The signing states were Argentina, Brazil, Chile, Columbia, Cuba, Dominican Republic, Ecuador, El Salvador, Guatemala, Haiti, Honduras, Mexico, Nicaragua, Panama, Paraguay, Peru, United States, Uruguay, Venezuela.

264 For a brief summary of the historical development of the concept of statehood see below § 3. D.

265 Similarly: see *Grote Stoutenburg* in: Gerrard/Wannier, 57 (61).

266 *Geiger*, para. 51.

267 *Isensee* in: HStR, para. 15, marginal no. 52.

268 *Grote Stoutenburg* in: Gerrard/Wannier, 57 (61).

The opinion to only require any land that is not (yet) uninhabitable even if predominantly, the territory is covered by water[269] is unconvincing. The view has been presented – with reference to the formerly sovereign state of Venice – that as long as there are buildings on stilts, a former state territory does not lose its legal quality in this respect.[270] Endangered states thus would sufficiently fulfil statehood criteria as long as they "enable an – even small – number of people to continue living on the remaining island territory as a community."[271] A community then would be sufficient to "form a 'population nucleus' capable of upholding the personal element of statehood."[272] In order to retain their state territory, endangered states thus only would have to ensure that some part of their land remains inhabitable.[273]

This very formal argument is not persuasive. A state territory has to be able to serve as a basis for a state, not for a community. Recall that international law is based on international consent – it is hard to imagine that the international community would be convinced by such a sleight of hand: In the extreme case an almost completely flooded island could continue qualifying as 'state territory' as long as a single hut on stilts is left standing.

Thus, the question still needs to be answered when a territory becomes uninhabitable in the sense of not qualifying as state territory anymore. A good argument can be made that this is the case from the very moment that the state apparatus can no longer be maintained properly or at least provisionally, provided this situation is permanent. This understanding should apply due to the following reasoning:

The three powers legislation, administration, and jurisdiction must be capable to fulfil their main tasks. As soon as one of these powers stops working properly, the state apparatus will collapse. If this is the result of (permanent) land loss, the state territory hence is incapable to serve as territorial basis for a state and thus cannot be considered to exist as such any longer.

This understanding corresponds to the competence theory: The regional competence of a state is to be understood in a way such that the state is also capable of exercising its competence. If this is not the case, and lastingly so, there is no territory for which the state is competent – hence there is no state territory.

---

269 See *Grote Stoutenburg* in: Gerrard/Wannier, 57 (62).

270 See *Kehrer*, p. 61.

271 *Grote Stoutenburg* in: Gerrard/Wannier, 57 (65).

272 *Grote Stoutenburg* in: Gerrard/Wannier, 57 (65).

273 See *Grote Stoutenburg* in: Gerrard/Wannier, 57 (62).

This scenario must be distinguished from other forms of state instability such as civil war, natural disasters, failed states, or governments in exile.[274] As mentioned, the criterion for this distinction should be permanence. What the above cases of instability have in common is that the unstable status is transitional. In contrast, sinking island nations whose state organs are unable to work, not even provisionally, do not have the prospect that this circumstance will change.[275] Amongst the various solutions conceivable, they could, for example, cooperate with other states to exercise their power – partially and provisionally – based in another territory. But this does not contradict the conclusion that the former state territory cannot be considered as such anymore when it becomes too small and/or too affected to serve as territorial basis for a state.

The permanent collapse of the state apparatus is a severe cesura and thus an appropriate occasion to determine the dissolution of the respective state territory.[276]

4. Legal Relationship between State Sovereignty and State Territory

As the competence theory illustrates, the two elements 'territory' and 'sovereignty' overlap in crucial areas. The territory is the sphere in which the respective state exercises the competences it deduces from its sovereignty. This raises the question as to whether these two elements condition each other such that a state losing its territory also loses its sovereignty – or major parts of it.

States are territorial entities that enjoy territorial sovereignty,[277] in which context the relationship between statehood and territorial sovereignty is of a special kind.[278] In the *Island of Palmas Case* (1928) the Swiss arbitrator *Huber* assumed that "it appears to follow that sovereignty in relation to a portion of the surface of the globe is the legal condition necessary for the inclusion of such portion in the territory of any particular state."[279] At first glance, this understanding suggests the *argumentum e contrario* that a particular state (or better: A particular subject of international law) having no portion of the globe's surface at all would not satisfy the requirements of sovereignty. This conclusion would result in a nexus

---

274 The latter two scenarios will be examined further below, see § 5. B. 1.

275 Unless the whole state moves elsewhere. The legal prerequisites for this strategy will be elaborated in detail in §§ 4 and 5.

276 Concerning the question if the respective state also ceases to exist in this case see below § 5. B.

277 See *Crawford*, p. 46.

278 See *Crawford*, p. 48.

279 *Island of Palmas Case*, 829 (838).

of the two elements 'state territory' and 'sovereignty' in a way that neither of the elements could exist without the existence of the respective counterpart.

Furthermore, the term 'territorial sovereignty' itself seems to imply that sovereignty is dependent on the territory. The state, at least, might have to consist of a certain coherent territory that is subject to effective governance.[280] As discussed above,[281] this conclusion is only partly correct: For the most part, internal sovereignty is exercisable only if the state has a territory on which a (at least predominantly) functioning state apparatus is installed. National jurisdiction, for example, cannot be exercised in a foreign country. The state's monopoly on the legitimate use of force ends at its boundaries. On the other hand, governmental administration is – at least partly and transitionally – imaginable without a state territory, if it is given contractual permission by other states to address administrative issues within their territories. The same applies for constitutional amendments – at least theoretically, this legislative procedure does not require a state territory in order to be exercised. Moreover, consular sections, as part of a national administration, are examples for a common exercise of internal sovereignty outside of a state's own territorial boundaries.

The external sovereignty does not necessarily require a certain territory for it to be exerted. A government can continue representing its people or concluding international treaties without the compulsory need to derive these competences from its territory. The term *external* sovereignty itself implies – contrary to its *internal* counterpart – a worldwide range. What is more, the international practice of acknowledging governments in exile[282] demonstrates that the loss of internal sovereignty does not necessarily lead to the loss of external sovereignty. The situation of a government in exile indeed differs from a government that cannot be associated with a certain state territory (any longer), yet it exemplifies that the theoretically close connection between the elements of a state can become frayed provided there is a certain degree of consent (and pragmatism) within the international community.

Accordingly, despite the term 'territorial sovereignty,' these two elements of a state do not depend on each other such that sovereignty can only exist as long as there is a state territory. If this were the case, the doctrine of three elements would actually be reduced to a doctrine of two elements, consisting of a people and territorial sovereignty.

---

280 See *Crawford*, p. 52.

281 See above § 3. B. 3. b.

282 Governments in exile will be addressed further below, see below § 5. B. 1.

C. Discussions with regard to other Criteria

In the broad field of international law, different opinions have been expressed on the issue of which further criteria are necessary in order to constitute a state. As none of these opinions have met with any greater degree of acceptance and thus the approaches are only of rather theoretical interest, only a few of them will be briefly highlighted here in order to document the ongoing debate about what is considered a state. The debate itself illustrates a certain flexible nature of statehood.

1. Recognition

The recognition of entities as states by already established states has frequently been focal in international law.[283] Effective 28 August 2011, 124 of the 193 UN member states (64%) have, as an example, recognised Palestine as a state, amongst them all ten of the most populated countries except for the USA.[284] Not uncommonly, entities try to prove their statehood by referring to the explicit or *de facto* recognition by other states.[285]

The ongoing debate regarding the importance of recognition must be differentiated, however: Firstly with regard to the question of whether recognition is a necessary pre-requisite for statehood to exist, and secondly concerning the question what the prerequisites are for recognition by other states.[286] Only the first question is of direct relevance for this thesis, yet the second question illustrates the political and indirect context: Any only 'formal' state would always seek recognition as a prerequisite for its participation within the international community.

---

283 See *Darsow*, p. 44; *Grant*, 37 Colum. J. Transnat'l L. 1998-1999, 403 (446).

284 See International Middle East Media Center, available at http://www.imemc.org/article/61902, last accessed 29 April 2014.

285 As it was the case with the self-appointed "Principality of Sealand," a shut-down AA gun emplacement located in the North Sea, which invoked the forthcoming recognition by the states Ceylon, Paraguay and Cyprus, see VG Köln, verdict from 3 May 1978, 9 K 2565/77, DVBl. 510 (511). Affirmatively and moreover *inter alia* referring to de-facto recognition by the United Kingdom and France due to (accidental) acceptance of Sealand passports: *Leisner*, Legal expert opinion on the jus gentium of the Principality of Sealand, 1975, available at http://www.principality-of-sealand.eu/pdf/e_opinion_leisner.pdf, last accessed 29 April 2014.

286 For a detailed description of this distinction and the discussion with regard to further criteria see Grant, 37 Colum. J. Transnat'l L. 1998-1999, 403 (437 et seqq.).

Recognition has been regarded either as a mere reflection, declaring a statehood that has already been achieved, or as constitutive element for a state – and in fact, it can hardly be denied that recognition will be important in the process of state creation, such as in the cases of Bosnia-Herzegovina and European Micro-States[287], where especially the United States and the European Community successfully set up a list of preconditions for their recognition.[288] Yet despite its political importance – or maybe in fact because of it – recognition has not gained acceptance as a constitutive element for a state, neither within the international community nor within the scientific community.[289] "An entity is not a State because it is recognised; it is recognised because it is a State."[290] Recognition is thus predominantly considered a performative statement, declaring that a certain entity fulfils the conditions of statehood as required by international law.[291] This understanding is also reflected by the MCRDS[292]: Its Article 3 commences with the statement that

> *"The political existence of the state is independent of recognition by the other states."*

The relevance of recognition is also referred to in Article 6:

> *"The recognition of a state merely signifies that the state which recognises it accepts the personality of the other with all the rights and duties determined by international law."*

This understanding strongly implies that the aspect of recognition is of political relevance alone.

2. Independence

The independence of a putative state has also been discussed as a further criterion. Despite the obvious overlap with the attribute 'sovereignty,'[293] authors found various approaches to define this alleged requirement. The sources argue, for

287 See *Grant*, 37 Colum. J. Transnat'l L. 1998-1999, 403 (440 et seq., 447).

288 See *Grant*, 37 Colum. J. Transnat'l L. 1998-1999, 403 (442 et seq.).

289 See *Kunig*, Jura 1986, 344 (346).

290 *Crawford*, p. 93, adding that entities that do not fulfil the criteria might nevertheless, under certain circumstances, still be recognised as states; *Sterio*, 39 Denv. J. Unt'l L. & Pol'y 2010-2011, 209 (215).

291 See *Lauterpacht*, 53 Yale L. J. 1943-1944, 385 (385).

292 For a brief summary of the history and relevance of the convention see below § 3. D. 3.

293 See *Huber* in the *Island of Palma Case*: "Sovereignty in the relations between States signifies independence," 2 RIAA 829, 838 (1928).

example, that the substantial illegality of origin, such as a formation of the putative state under belligerent occupation, would cast doubts on independence.[294] However, independence as a fairly indeterminate criterion has been criticised as being of little help: On the one hand with regard to the growing importance of supranational (and at times superordinate) organisations such as the UN, on the other hand with the thought that if political and military independence is also required, there would be a considerable number of entities currently classified as states which might not be properly defined as such.[295]

3. Claim to Statehood

The American Law Institute proposed, in its *Restatement (Third),* that it should be required additionally that an entity must claim to be a state before it can be considered a state.[296] This approach seeks to reflect the situation of Taiwan, claiming to be the Republic of China (and not claiming to be the state of Taiwan) with the result that most of the states in the world do not recognise Taiwan although it meets the criteria.[297] However, this lack of acceptance has little to do with theoretical difficulties. Rather, it can be traced back to the One-China policy of the People's Republic of China, which imposes the condition on its fellow states to break official relations with the Republic of China.[298] Solving this protracted conflict by amending the term 'statehood' does not seem convincing.

4. Other Criteria

Numerous other suggestions have been made to further shape the concept of states, amongst them the need for a popular process as the source of a claim to statehood, external legality (compliance with *jus cogens*) and/or internal legality (democracy and minority rights), organic bonds within the community claiming statehood, and United Nations membership.[299] In some cases, these criteria overlap quite significantly. Some of them alternatively have been named as prerequisites for recognition.[300]

---

294 See *Crawford*, p. 71.

295 See *Grant*, 37 Colum. J. Transnat'l L. 1998-1999, 403 (438).

296 See Restatement 3rd, § 201 cmt. f.

297 See *Grant*, 37 Colum. J. Transnat'l L. 1998-1999, 403 (439).

298 See Restatement 3rd, § 201 cmt. f.

299 For a list with further comments see *Grant*, 37 Colum. J. Transnat'l L. 1998-1999, 403 (450 et seq.).

300 See *Grant*, 37 Colum. J. Transnat'l L. 1998-1999, 403 (446).

5. Interim Result

The approaches cited have not made any significant contribution to amending the common international understanding of what is to be considered a state. The failure to establish the above-mentioned criteria can essentially be explained by one basic argument: The recurring attempts at implementing or adding a principle of legitimacy do not correspond with international reality: The ideological fragmentation of the contemporary international community leaves no room for consent over what is to be considered legitimate.[301] For an internationally accepted definition to be codified in a convention, treaty, or resolution, a political level of agreement would be required that has not existed during the last decades.[302] Beyond that, any codified amendment of the statehood criteria might well be reassuring and convenient, but would also likely be either over-inclusive or under-inclusive – and above all it would be challenging to reflect the fluid and controversial character of the definition of statehood: While the use of the term 'state' is historically contingent, its criteria vary over time.[303]

Nevertheless, the doctrine of three elements is still dominant (but not unopposed)[304] in international law. The ongoing discussion itself proves, to a certain extent, the dynamic nature of the concept of state. Additionally, the conserving character of international law with respect to states is another significant factor: Even if a state loses significant characteristics, it usually does not lose its legal status.[305]

D. History

Müller wrote in 1808/09 that there is no concept of state – the state, like all significant abstract ideas, cannot be shoe-horned into a definition.[306] Every new generation gives new shape to the idea, amending or overruling the established understanding of old.[307] Thus, our common state theories are nothing but dead

---

301 *Isensee* in: HStR, para. 15, marginal no. 50.

302 *See Crawford*, p. 31; for further explanation with regard on the Montevideo Convention as the only noteworthy codification of what is required to speak of a state in international law see below § 3. D. 3.

303 See *Grant*, 37 Colum. J. Transnat'l L. 1998-1999, 403 (408, 457).

304 E.g. *Smend*, p. 129 et seqq., criticises this simplifying and naturalistic approach as not suitable for the developing nature of states (p. 169); affirmative: *Krüger*, p. 146.

305 See *Kunig*, Jura 1986, 344 (346). This thought will be examined in more detail further below with regard to failed states and governments in exile, see § 5. B. 1.

306 See *Müller*, p. 16.

307 See *Müller*, p. 16.

and impractical accumulations of concepts which cannot keep pace with life because they are based on the illusion that it is possible to comprehend the state once and for all, whilst the state, in fact, proceeds *ad infinitum*.[308]

To furthermore comprehend the dynamic nature of the concept of state implied by this statement, it is helpful to briefly regard its historical development.

1. Genesis of the Modern State

As early as 1500 years B.C., autonomous units of rule (especially in the Mediterranean region) concluded treaties similar to those in today's international law.[309] The organisation of societies into entities referred to as states was established much later within Europe.[310] The so-called modern state is, according to *Hobbes*, a construct humans created in the quest of peace and for the purpose of ensuring their existence on earth.[311] *Hobbes* used the term 'Leviathan' as a synonym for the state, an artificial 'mortal god' that shapes the will of its members and protects them from their enemies.[312]

The term 'state' in its current meaning is not older than the modern state and derives its origin from the Italian Renaissance,[313] when *Machiavelli* in 1513 opened the Chapter 1 of his "Il Principe" with the observation that all states ("tuttu li stati") and all forces which have or had power over human beings were either republics or monarchies.[314] In this context, 'stato' is to be understood as an abstract term comprising the different forms of government, whereas originally, the corresponding Latin term *status* meant charge, degree, rank, status.[315]

2. The Development of the Modern State towards the Welfare State

Due to its monopoly on the legitimate use of force, the original modern state ensured safety amongst its citizens – a central achievement of the

308 See *Müller*, p. 17.
309 See *Ipsen* in: id., para. 2, marginal no. 3.
310 See *Ipsen* in: id., para. 2, marginal no. 13-20 with an overview of the historical development of states.
311 See *Hobbes*, p. 106.
312 See *Hobbes*, p. 106.
313 See *Jellinek*, p. 131 et seq.; for a detailed exposition with regard to the etymology and the history of the term "state" see *Weinacht* (description of the usage in its current meaning: p. 60 et seqq.).
314 See *Machiavelli*, Chapter 1 p. 3: "*Tutti li stati, tutti e' dominii che hanno avuto et hanno imperio sopra li uomini, sono stati e sono o repubbliche o principati.*"
315 See *Isensee* in: HStR, para. 15, marginal no. 63.

16th century.[316] After this had been achieved, the principle of the rule of law was and is to answer to the citizens' need to be protected against the mighty state itself and to be provided with liberty – hence human rights, division of powers, and democracy began to be implemented, especially during the 18th century.[317] The liberalisation of society and the industrialisation subsequently lead to the necessity to protect citizens from the risks of a free market – a precondition for the development of the welfare state which has its origins in the 19th century.[318]

3. Montevideo-Convention

a) Content

The MCRDS from 26 December 1933 is the most widely accepted source providing a definition of statehood.[319] It was signed by the representatives of 19 pan-American states, and was ratified by only five of them.[320] It is referred to as (mere) codification of customary international law, or "soft law."[321] One of its purposes was to set up clear attributes for a state in order to establish a distinction between an intentional legal theory and mere political influences, especially from powerful states.[322] Its key declaration, Article 1, reads as follows:

> "*The state as a person of international law should possess the following qualifications: (a) a permanent population; (b) a defined territory; (c) government; and (d) capacity to enter into relations with the other states.*"

Though it primarily reflects the attributes also included in the doctrine of three elements, the achievement of the codification of statehood has been described as a significant touchstone reflecting ideas prevalent at the time of the convention's framing.[323]

---

316 See *Isensee* in: HStR, para. 15, marginal no. 118.

317 See *Isensee* in: HStR, para. 15, marginal no. 118.

318 See *Jellinek*, p. 174 et. seqq.; *Isensee* in: HStR, para. 15, marginal no. 118.

319 See *Grant*, 37 Colum. J. Transnat'l L. 1998-1999, 403 (403).

320 See *Grant*, 37 Colum. J. Transnat'l L. 1998-1999, 403 (456). The signing states were Argentina, Brazil, Chile, Columbia, Cuba, Dominican Republic, Ecuador, El Salvador, Guatemala, Haiti, Honduras, Mexico, Nicaragua, Panama, Paraguay, Peru, United States, Uruguay, Venezuela.

321 See *Grant*, 37 Colum. J. Transnat'l L. 1998-1999, 403 (456).

322 See *Sterio*, 39 Denv. J. Unt'l L. & Pol'y 2010 2011, 209 (215 et seq.).

323 See *Grant*, 37 Colum. J. Transnat'l L. 1998-1999, 403 (416).

b) Criticism

The criterion (d), the "capacity to enter into relations with the other states," has received the most scrutiny amongst scholars, *inter alia* for the reason that it is a consequence of statehood depending on the status and the situation of particular states, rather than a prerequisite for statehood.[324] Indeed, it is unclear in which practical situation a sovereign state might not be able to enter into relations with other states – except for those cases in which the other states refuse to establish diplomatic relations.[325] In this instance, however, it is not the *capacity* of the respective entity to build up such relations that is in question, but rather the actual *possibility*. Beside this fairly vague criterion, the remaining attributes (a), (b), and (c) reflect the previously mentioned criteria of people, territory, and sovereignty.

c) Relevance for Sinking Islands States

The MCRDS binds no-one but its signatories and thus does not exert any binding force for more than 90% of the states worldwide. Beyond that, even within the group of signatory states, the degree of obligation is low: The wording "*should* possess" in Article 1 MCRDS[326] indicates a non-binding nature of this agreement – as opposed to what the terms 'has to' or 'shall' would imply. Yet it cannot be denied that despite considerable criticism, the MCRDS as the sole codification of the criteria for statehood is quoted frequently even by its critics and thus sets standards in international law.[327]

Hence, (only) the indirect impact of the MCRDS is relevant in the context of sinking islands states. Put in more concrete terms, out of the four elements only (b), "a defined territory,"[328] is central in the context of this thesis. The MCRDS thus does not provide any theoretical difficulties for the present study that would extent beyond those given in the doctrine of three elements.[329]

Furthermore, one crucial circumstance must be taken into account: The MCRDS was only meant to set up rules on how new states were created, not on the question under which conditions an already established and recognised state

---

324 See *Crawford*, p. 69.

325 Yet for the purpose of clarification it has to be added that this criterion is meant to ensure the capacity to fulfil international treaty obligations, *Grant*, 37 Colum. J. Transnat'l L. 1998-1999, 403 (414).

326 Italics added.

327 See *Grant*, 37 Colum. J. Transnat'l L. 1998-1999, 403 (408).

328 Art. 1 MCRDS.

329 Thus, the question if the MCRDS set rules of customary law need not be answered.

could lose its statehood.[330] The overall view therefore suggests the assumption that the criteria of the MCRDS are not to be considered as *jus cogens* for the question of whether a sinking island state ceases to exist as a state.

4. San Francisco Conference

The San Francisco Conference was held from 25 April 1945 to 26 June 1945 to develop the UN Charter which was then signed by 50 states.

The second committee of the first commission, responsible for questions concerning the membership in the UN, did not lead a discussion about the concept of states – although the delegate of Uruguay did point out the necessity of a precise legal definition of that term.[331] The explanation basically is the same as for the failure to establish a further constitutive criterion for what is to be considered a state[332]: The difficulties with regard to diverging understandings of an appropriate concept of state could not be overcome.[333] Yet, already in the foundation period of the United Nations, we see evidence of the question of what is to be considered a state being answered on a consensual rather than a theoretical basis: Amongst the founding members were Belarus and Ukraine, two member states of the former USSR, which *de facto* were not sovereign. Yet their membership was accepted as a result of negotiations – initially, the USSR had claimed the membership of all 16 Soviet republics.[334]

Furthermore, India did not gain independence until Great Britain's 'India Independence Act' was passed on 18 July 1947. Nevertheless, it has been a comprehensively recognised member of the United Nations since 1945.[335]

The delegate of the Philippines tried to introduce the concept of 'nation' instead of 'state' because the latter would not allow the Philippines to become a member of the United Nations at the time.[336] The Philippines did not gain independence until later, when the Treaty of General Relations and Protocol between the USA and the Philippines was signed in Manila on 4 July 1946.[337] Nevertheless,

330 See *Grant*, 37 Colum. J. Transnat'l L. 1998-1999, 403 (435).
331 See *Darsow*, p. 112.
332 See above § 3. C. 5.
333 See *Darsow*, p. 112.
334 See *Darsow*, p. 116.
335 See *Verdross/Simma*, § 394.
336 See *Darsow*, p. 117.
337 Its full text is accessible at http://treaties.un.org/doc/Publication/UNTS/Volume 7/v7.pdf, pp. 3-13, last accessed 29 April 2014.

the Philippines became a founding member of the UN and were referred to – in spite of their lack of sovereignty – as one of the founding 'states.'

In light of these cases, one important fact should be stressed: The founding members, of course, did not decide that Belarus and Ukraine, for example, should be founding members despite their not sufficiently meeting statehood criteria. Instead, a very formal solution was found for considering these states as sovereign despite their current dependence on the USSR: The delegate of the USSR stressed the right (in those days very theoretical) of these two 'states' to leave the USSR.[338] This was sufficient in the end. Conversely, we have an example for not acknowledging statehood despite the fulfilment of the criteria in South Rhodesia: When the white minority regime proclaimed its independence in 1965, no state recognised the entity as a state since it violated principles of legal justice and self-determination.[339]

In most cases, international practice is aligned with the legal criteria of international law.[340] Yet in some cases political interests – i.e. a broad consensus – supersede international principles.[341]

5. Growing Importance of Statehood

The still valid understanding of a state based on the doctrine of three elements gained worldwide acceptance during the 20th century – especially younger states in Africa and Asia adopted it because it corresponded to their desire for independence and participation in international communication.[342] Today, the earth's territory is almost completely allocated to states, virtually no *terra nullius* is left.[343]

In the 60 years since the UN Charter was signed in 1945, there have been fewer than ten state extinctions, most of them voluntary, such as the GDR in 1990.[344] During the same period, 128 states (more than 60% of the current UN member states) have been reconstituted or were founded, among them many as a consequence of decolonisation and the collapse of the Soviet Union.[345]

---

338 See *Darsow*, p. 116.
339 See *Verdross/Simma*, § 386.
340 See *Verdross/Simma*, § 385.
341 See *Kriele*, § 18, p. 82; *Verdross/Simma*, § 385.
342 See *Isensee* in: HStR, para. 15 No. 54.
343 See *Shaw*, NYIL 13 (1982), 61 (82).
344 See *Crawford*, p. 715, see also a list of the respective states on p. 716.
345 See *Crawford*, p. 715.

The number of entities concerned has thus risen vastly in recent history. In like manner, the spectrum of concurrent and contradictory interests and viewpoints has become wider and less lucid.

E. Interim result

Two key statements can be made with regard to the concept of states:

First, since the existence of statehood, the notion of the 'state' has evolved. The contemporary understanding is a result of centuries of evolution and state theory. International law has always been a flexible instrument against the background of historical developments of the international community and mankind itself. Already more than a century ago, the understanding of the state was fluid, notwithstanding a quest for consistency: *Adam Müller* commented that, referring to the notion 'state', the essential fidelity and tranquility can only be shown by movement, while a firm heart requires versatility.[346] He thereby pointed out the necessity of adaptability in the context of defining statehood.

Second, the ongoing debate about statehood criteria proves that the evolution of the concept of states has not come to an end. The notion remains flexible and open to current and future developments in international law.

It furthermore bears noting at this juncture that up until now, state theories primarily had to answer the question of how states are formed and under which circumstances they begin to exist. Additionally, international law has found answers to the extinction of states – for example as a result of succession or annexation.[347] The title of the most comprehensive and most frequently quoted work with regard to international theory of the state, *Crawford*'s 'The Creation of States in International Law,' is evidence of the fact that mainly the *genesis* of states has been at the focus of discussion. A state's *extinction* due to sea level rise – or, to put it more abstractly, due to predominantly anthropogenic circumstances[348] – has no precedent in international law and in the history of states.

It is beyond noteworthy to point to the comprehensive discontent with the current understanding of statehood as well as to the lack of a binding codification of statehood in international law.[349]

346 See *Müller*, p. 19.

347 See *Isensee* in: HStR, para. 15 No. 63.

348 See *Jarvis*, 9 Seattle J. Soc. Just. 2010-2011, 447 (455).

349 See *Grant*, Colum. J. Transnat'l L. 1998-1999, 403 (447).

§ 4. Claim to a New State Territory?

A. Introduction

1. Preliminary Remarks

Two major findings from the previous chapters shall be highlighted: Firstly, in all probability various territories will lose their legal quality as 'state territory' within this century. This development will be the result of an expected sea level rise caused by an increase in temperature and thus a change in climate.

Secondly, the contemporary concept of states requires sovereignty, people, and a state territory. This concept is not without opposition and has undergone various modifications over time. It has never been codified in a mandatory fashion. Furthermore, it has thus far primarily been applied to the genesis of states.

This situation can result in two alternative legal consequences with regard to the precise moment in which a state ceases to have a state territory: On the one hand, the state either ceases to exist due to the loss of one of its constitutive elements. It would become a *sui generis* subject of international law, and at the moment it would be unclear which of its former rights and duties would still exist. It is being argued, for example, to accommodate the 'Nation Ex-Situ' as a new category of international actors.[350] Or on the other hand, the state would alternatively maintain its legal status as such despite the loss of its territory. The latter option is only conceivable if the purpose of the state is continued existence. If a state were to be liquidated without legal successor, it would (probably) be dissolved step by step. A preservation of its legal status 'state' would in this case be unconvincing.

The continued existence of a state despite its having permanently lost its territory would thus require two conditions to be satisfied: First, the state would need to have the allocation of a new state territory as a perspective. As all territory on earth is assigned to a state, this territory would have to be transferred from another state or would have to be built artificially. Secondly, a state relocation (and thus the continued existence of the state as an identical legal entity at another location) would have to be possible under international law. This chapter will address the first prerequisite, while the second one will be examined in § 5.

---

350 See *Burkett* in: Gerrard/Wannier, 89 (89 et seq.). This approach will be addressed in more detail further below, see § 5. B. 4.

At first glance, the idea of a state's physical relocation appears to be quite radical. Yet there is only a narrow range of opportunities.[351] This option is one of only two possible adaption strategies.[352] The other alternative would be what *Jarvis* calls an "immigration strategy" according to which the entire population of the respective endangered state would have to immigrate into other states.[353] This solution also would entail most serious legal and political challenges for all parties concerned. So far it is not clear whether the migration would be conducted on the basis of an elaborated strategy or would proceed unregulated. A framework based on which the migration of climate refugees to safer territory could be organized does not exist as of yet.[354] Hence, this thesis will speak of an 'immigration scenario' instead of 'immigration strategy.' Both the 'relocation strategy' and the 'immigration scenario' will be referred to as 'adaption scenarios.'

Considering the first adaption scenario, the relocation of entire states while maintaining their legal status, the required state territory can be transferred to the respective nation either voluntarily or to settle a claim. The first option, a voluntary transaction, is highly unlikely – albeit not impossible. The second option, the settlement of a claim, requires the existence of such a claim.[355]

Such a claim could either stem from a contract under international law or it could be deduced from non-contractual international law. Contractual transfers from one state to another have been the main area of application so far.[356] Yet a contract according to which a certain state commits itself to assigning a part of its territory to an endangered state for the purpose of state relocation does not exist so far.

Hence, in this chapter international law shall be examined with regard to arguments and counter-arguments for a potential claim of endangered states to a new state territory.

351 See *Brunnée* et al. in: Lord et al., 1 (1) para. 1.01.

352 See *Jarvis*, 9 Seattle J. Soc. Just. 2010-2011, 447 (449).

353 See *Jarvis*, 9 Seattle J. Soc. Just. 2010-2011, 447 (449); a detailed comparison of the "Global Immigration Adaptation Strategy" and the "Relocation Adaptation Strategy" can be found at p. 462 et seqq.

354 See *Millar et al.* in: Gerrard/Wannier, 433 (433).

355 In U.N. Doc. E/CN.4/Sub.2/AC.4/2004/CRP.1, p. 4, para. 10 the author poses the question of whether the population of a state has a right to remain a collectivity.

356 See *Graf Vitzthum* in: HStR, § 16 No. 10.

2. Relevant Legal Sources of International Law

First, a brief description of the legal sources in this field of international law is provided to outline its peculiarities for the present study and elucidate the subsequent structure of examination.

International law related to the protection of mankind against threats caused by climate change has become a distinct field, also being referred to as 'climate change law,' or with regard to states' responsibility 'climate change liability,'[357] respectively.

Art. 38(1)(a)-(d) Statute of the ICJ lists four sources of international law. These sources can be summarised as treaties, international customs, general principles of law and several subsidiary sources.[358] Beyond that, binding decisions of international organisations and judgments of international courts or tribunals shape international environmental law.[359]

These five sources, however, only describe what is being referred to as 'hard' law, i.e. law with the purpose of creating binding obligations.[360] Besides these binding obligations, international law comprises non-binding rules. This so-called 'soft' law consists of treaties with soft obligations (legal soft law), non-binding or voluntary resolutions and codes of conduct formulated and accepted by international and regional organisations (non-legal soft law) as well as statements prepared by individuals in a non-governmental capacity, but which purport to lay down international principles.[361]

This latter field of soft law is often underestimated.[362] Here, consideration shall also be given to it for the following reasons: Firstly, at least with regard to the adequate expectation of compliance, there is no need to distinguish between the categories of 'hard' and 'soft' law.[363] Secondly, soft law establishes rules of behaviour and thereby points towards the direction of formally binding obligations[364]

---

357 On "climate change law," see *Verheyen*, p. 138. On "climate change liability," see *Brunnée* et al., in Lord et al., 23 (23) para. 3.02.

358 See *Sands*, p. 94.

359 See *Sands*, p. 94. The reference quoted there (*International Law Commission, Draft Articles on State Responsibility, Part 2, Art. 5 (1), "Report of the ILC to the United Nations General Assembly," U.N. Doc. A/44/10, 218 (1989)*) does not, however, comprise the cited information.

360 See *Sands*, p. 95.

361 See *Chinkin*, 38 Int'l & Comp. L.Q. 1989, 850 (851).

362 See *Brunnée et al.* in: Lord et al., 23 (42).

363 See *Lowe* in: Boyle/Freestone, 19 (30).

364 See *Peel* in: Axelrod et al., 48 (57); *Chinkin*, 38 Int'l & Comp. L.Q. 1989, 850 (856 et seqq.).

(although common claims that former soft law has morphed into customary law have to be treated with caution)[365]. The present study deals with a problem that has not yet occurred, but will most likely transpire in the future – at a stage when today's soft law will most likely have become binding to some extent. The future of international law cannot be predicted, but the quickly evolving nature especially of its complex environmental scope[366] has to be taken into account.

With regard to international treaties – especially those concluded in the field of environmental law – and principles in this field, the following general and specific remarks shall be highlighted.

Treaties can be concluded bilaterally or multilaterally.[367] Art. 2(1)(a) of the 1969 Vienna Convention on the Law of Treaties defines a 'treaty' as "*an international agreement concluded between States in written form and governed by international law, whether embodied in a single instrument or in two or more related instruments and whatever its particular designation.*" The question of whether or not a treaty establishes obligatory duties has to be considered in each individual case – many treaties are non-binding declarations of goodwill, which nevertheless can contribute to the evolution of customary international law.[368]

The number of international treaties relating to the environment increased significantly after the 1980s but has slowed down recently.[369] In the year 2005, a total of 272 treaties and other agreements existed in the field of the environment.[370] In addition, a considerable number of over 2,000 bilateral environmental agreements existed at that time.[371] However, within the regime of international environmental law there is no treaty (equivalent, for example, to the Universal Declaration of Human Rights) summarising the general rights and obligations of the international community with respect to environmental matters.[372] Therefore, the question of whether the treaties dealing with environmental duties of states are to be considered 'self-contained regimes,' which preclude the applicability of general customary law between the parties, does not seriously

365 See *Chinkin*, 38 Int'l & Comp. L.Q. 1989, 850 (856).
366 See *Brunnée* et al., in Lord et al., 1 (1) para. 1.02.
367 See *Sands*, p. 96.
368 See *Wolfrum*, DVBl. 1984, 493 (494).
369 See *Sands*, p. 97.
370 See U.N. Doc. UNEP/Env.Law/2005/3, p. iii.
371 See *Sands*, p. 98.
372 See *Tomuschat* in: Hestermeyer et al., 3 (6); *Sands*, p. 190. Remarks on the Kyoto Protocol and The United Nations Convention on Climate Change will be made below, see § 4. B. 4. e.

arise.[373] This can only be the case when there is a distinct set of primary rules that precludes general rules in accordance with the dictum *lex specialis derogat legi generali* (a law governing a specific matter takes precedents over a law governing a general matter), which is applicable in international law.[374] Environmental treaties can, together with existing institutions and additional decisions in the field of climate change, as a whole be referred to as legal regime; this, however, does not exclude the application of customary environmental law.[375]

In this context, some SIDS anticipated problems when signing or ratifying the UNFCCC[376] and thus stressed that joining this framework

> *"shall, in no way, constitute a renunciation of any rights under international law concerning state responsibility for the adverse effects of climate change, and that no provisions in the Convention can be interpreted as derogating from the principles of general international law."*[377]

Environmental treaties, which aim to impose duties on signatory states so far predominantly focus on mitigation strategies instead of concretising adaption obligations[378] or loss and damage. Despite their recognition as important elements of the climate regime since its inception, so far treaties have been constrained by procedural and especially by political factors.[379]

Customary international environmental law thus has to deal with those problems that are not solved satisfactorily (e.g. by means of a treaty) by ecological policy.[380] This especially applies to 'loss and damage' strategies such as liability.

Therefore, general rules and principles (which are also referred to in relevant treaties) shape and characterise international environmental law, structure this part of law by providing the common scaffolding,[381] and – with regard to adaption as

---

373 Yet *Voigt*, 77 Nordic J. of Int. L. 2008, 1 (3 et seq.) addresses this question in a brief subchapter with the same result.

374 See *Simma/Pulkowski*, EJIL 2006, (485 et seqq.).

375 See *Verheyen*, p. 139.

376 See *Werksman* in: Gerrard/Wannier, 409 (415).

377 Declaration by Parties, UNFCCC, Fiji. Kiribati, Nauru, and Papua New Guinea made similar remarks. Declarations available at http://unfccc.int/essential background/convention/items/5410.php, last accessed 29 April 2014.

378 See *Verheyen*, pp. 138, 142; *Voigt*, 77 Nordic J. of Int. L. 2008, 1 (4 et seq.), both of whom point at the Kyoto Protocol and the UNFCCC as the most noteworthy legal regimes with regard to climate change prevention.

379 See *Yamin/Depledge*, p. 213.

380 See *Epiney*, AVR 1995, 309 (311).

381 See *Peel* in: Axelrod et al., 48 (57).

well as loss and damage strategies this thesis is focussing on – play a more significant role than international treaty law. These general rules and principles can be established rules as well as emerging soft law.[382] A clear demarcation is not possible.[383] This makes it necessary to examine their characteristics.

3. Legal Nature of Rules and Principles

Although rules and principles in both general and environmental international law are considerably advanced, liability rules in this field are still in their formation process and need to be developed further.[384] This development, however, faces considerable difficulties regarding a categorisation of environmental customary and soft law.[385] Overall, there is a high degree of legal uncertainty regarding status, content, and legal consequences of this crucial part of environmental law.[386] This is also due to the absence of clear judicial authority and to conflicting interpretations of the numerous actors – not only authors – involved.[387] The environmental scope of international law, thus, is currently a *laissez-faire* system with rare explicit constraints on state sovereignty.[388] Several factors which have to be given consideration for the purpose of interpretation make it more difficult to shape these legal concepts: The source of the principle can be relevant, as can the facts and circumstances of each case, especially the environmental and other consequences of the particular incident or activity.[389] Generally, principles in international environmental law are of quite an abstract nature and serve as guidelines rather than provide clearly defined regulations.[390]

Nevertheless, the general applicability of principles in international jurisdiction has been stressed, *inter alia*, in the *Iron Rhine Case*, where the arbitral tribunal confirmed the existence and applicability of 'principles of international environmental law.'[391] Recalling Art. 31(3)(c) of the Vienna Convention on the Law of Treaties, according to which "any relevant rules of international law applicable in

382 See *Beyerlin*, OYIL 2007, 425 (447).
383 See *Beyerlin*, OYIL 2007, 425 (447).
384 See *Tomuschat* in: Hestermeyer et al., 3 (6); *Epiney*, AVR 1995, 309 (311 et seqq.).
385 A descriptive summary regarding the status of academic discussion in that regard is made by *Beyerlin*, OYIL 2007, 425 (429-433).
386 See *Beyerlin*, OYIL 2007, 425 (446).
387 See *Sands*, p. 187; *Iron Rhine Case*, para. 58.
388 See *Birnie* et al., p. 2.
389 See *Sands*, p. 187 et seq.
390 See *Hobe*, p. 519.
391 See *Iron Rhine Case*, para. 223.

the relations between the parties" shall be taken into account for the purpose of interpretation, the arbitrators pointed out that provisions of general (and thus also environmental) international law are applicable to the relation between parties.[392]

In the *Gentini Case*, the appellate body distinguished rules and principles in the following way: Rules can be divided into rules of arts and rules of government, are essentially practical, and, most notably, binding.[393] They are applicable in an all-or-nothing-fashion.[394] A rule can thus be divided into certain objective elements whose cumulative existence leads to a defined legal consequence. A principle, on the contrary, expresses a general truth by which our actions are guided; it serves as a theoretical base for the various acts of life – applied to reality it can lead to one consequence or another.[395] Principles, therefore, do not necessarily point to only one possible result but can be used to argue in a specific direction – whereas another principle might be used to argue in the opposite direction.[396] Nevertheless, principles – just like rules – can have international legal consequences (which is what makes the pricinple appealing particularly for developing countries in order to support their inclusion into international environmental treaties).[397] In contrast to mere preambular statements, principles embody legal standards of a more general nature than commitments as they do not specify particular actions.[398]

However, even amongst those authors using the terminology 'rules' and 'principles,' these distinctions are not consistently obeyed.[399] In this thesis, the term 'principle' or 'rule' shall therefore not prejudge the status of the respective legal statement. This only leads to "utter confusion."[400] The "no harm rule," for example, is also referred to as the "no harm principle."[401] The crucial issue here is the proper identification of the characteristics of a special legal instrument rather than the assignment to a certain category.[402] Thus, in the present thesis, the legal

392 See *Iron Rhine Case*, para. 58.

393 See *Gentini Case*, p. 556; the umpire Ralston at this point translates the entry of "règle" in the Bourguignon & Bergerol's Dictionnaire des Synonyms.

394 See *Dworkin*, p. 24.

395 See *Gentini Case*, p. 556.

396 See *Dworkin*, p 26.

397 See *Sands*, p. 189.

398 See *Bodansky*, 18 Yale J. Int'l L. 1993, 451 (501).

399 See the summary of *Beyerlin*, OYIL 2007, 425 (429-433).

400 *Beyerlin*, OYIL 2007, 425 (433).

401 "No harm rule": *Voigt*, 77 Nordic J. of Int. L. 2008, 1 (7).; "no harm principle": *Brunnée* et al. in Lord et al., Policy Considerations, 50 (53) para. 4.06. The no harm rule will be examined in detail further below, see § 4 B. 4.

402 See *Beyerlin*, OYIL 2007, 425 (432 et seq.).

quality of each legal instrument under investigation will have to be examined individually, as in almost every case the opinions are considerably divided.

B. The No Harm Rule – Classical Approach

1. Introduction

The most obvious basis for a claim based on transboundary pollution – in the present case by means of GHG emissions – is the so-called no harm rule. It has the same legal effects as Principle 21 of the Stockholm Declaration,[403] which reads as follows:

> *"States have, in accordance with the Charter of the United Nations and the principles of international law, the sovereign right to exploit their own resources pursuant to their own environmental policies, and the responsibility to ensure that activities within their jurisdiction or control do not cause damage to the environment of other States or of areas beyond the limits of national jurisdiction."*[404]

It was described as *the* cornerstone of international environmental law and was reiterated almost verbatim 20 years later in Principle 2 of the Rio Declaration.[405] The principle is the starting point and the basis of international law responding to climate change.[406] The very similar principle *sic utere tuo ut alienum non laedes* ("use your own property so as not to injure that of another") is understood to be equivalent to the no harm rule.[407] Rooted in Roman law, it is one of the oldest concepts available in interstate disputes and does not trigger any specific legal consequence exceeding Principle 21 or the no harm rule.[408] It nevertheless is revealing proof that the ideas expressed in Principle 21 and the no harm rule are by no means a recent development in international law.

Before addressing the question of whether the legal prerequisites of the no harm rule are met in the present case, some general observations will be made with regard to this legal instrument and its codification, Principle 21.

403 See *Tanaka*, ZaöRV 2006, 535 (537), *Beyerlin*, OYIL 2007, 425 (439).

404 Hereinafter: Principle 21.

405 On Principle 21 being the cornerstone of international environmental law see *Sands*, p. 191; *Peel* in: Axelrod, 48 (57 et seq.); *Yamin/Depledge*, p. 68. In Principle 2 of the Rio Declaration, only the following italicized words have been added: "pursuant to their own environmental *and developmental* policies."

406 See *Nanda* in: WJU 2010, 42 (44).

407 See *Tanaka*, ZaöRV 2006, 535 (537).

408 See *Birnie et al.*, p. 216; *Beyerlin* in: FS Doehring, p. 59.

2. Content and History

Principle 21 contains two elements that must not be separated: The sovereign right of states to exploit their own resources and the duty to not cause environmental damage to other states.[409]

The first element is rooted in the principle of permanent sovereignty over natural resources that was already established before the Stockholm Declaration.[410] It includes a state's right to be free from external interference in its own exploitation of resources.[411] The recognition of the international community that it is necessary to co-operate in order to protect the environment lead to the second element, namely responsibility for the environment.[412]

The second element can also be considered as *lex specialis* of the older principle of international law according to which states are obliged to respect the territorial integrity of other states – in the words of the *Island of Palmas Case* from 1928, "the obligation to protect within the territory the rights of other states, in particular their right to integrity and inviolability in peace and war."[413]

The landmark case regarding international environmental law with regard to transboundary harm is the *Trail Smelter Case* from 1941,[414] which included the following key statement:

> "*Under the principles of international law [...] no state has the right to use or permit the use of its territory in such a manner as to cause injury by fumes in or to the territory of another or the properties or persons therein, when the case is of serious consequence and the injury is established by clear and convincing evidence.*"[415]

The *Trail Smelter Case* thus determines two prerequisites for certain pollution to be prohibited by international law.[416] First, substantial damage must have occurred in another state, and second, causation has to be proven unequivocally.[417]

---

409 See *Sands*, p. 191.

410 See *Sands*, p. 191.

411 See *Sands*, p. 192.

412 See *Sands*, p. 192.

413 *Island of Palmas Case*, 829 (838).

414 Confirming the importance of this verdict: see *Bothe* in: FS Steinberger, 83 (92); *Voigt*, 77 Nordic J. of Int. L. 2008, 1 (7), *Birnie et al.*, p. 216; *Tomuschat* in: Hestermeyer et al., 3 (7).

415 *Trail Smelter Case*, 1905 (1965).

416 See *Hinds*, p. 308.

417 See *Hinds*, p. 308.

This precept is referred to as the "principle not to cause transboundary environmental damage," as the "no harm rule" or the "no harm principle."[418] It is of paramount importance for the present study.[419] However, it has to be emphasised that the detailed criteria of this principle are being discussed controversially.[420]

The concept of Principle 21 outlines the idea that a state's sovereignty ends where it infringes upon the territorial sovereignty of another state.[421] This concept has been constantly reiterated on numerous occasions, e.g. in Article 30 of the Charter of Economic Rights and Duties of States[422], which additionally explicates the obligation of all states to enhance their own environmental and developmental policies with regard to their responsibility previously mentioned. Moreover, they are to "enhance and not adversely affect the present and future development potential of developing countries."[423]

Also, in the UN General Assembly resolution 2996 of 1972, the Principles 21 and 22 are reiterated as basic rules with regard to the international responsibility of States concerning environmental matters.[424] Principle 22 of the Stockholm Declaration reads as follows:

> "*States shall cooperate to develop further the international law regarding liability and compensation for the victims of pollution and other environmental damage caused by activities within the jurisdiction or control of such States to areas beyond their jurisdiction.*"

Furthermore, the UN General Assembly reiterated the principle in a more environmental context (with regard to radioactive fallout) in 1961, declaring that

> "*both concern for the future of mankind and the fundamental principles of international law impose a responsibility on all States concerning actions which might have harmful biological consequences for the existing and future generations of peoples of other States.*"[425]

---

418 On the principle not to cause transboundary environmental damage see *Beyerlin*, OYIL 2007, 425 (439). On the no harm rule see *Voigt*, 77 Nordic J. of Int. L. 2008, 1 (7). On the no harm principle see *Brunnée* et al. in Lord et al., Policy Considerations, 50 (53) para. 4.06.

419 *Voigt*, 77 Nordic J. of Int. L. 2008, 1 (17), describes this principle as the "most important primary rule" in the context of state responsibility for environmental damages.

420 See *Clarkson/Wood*, p. 116. For a detailed analysis of this principle see below § 4 B. 4.

421 See *Epiney*, AVR 1995, 309 (320).

422 Hereinafter, the Charter of Economic Rights and Duties of States will be referred to as CERDS, available at http://www.un-documents.net/a29r3281.htm, last accessed 29 April 2014.

423 Art. 30 CERDS.

424 See UNGA-Res. 2996.

425 UNGA-Res. 1629, I. 1.

There is a long list of references to Principle 21, its quotations and the usage of its language.[426] Two further noteworthy examples shall be highlighted: The first time the language was fully incorporated into the operational part of a treaty was the Convention of Biological Diversity from 1992[427] without expressing that this principle's applicability is limited to the scope of the Convention.[428] The second example is Art. 193 UNCLOS:

> *"States have the sovereign right to exploit their natural resources pursuant to their environmental policies and in accordance with their duty to protect and preserve the marine environment."*

In this text similar to Principle 21, the word 'responsibility' has been replaced by 'duty.' Based on this wording and the historical context this could imply a higher degree of obligation. This implies a shift from a negative obligation to prevent harm to a positive commitment to preserve and protect the environment.[429] Yet it also has to be noted that this Article is not referring expressly to the environment of other states. This affirmation is, however, made in the following Art. 194(2) UNCLOS:

> *"States shall take all measures necessary to ensure that activities under their jurisdiction or control are so conducted as not to cause damage by pollution to other States and their environment, and that pollution arising from incidents or activities under their jurisdiction or control does not spread beyond the areas where they exercise sovereign rights in accordance with this Convention."*

This overall impression leads to the conclusion that the degree of commitment arising from the no harm rule has so far been increasing rather than decreasing with time. This suggests that the legal consequences of an infringement of this principle are also following increasingly strict standards. A possible future development is that state liability might follow stricter rules rather than more tentative ones – although this development might take place very slowly.

3. Legal Status

As pointed out by the ICJ in 1996, Principle 21 reflects that the environment is not an abstract concept but represents the living space and thereby quality of life

---

426 For further examples see *Epiney*, AVR 1995, 309 (317), footnotes 34-36; *Sands*, pp. 198 et seqq.

427 Art. 3, full text available at http://www.cbd.int/doc/legal/cbd-en.pdf, last accessed 29 April 2014.

428 See *Sands*, p. 198.

429 See *Sands*, p. 198 et seq.

for current and future generations.[430] The existing general obligation of states to ensure that activities within their jurisdiction respect the inviolability of the environment of other states has by now been incorporated into international environmental law,[431] which is why it is to be considered customary law.[432] Also, the coexistent no harm rule, as elucidated in the *Trial Smelter Case*, is generally accepted as a rule of customary law and can be described as an extension of the principle of neighbourliness, which is also reflected in Art. 74 UN-Charter.[433]

The ICJ in the *Corfu Channel Case* of 1949 again stressed this understanding, emphasising "every State's obligation not to allow knowingly its territory to be used for acts contrary to the rights of other States."[434]

The limitation of a state's sovereignty reflected in Principle 21 (respectively in the no harm rule), however, is not only a rule of recent customary international law, but also an essence of international law specifying the principle of sovereign equality of states.[435] As all states share the rights of sovereign equality, the sovereignty of one state is always limited by the sovereignty of other states.[436] The obligation to respect other states' territorial integrity therefore is a part of the concept of sovereignty.[437] The balancing of these interests emerges from the law of war and peace.[438] It is thus rooted into the core of international law.[439] Based on the principle of territorial sovereignty, a state can make use of its territory at its own discretion.[440] The principle of territorial integrity on the contrary allows states to defend themselves against adverse impacts on their respective territory, including environmental damage.[441] As both principles are inconsistent when taken as absolute, Principle 21 outlines a balance of interests as originated within general international law.[442]

---

430 See *Legality of the Threat or Use of Nuclear Weapons Case*, p. 241, para. 29.
431 See *Legality of the Threat or Use of Nuclear Weapons Case*, p. 241 et seq., para 29.
432 See *Sands*, p. 191; *Beyerlin*, OYIL 2007, 425 (439).
433 On the acceptance of the no harm rule as customary law, see *Epiney*, AVR 1995, 309 (318). On See *Sands*, p. 197.
434 *Corfu Channel Case*, p. 22.
435 See *Wolfrum*, DVBl. 1984, 493 (494); *Epiney*, AVR 1995, 309 (321 et seqq.); also: *Voigt*, 77 Nordic J. of Int. L. 2008, 1 (9). Further remarks on the principle of sovereign equality will be made further below, see § 4. C. 3. e. bb.
436 See *Epiney*, AVR 1995, 309 (321).
437 See *Epiney*, AVR 1995, 309 (321).
438 See *Verheyen*, p. 146.
439 See *Epiney*, AVR 1995, 309 (321), *Verheyen*, p. 146.
440 See *Wolfrum*, DVBl. 1984, 493 (494).
441 See *Wolfrum*, DVBl. 1984, 493 (494).
442 See *Wolfrum*, DVBl. 1984,. 493 (494 et seq.).

Nevertheless, international environmental case law remains scarce and imprecise, leading to various legal uncertainties.[443] In practice, so far states have only rarely and in very clear cases referred to the no harm rule.[444] This does however not necessarily lead to the conclusion that the degree of obligation is low: International law cannot only be based on an already established practice solely, but also emerges from theoretical reasoning that follows the rules of prudence and logic.[445] The existence of a liability to principally compensate for damage caused by transboundary harm is not questioned and reflects what is being codified in Principle 13 of the Rio Declaration as well as Principle 22 of the Stockholm Declaration.[446]

4. Elements of the No Harm Rule

Given that it is the most important primary rule for a state to be liable for environmental harm,[447] the no harm rule will be examined in the following. This analysation will initially focus on the no harm rule only, i.e. not in the context of other rules, principles, or aspects of general and environmental international law.

The structure of examination will primarily follow the specifications of the no harm rule. This legal instrument concentrates on customary international law in the way the above-mentioned treaties (most notably Principle 21 of the Stockholm Declaration) as well as international case law (most notably the *Trail Smelter Case*) have shaped it.

The criteria of this legal instrument are environmental damage, border crossing, substantiality (i.e. no minor strains), causation, and non-compliance with due diligence.[448]

a. Environmental Damage

Uninhabitability of the claimant's territory due to the rising sea level would need to be understood as environmental damage. Various approaches have tried to establish pre-requisites for this criterion: A narrow definition states that only damage to natural resources (like air, water, soil, fauna, and flora) will constitute

443 See *Epiney*, AVR 1995, 309 (319).
444 See *Epiney*, AVR 1995, 309 (325).
445 See *Epiney*, AVR 1995, 309 (326).
446 See *Voigt*, 77 Nordic J. of Int. L. 2008, 1 (9), see also footnote 18 of this source.
447 See *Voigt*, 77 Nordic J. of Int. L. 2008, 1 (17).
448 See *Epiney*, AVR 1995, 309 (326 et seqq.).

environmental damage.[449] The most extensive understanding,[450] stated in the ILC Draft Principles on the Allocation of Loss in the Case of Transboundary Harm Arising out of Hazardous Activities, reads as follows:

> "*For the purposes of the present draft principles:*
> *(a) 'damage' means significant damage caused to persons, property or the environment; and includes:*
>
> *(i) loss of life or personal injury;*
> *(ii) loss of, or damage to, property, including property which forms part of the cultural heritage;*
> *(iii) loss or damage by impairment of the environment;*
> *(iv) the costs of reasonable measures of reinstatement of the property, or environment, including natural resources;*
> *(v) the costs of reasonable response measures;*
>
> *(b) 'environment' includes natural resources, both abiotic and biotic, such as air, water, soil, fauna and flora and the interaction between the same factors, and the characteristic aspects of the landscape.*"[451]

Noteworthy in this context and closely connected to the understanding of environmental damages is the following definition of 'adverse effects' in the 1985 Vienna Convention for the Protection of the Ozone Layer:

> "*'Adverse effects' means changes in the physical environment or biota, including changes in climate, which have significant deleterious effects on human health or on the composition, resilience and productivity of natural and managed ecosystems, or on materials useful to mankind.*"[452]

This language has been used with only marginal amendments in the UNFCCC to define 'adverse effects of climate change.'[453]

The territories of the endangered states undoubtedly count as environment as they comprise most of the criteria of the narrow definition (i.e. soil, fauna, and flora) as well as additional criteria of the ILC definition (natural resources,

---

449 See *Sands*, p. 706.

450 According to *Sands*, p. 706.

451 Principle 2 of the ILC Draft Principles on the Allocation of Loss in the Case of Transboundary Harm Arising out of Hazardous Activities, available at http://legal.un.org/ilc/texts/instruments/english/draft%20articles/9_10_2006.pdf, last accessed 29 April 2014.

452 Art. 1(2) of the 1985 Vienna Convention for the Protection of the Ozone Layer, hereinafter: Vienna Convention 1985. Available at http://ozone.unep.org/pdfs/viennaconvention2002.pdf, last accessed 29 April 2014.

453 Art. 1(1) UNFCCC.

both abiotic and biotic, the characteristic aspects of the landscape). With regard to the required damage, a detailed elaboration is unnecessary: A total loss of the environmental attributes mentioned above and thus a substantial destruction of a state's environment is the most severe kind of damage possible. The term 'loss' is also used to define 'damage' in the above-cited principle 2 lit. (a) (i)-(iii).

The endangered states' potential future loss of their respective territories thus constitutes environmental damage. This applies especially with a view to the roots of this principle in the context of the principle of territorial sovereignty. Uninhabitability and thus loss of state territory[454] are the most severe infringements possible with regard to territorial sovereignty, as they appear to be irreversible.

b. Border Crossing

The act causing the environmental damage has to be of a transboundary nature to affect the territorial integrity of another state.[455] As illustrated, the effects of climate change are caused by everybody in the world[456] yet only states, the key players in international law, can be held responsible with regard to potential breaches of their duty to control emission activities within their territories.[457]

It is not possible to comparatively assess the potential negligence of endangered states in this regard: Amongst the threatened states, the Maldives are the largest nation with close to 400,000 citizens in 2011,[458] which is less than 0.01 % of the emitting world population. The Bahamas are the largest economy amongst the states considered endangered; their GDP amounts to slightly more than 8 billion USD in 2011, making them no. 151 of the world's economies in this respect.[459] That is quite precisely 0.01 % of the world's economy.[460] It is therefore a matter of course that the respective minute share of causation on the part of the endangered state itself should not be held against it.

---

454 See above § 3. B. 3. b. bb.

455 See *Epiney*, AVR 1995, (309) 357.

456 See *Tomuschat* in: Hestermeyer et al., p. 4; *Jarvis*, 9 Seattle J. Soc. Just. 2010-2011, 447 (455).

457 See *Voigt*, 77 Nordic J. of Int. L. 2008, 1 (9).

458 According to the CIA World Factbook, available at https://www.cia.gov/library/publications/the-world-factbook/geos/mv.html, last accessed 29 April 2014.

459 See CIA Wold Factbook, available at https://www.cia.gov/library/publications/the-world-factbook/geos/mv.html, last accessed 29 April 2014.

460 See CIA World Factbook, https://www.cia.gov/library/publications/the-world-factbook/geos/xx.html, last accessed 29 April 2014.

Also, despite its being tied to the rules of neighbourliness, the no harm rule is not limited to protection of the sovereignty of immediate neighbouring countries – simply because there would be no reasonable justification for this kind of limitation.[461] The crux is that one state's exercise of territorial sovereignty adversely affects other states' territorial integrity; the distance between the places of cause and effect does not matter.[462]

The causes for the environmental damage, i.e. GHG emissions, hence are of a transboundary nature.

c. *Substantiality*

There is a fairly broad consent that the no harm rule does not prohibit just any kind of harm, but only harm that is 'serious,' 'significant,' 'substantial,' 'appreciable,' or similarly qualified.[463] This threshold has to be outlined in order to determine whether this criterion is met with regard to endangered states.

There is no agreed-upon international standard establishing clear rules for environmental damage that triggers liability.[464] Yet intent on the part of the liable party can be excluded from the catalogue of criteria deemed necessary[465] – establishing intent as a necessary criterion would, especially in the case of GHG emissions, undermine any potential claim and thereby run contrary to the purpose of a balance of interests in the way Principle 21 suggests.[466]

Despite problems to define the level of harm in a precise way and subsequent problems in state practice, there can be no doubt that any required level of substantiality is met in the present case: There is no potential balance of interest between territorial sovereignty and territorial integrity that would result in an outcome where the total loss of territorial integrity would not constitute a substantial impact on the infringed party.

d. *Causation*

Causation has been, to some extent, a crucial point in literature discussing compensation for environmental damages based on climate change. In case of a lawsuit, the onus of proving causation – like all elements and facts of an alleged

---

461 See *Beyerlin* in: FS Doehring, 37 (46).
462 See *Beyerlin* in: FS Doehring, 37 (46).
463 See *Handl*, OYIL 2007, 531 (535).
464 See *Sands*, p. 708 et seqq.
465 See *Birnie et al.*, p. 215; *Verheyen*, p. 150.
466 See *Epiney*, AVR 1995, (309) 335.

title – would, according to general international law, lie with the party claiming it.[467] The degree of attention given to this legal prerequisite has experienced considerable variation. *Kehrer* in her thesis "Staatenverantwortlichkeit und Meeresspiegelanstieg" ['State Responsibility and Sea Level Rise'], for example, addresses the problem of proving causation between the action/omission of potential injuring states and occurring environmental damages in a comprehensive chapter on more than 100 pages.[468] Three years later, *Voigt* e.g. simply states that "[t]his causation chain is not discussed here as almost universal international scientific consensus exists on these issues," citing the IPCC-Report from 2007[469] which is also quoted in *Kehrer's* thesis.[470]

For the purpose of this thesis, the present work will distinguish (following both authors referred to above) between problems with regard to the chain of causation (see under aa.) and questions with regard to cumulative causation (see under bb.).

aa. Chain of Causation

(1) Ongoing Discussion and Scientific Level of Knowledge

With regard to the problems concerning the linkage between GHG emissions and (current and prospective) sea level rise, *Voigt's* approach seems for the most part more up-to-date than *Kehrer's* fairly excessive problem description. Most authors come to the same conclusion: The nexus between GHG emissions, climate change, and sea level rise is sufficiently proven.[471] As *Tomuschat* puts it: "That climate change is to be traced back to human activity must be accepted as a simple truth which can no longer be talked away."[472] Today there is no longer any question that global warming is taking place – and that the causation is predominantly anthropogenic.[473] Whereas the causation issue was once the most

---

467 See e.g. *Minquiers and Ecrehos Case*, 47 (52).

468 See *Kehrer*, § 7, pp. 228-332 (i.e. approximately a third of her thesis).

469 *Voigt*, 77 Nordic J. of Int. L. 2008, 1 (15). It has to be added that *Voigt* was only referring to problems with regard to a causation chain between emission of GHG and sea level rise. *Kehrer* considers this specific problem on more than 70 pages.

470 See e.g. *Kehrer*, p. 4, footnote 10.

471 See e.g. *Oschmann/Rostankowski*, ZUR 2010, 59 (63), *Werksman* in: Gerrard/Wannier, 409 (412).

472 *Tomuschat* in: Hestermeyer et al., 3 (3). This quotation however does only touch one single link of the causation chain as will be elucidated in the following.

473 See *Gordon*, 78 U. Colo. L. Rev. 2007, 1559 (1559).

significant obstacle to be overcome in a climate-change suit, it is no longer considered to be impossible to prove.[474]

Nevertheless, a considerable amount of doubt remains regarding causation. One important distinction between the present case (state inundation) and the discussion about a *general* climate change liability, e.g. for certain serious weather events, shall be stressed at this point: According to a recent World Bank Report (and in line with the opposing view of liability for climate change damages), "[a]ttributing causality of disasters to climate change remains intrinsically difficult due to the uncertainties, and complex and dynamic interactions between development patterns, the environment and the climate."[475] This is different in the case of endangered states. Their threat is caused by sea level rise. Causation between climate change and sea level rise does not inherit the aforementioned uncertainties, the complexity, and the dynamic interactions between development patterns, the environment and the climate.

Moreover, the condition is met that the potential damage must be caused by and attributable to the opponent. Art. 2 (a) of the Articles on Responsibility of States for Internationally Wrongful Acts also reflects this requirement.[476] Essentially, emissions are caused only to the smallest degree by a state itself; rather, they are predominantly caused by industrial installations, traffic, households, farming practices, forestry etc., which can be attributed to private actors within said state.[477] Still, in the scope of international law it is the respective state's responsibility to control such activities of private actors.[478] If a state fails to appropriately satisfy such an obligation, it can be held liable for this omission.[479]

To address remaining doubts, the steps within the chain of causation shall subsequently be examined on the basis of the 5th and most recent IPCC-Report. The question is whether sea level rise can be traced back to human activities – basically GHG emissions – and what degree of certainty exists regarding the respective chain link in this causation chain.

The causation chain is established as follows: The increasing emissions of GHG lead to an increase in average temperature worldwide (**step 1**). This

474 See *Faure/Peeters* in: id., 255 (267).

475 *Gitay et al.*, World Bank Report 2013, Executive Summary, p. vii.

476 The Articles on Responsibility of States for Internationally Wrongful Acts will be referred to hereinafter as ARS, available at http://legal.un.org/avl/ha/rsiwa/rsiwa.html, last accessed 29 April 2014.

477 See *Voigt*, 77 Nordic J. of Int. L. 2008, 1 (9).

478 See *Voigt*, 77 Nordic J. of Int. L. 2008, 1 (9).

479 See *Voigt*, 77 Nordic J. of Int. L. 2008, 1 (9).

temperature rise can be traced back (almost) exclusively to human activities, meaning that natural factors are at most a minor secondary cause (**step 2**). The increase of the average temperature leads to a sea level rise (**step 3**).

The warming of the climate is an unequivocal fact.[480] This has led to an average annual sea level rise of 1.7 mm between 1901 and 2010, respectively an average of 3.2 mm between 1993 and 2010 which can be traced back to the rising temperature.[481]

The various factors contributing to sea level rise are primarily thermal expansion of the oceans as well as the transfer to the ocean of water currently stored on land (particularly from glaciers and ice sheets).[482] All these causes can be traced back to a warmer climate (**step 3**).

With regard to **step 1**, the 4th IPCC-Report emphasizes its "*very high confidence* that the global average net effect of human activities since 1750 has been one of warming"[483]. "Very high confidence" means that at least 9 out of 10 experts who assessed the correctness of the underlying data, models, or analysis agreed with a finding.[484] It is the maximum level in the respective scale, there is no category with a higher likelihood. The Summary for Policymakers of the 5th IPCC-Report states that it is "*extremely likely* [i.e. 95-100% probability[485]] that more than half of the observed increase in global average surface temperature from 1951 to 2010 was caused by the anthropogenic increase in GHG concentrations and other anthropogenic forcings together."[486]

In respect of **step 2**, the IPCC-Reports clarify that natural factors only play a minor role. According to the 4th IPCC-Report, the influence of natural impacts (solar and volcanic forcings) on the world climate has *likely* (i.e. 66-100% probability[487]) been a cooling one over the last 50 years.[488] The Summary for Policy Makers of the 5th IPCC-Report concurs that " [t]here is *high confidence* that changes in total solar irradiance have not contributed to the increase in global mean surface temperature over the period 1986 to 2008."[489]

---

480 See 5th IPCC-Report (2013), Summary for Policymakers, p. 2.
481 See 5th IPCC-Report (2013), draft, p. TS-12.
482 See 5th IPCC-Report (2013), draft, p. TS-13.
483 4th IPCC-Report (2007), p. 37, original italics.
484 See 4th IPCC-Report (2007), p. 27.
485 See 5th IPCC-Report (2013), Summary for Policymakers, p. 2, footnote 2.
486 5th IPCC-Report (2013), Summary for Policymakers, p. 15, original italics.
487 See 4th IPCC-Report (2007), p. 27.
488 See 4th IPCC-Report (2007), p. 39.
489 5th IPCC-Report (2013), Summary for Policymakers, p. 17, original italics.

Overall, "[i]t is *very likely* (i.e. 90-100% probability[490]) that there is a substantial anthropogenic contribution to the global mean sea level rise since the 1970s."[491]

These summarised basic findings of the IPCC-Reports, however, fail to convince all lawyers in the field of environmental law. It is especially questioned to what extent a natural cycle of planet Earth might also contribute to climate change.[492] Given the findings of the IPCC just cited, this point of view is hard to comprehend. Based on the data provided, a *cooling* effect of natural impacts has a likelihood of 66-100%, i.e. 83% +/- 17%.[493] Employing the *argumentum e contrario*, this means that a scenario of natural sources having no effect or a warming one has a likelihood of 17% +/- 17%. The overall likelihood has to be considered in light of the Gaussian distribution[494] – that means that in the (unlikely) case of any warming effect of natural sources, it is substantially more probable that this effect is very small. It is, based on the same thought, thus highly unlikely that a natural cycle contributes substantially to climate change.

This ultimately means that there is a very high degree of likelihood that the assumptions of **step 1** and **step 2** are true. At least 9 out of 10 experts consider **step 1** as proven.[495] Thus it is almost certain that this causal step could be proven also in a lawsuit based on expert opinions as a means of evidence. There is a likelihood of 90% to 100 % that **step 2** is a matter of fact.[496] There is no absolute certainty. Yet absolute certainty is not necessary.[497] The ICJ stated that, regarding requirements of evidence, it is certainly aware that

> "*within the limits of its Statute and Rules, it has freedom in estimating the value of the various elements of evidence, though it is clear that general principles of judicial procedure necessarily govern the determination of what can be regarded as proved.*"[498]

---

490 See 5th IPCC-Report (2013), Summary for Policymakers, p. 2, footnote 2.

491 5th IPCC-Report (2013), Summary for Policymakers, p. 15.

492 See *Tomuschat* in: Hestermeyer et al., 3 (3).

493 See 4th IPCC-Report (2007), p. 39.

494 This approach is not entirely accurate mathematically; however, it rather aims at highlighting the very low likelihood that mankind is responsible for climate change only to a small degree.

495 4th IPCC-Report (2007), p. 37.

496 See 5th IPCC-Report (2013), Summary for Policymakers, p. 15.

497 See *Kehrer*, p. 229.

498 *Nicaragua Case*, 14 (40), para. 60.

However, international case law is not consistent regarding the burden of proof in general, and even less so when it comes to causation issues in particular.[499] Nevertheless, in various cases judges did not demand a full burden of proof.[500]

In the *Trail Smelter Case*, the arbitrators considered it very likely that a natural cause – namely lack of sufficient rainfall – also contributed to the damage.[501] This did not change their persuasion that compensation still had to be paid.[502] The only difference between global warming and the *Trail Smelter Case* is the even higher degree of likelihood in the latter case that an additional natural factor amplified the damage. In the case of climate change, it is – as already mentioned – even more likely that natural factors *lessen* anthropogenic factors.[503]

The argument can therefore convincingly be made that causation is sufficiently proven.[504] This would be consistent with the *Trial Smelter Case*. This conclusion applies especially with an eye towards the tremendous effort made to set up a scientific basis *inter alia* for determining human and state responsibility. The scientific level of knowledge has increased significantly. Technological progress, moreover, makes it increasingly easy to furnish the necessary proof even when very strict standards are required.[505]

Nevertheless, whether or not the chain of causation has been proven conclusively is disputed. This leaves a degree of uncertainty whether endangered states could prove this element of the no harm rule in court. Accordingly, states thus far have mostly limited lawsuits based on the no harm rule on very clear cases of causation.[506]

(2) Precautionary Principle

(a) Introduction

The precautionary principle might further contribute to the question of how to legally assess remaining minor scientific uncertainties with regard to causation.

The principle is also referred to as "precautionary action"[507] or "precautionary approach."[508] It is codified in Principle 15 of the Rio Declaration as follows:

---

499 See *Kehrer*, p. 264.
500 See *Kehrer*, p. 264.
501 See *Trail Smelter Case*, 1905 (1930).
502 See *Trail Smelter Case*, 1905 (1930 et seqq.).
503 See 4th IPCC-Report (2007), p. 27.
504 See e.g. *Voigt*, 77 Nordic J. of Int. L. 2008, 1 (15); *Oschmann/Rostankowski*, ZUR 2010, 59 (62).
505 See *Birnie et al.*, p. 217.
506 See *Epiney*, AVR 1995, (309) 352, footnote 185; *Birnie et al.*, p. 212.
507 *Beyerlin*, OYIL 2007, 425 (440).
508 *Zander*, p. 35; *Birnie et al.*, p 136.

"In order to protect the environment, the precautionary approach shall be widely applied by States according to their capabilities. Where there are threats of serious or irreversible damage, lack of full scientific certainty shall not be used as a reason for postponing cost-effective measures to prevent environmental degradation."

The second sentence of this principle is meant to provide a basis for early international legal action to address serious environmental threats despite a lack of full scientific certainty.[509] This sentence, in particular, is referred to as the precautionary principle.[510] The principle is particularly significant in cases where serious and irreversible damages – like those caused by climate change, for example – are impending.[511] It is potentially the most radical of environmental principles.[512] Along with the principle of sustainable development, it is called one of the two most relevant principles in the framework of international environmental law.[513] The principle has been incorporated in numerous international treaties, which often do not, however, explicitly define this principle.[514]

(b) Content and History

The precautionary principle emerged in international environmental law in the mid-1980s.[515] Accordingly, it is one of the younger principles and has since spread throughout the world.[516] Its underlying idea – namely that full (scientific) proof need not be given in case of dangers of wide impact – was already established in 1969 when the international community passed the 'International Convention Relating to Intervention on the High Seas in Cases of Oil Pollution Casualties,' according to which account shall be taken of "the extent and probability of imminent damage if those measures [to prevent, mitigate or eliminate grave and imminent danger] are not taken."[517]

---

509 See *Wold et al.*, p. 166; *Beyerlin*, OYIL 2007, 425 (440), *Yamin/Depledge*, p. 70 et seq.

510 See *Wold et al.*, p. 166; *Yamin/Depledge*, p. 70 et seq.

511 See *Birnie et al.*, p. 137.

512 See *Peel* in: Axelrod, 48 (61).

513 See *Sands*, p. 237. The principle of sustainable development will be addressed further below, see § 4. C. 2. c.

514 See *Zander*, p. 35. A comprehensive analysis of the precautionary principle in international treaties can be found at *Sands*, p. 218 et seqq.

515 See *Sands*, p. 217 et seq.

516 See *Haritz*, p. 136.

517 Art. V(3)(a). Article I of said Convention defines the measures to which the cited Article refers as "such measures on the high seas as may be necessary to prevent, mitigate or eliminate grave and imminent danger to their coastline or related interests from pollution or threat of pollution of the sea by oil, following upon a

In the mid-1980s, the idea was introduced that precautionary action may be justified also from an economic perspective.[518] This approach is taken by the *Stern Review*, for example. In 2006, this comprehensive study compared the costs of preventing global warming with the costs of adapting to its consequences. So far, it is the most comprehensive economic study of climate change.[519] This study concludes that effective prevention of the worst impacts of climate change would cost around 1% of the global GDP annually, compared with a scenario of no action in which the overall costs and risks of climate change will amount to at least 5% of the global GDP each year.[520] If a wider range of risks and impacts is taken into account, these costs could even amount to 20% or more of the global GDP per year.[521] Therefore, the respective necessary actions within the next 10-20 years (based on 2006) will be crucial for the time between 2050-2100, as a lack of action could result in social and economic consequences comparable with those of the World Wars and the economic depression in the 20th century.[522] These findings support the argument for prevention, even despite possible uncertainty, just like the precautionary principle argues.

The precautionary principle is focussing on avoiding delay in action, i.e. it specifies *when* policy measures should be taken rather than of what *type* these measures should be.[523] In 2006, the Stern Review referred to 10-20 years as an adequate timeframe for appropriate measures.[524] Now almost half of this time has passed without substantial progress in addressing climate change. The findings of the study combined with the lack of subsequent progress demonstrate the importance and urgency of the approach taken by the precautionary principle, which accounts for the potential risks stemming from a discrepancy between the emergence of a risk and its having been fully understood.[525] Therefore, precaution is reasonable both legally and economicly.

---

maritime casualty or acts related to such a casualty, which may reasonably be expected to result in major harmful consequences" (Art. I). Other examples for early implementation are listed by *Zander*, p. 34.

518 See *Sands*, p. 219.

519 See *Würtenberger*, ZUR 2009, 171 (171).

520 See *Stern Review*, Summary of Conclusions, p. vi.

521 See *Stern Review*, Summary of Conclusions, p. vi.

522 See *Stern Review*, Summary of Conclusions, p. vi.

523 See *Wold et al.*, p. 167. For a fairly comprehensive elaboration, see *Epiney/Scheyli*, p. 89 et seqq., p. 103 et seqq.

524 See *Stern Review*, Summary of Conclusions, p. vi.

525 See *Haritz*, p. 75.

(c) Legal Status

The legal status of the precautionary principle is rather unclear.

To different degrees, authors argue for a binding legal status. The Rio Declaration's language that "full scientific certainty *shall not be used* as a reason for postponing cost-effective measures"[526] is interpreted to imply the principle's mandatory character.[527] Other authors consider the principle as an obligatory rule of customary law only in cases when it is connected to transboundary harm.[528] Also, the principle is being interpreted as a case of the rule of prior restraint, leading to direct liability for current activities that potentially lead to future damages.[529] Its integration into the Rio Declaration establishes a widely accepted minimum precautionary approach; at the same time, however, authors stress that it is not a binding instrument.[530]

Sunstein concludes that a rational system of risk regulation should not adopt the precautionary principle at all.[531] According to him, the principle encourages decision-making that is not based on facts, but on emotions instead.[532] Probability of harm is, however, a sufficient reason to act.[533] But the principle considers only the severity of possible outcomes rather than to take into account how likely these outcomes are.[534] The precautionary principle can be made operational only because of identifiable cognitive mechanisms like loss aversion.[535] The principle is, according to this view, frequently underwritten by probability neglect.[536] In the context of climate change, this approach would pursue redistribution goals from wealthier countries to poorer ones, an outcome allegedly intended by interest-group manipulation.[537]

For other authors, it remains unclear whether or not the precautionary principle has (already) become a part of customary international law.[538]

526 Principle 15 Rio Declaration, emphasis added.
527 See *Sands*, p. 222.
528 See *Birnie et al.*, p. 143.
529 See *Jacobs*, 14 Pac. Rim L. & Pol'y J. 2005, 103 (127).
530 See *Zander*, p. 37.
531 See *Sunstein*, p. 45.
532 See *Sunstein*, p. 42 et seq.
533 See *Sunstein*, p. 43.
534 See *Sunstein*, p. 43.
535 See *Sunstein*, p. 43.
536 See *Sunstein*, p. 43.
537 See *Sunstein*, p. 45.
538 See *Beyerlin*, OYIL 2007, 425 (440 et seq.); *Jacobs*, 14 Pac. Rim L. & Pol'y J. 2005, 103 (122), footnote 124.

At the other side of the spectrum of opinions it is being argued that the principle shifts the burden of proof as it shortens the time period between the identification of a potential environmental threat and the development of a legal response.[539]

Case law with regard to the principle is also not clear. The ICJ first addressed the precautionary principle in the 1995 *French Nuclear Test II Case*.[540] The court, however, dismissed the case due to formal reasons.[541] This is only one example for the reluctance of international tribunals to base rulings in which the principle is interpreted as a general principle of international law.[542]

In 1998, the Appellate Body of the WTO had to decide a case between the European Community and the United States as well as Canada on hormones in meat.[543] The European Community was of the opinion that the precautionary principle is "a general customary rule of international law or at least a general principle of law"[544] whereas the United States clearly rejected this interpretation and added that "it may be characterised as an 'approach' – the content of which may vary from context to context."[545] Canada concurred, interpreting the "precautionary approach or concept as an emerging principle of international law, which may in the future crystallise into one of the general principles of law recognised by civilised nations."[546] The Appellate Body recognised the ongoing discussion about the status of the precautionary principle in international law.[547] It considered a decision about this important but abstract question not necessary and "probably imprudent" for the Appellate Body.[548]

More recently, in the Advisory Opinion 2011 of the International Tribunal for the Law of the Sea, the Chamber highlighted the numerous incorporations of the precautionary principle into international treaties.[549] It therefore concluded that "this has initiated a trend towards making this approach part of customary

---

539 See *Wold et al.*, p. 167.

540 See *Zander*, p. 37.

541 See *Nuclear Test II Case*, 288 (306 para. 64, 307 et seq. para. 68).

542 See *Zander*, p. 72; see also *Peel* in: Axelrod, 48 (61), with further examples of judicial cautiousness.

543 See WT/DS26/AB/R.

544 WT/DS26/AB/R, p. 6 et seq., para. 16.

545 WT/DS26/AB/R, p. 17 et seq., para. 43.

546 WT/DS26/AB/R, p. 22 et seq., para. 60.

547 See WT/DS26/AB/R, p. 45, para. 123.

548 See WT/DS26/AB/R, p. 45 et seq., para. 123.

549 Hereinafter, the International Tribunal for the Law of the Sea will be referred to as ITLOS. See ITLOS Advisory Opinion 2011, p. 41 para. 135.

international law."[550] The Chamber furthermore called it "appropriate to point out that the precautionary approach is also an integral part of the general obligation of due diligence [...], which is applicable even outside the scope of the Regulations."[551]

The ICJ in the recent *Pulp Mills Case* stated, slightly more ambiguously, "the Court considers that while a precautionary approach may be relevant in the interpretation and application of the provisions of the Statute, it does not follow that it operates as a reversal of the burden of proof."[552]

The current status of the precautionary principle is thus difficult to determine. International case law once again is cautious. *Sunstein*'s approach, though, has to be contradicted. He misinterprets the current understanding of the principle. He is right in pointing out the danger imminent to aspects such as climate change: Abstract apocalyptic threats might lead to imprudent decisions. There is, especially in the context of climate change, a huge danger of lack of objectivity – so he is right in stressing that only facts matter.[553] Yet he seems to interpret the principle in a way that given an abstract risk like climate change, decisions are not based on science, but rather on irrational emotions. He thereby not only underestimates especially the rationality of judges who make decisions and in doing so are cautious in adopting principles. He also focuses very much on the question whether there is an obligation to act. The precautionary principle, however, has a broader scope. The ICJ, as just referred to, does not agree that it causes a reversal of the burden of proof.[554] The court thereby, however, seems to recognise that the principle is not without legal effect, even if it is a minor one.[555] It could e.g. possibly argue for an alleviation of the standard of proof.[556]

In conclusion, the considerable differences among the interpretations of the precautionary principle show that it is impossible to determine the clear current legal status of this legal instrument. These differences are, however, not to be

550 ITLOS Advisory Opinion 2011, p. 41 para. 135.

551 ITLOS Advisory Opinion 2011, p. 40 para. 131.

552 *Pulp Mills Case*, p. 71 para. 164. *Sands*, p. 222 et seq., nevertheless seems to argue for such a shift of burden of proof.

553 See *Sunstein*, p. 45.

554 *Pulp Mills Case*, p. 71 para. 164; different view: *Sands*, p. 237.

555 See *Sands*, p. 224.

556 *Haritz*, pp. 372, 381 summarises her comprehensive elaboration of the precautionary principle *inter alia* by pointing out such an alleviation of proof. *Sands*, p. 222 et seq., even seems to argue for a shift of burden of proof – despite acknowledging that the ICJ ruled differently in the *Pulp Mills Case*.

considered as obstacles towards the principle's application.[557] At the very least it can be inferred that the principle is adequate to act as a guideline for the interpretation of international instruments in cases of scientific uncertainty.[558]

(d) Implications for this Study

The precautionary principle reads as if being shaped exactly for the case of climate change. Global warming causes serious and irreversible threats. The required minimum level of risk to engage in precautionary measures is definitely reached in the case of climate change.[559] With regard to a remaining lack of full scientific certainty, the remarks made above with respect to causation shall be re-emphasised.[560] The uncertainties within the causation chain are becoming fewer and fewer – a development which might already have made it redundant to even resort to the precautionary principle.

Sunstein's concern that the potential of damages linked e.g. to climate change is so alarming that it might lead to dangerous precipitancy is unconvincing. Case law indicates that these worries are unfounded considering international practice.

The precautionary principle is an undeniably important element within the framework of international environmental law. It might not be approved customary law (yet). However, there is no doubt that even as a mere part of international soft law, the principle can give guidance for interpretation – in the present case regarding the requirements for proving conclusively that causation as an element of the no harm rule exists.

Of course, the precautionary principle primarily points at prevention rather than compensation. It aims at protecting the environment, which in the scenario of this thesis is already (about to be) destroyed. The term 'precaution' itself implies mitigation rather than adaption or loss and damage. The precautionary principle however also has to be taken into account in the context of adaption strategies such as compensation.[561] If this is meant to indicate that the principle can serve as immediate cause of action for compensation, this conclusion appears to overstretch both the legal potential as well as the purpose of the precautionary

557 See *Haritz*, p. 373.

558 See *Sands*, p. 228.

559 See *Zander*, p. 36.

560 See above § 4 B. 4. d. aa.

561 *Haritz*, p. 382, draws the same conclusion, namely that the original purpose of the precautionary principle does not hinder its application to the scope of compensation for climate change damages.

principle. However, it can, when appropriate, give guidance also in the context of compensation.

Concerning the question as to its effect as an 'interpretational guideline' in the context of causation as an element of the no harm rule, the following consequences have to be mentioned: In terms of remaining doubts with regard to the chain of causation and its proof, the precautionary principle strongly argues that these slight uncertainties should not lead to denial of the proof of causation. One has to take into account the considerable amount of evidence regarding the causation chain between human GHG emissions and the respective loss of state territory.[562] Remaining uncertainties in terms of causation can be overcome by resorting to the precautionary principle. In this context, it shall be argued for a decent alleviation of the standard of proof regarding possible remaining, minor doubts within the causation chain.[563] This would also be in line with the encouragement proferred in Principle 15 of the Rio Declaration that the precautionary principle shall be widely applied by states.

Most notably, this understanding would also be in line with the following guideline of the World Charter for Nature from 1982:

> "*Activities which are likely to pose a significant risk to nature shall be preceded by an exhaustive examination; their proponents shall demonstrate that expected benefits outweigh potential damage to nature, and where potential adverse effects are not fully understood, the activities should not proceed.*"[564]

In regards to environmental risks, the burden of proof can be reversed so that the benefits of a certain proposed activity are proven to outweigh the potential risk.[565] The precautionary principle argues for a similar approach regarding the proof of causation. It bears repeating that there is no international consensus regarding a reversal of the burden of proof based on the precautionary principle.[566] This thesis does not argue for such a view, based on its recent denial by the ICJ.[567] However, a decent alleviation of the standard of proof based on the precautionary principle is argued for[568] amongst those who view the remaining

562 See above § 4. B. 4. d. aa. (1).
563 See Similar: *Jacobs*, 14 Pac. Rim L. & Pol'y J. 2005, 103 (127).
564 U.N. Doc. A/RES/37/7 para. 11(b).
565 See *Zander*, p. 37.
566 See *Zander*, p. 72.
567 See *Pulp Mills Case*, p. 71 para. 164.
568 *Haritz*, p. 372, 381 likewise summarises her comprehensive examination of the precautionary principle with the finding that it is capable to alleviate the burden of proof in the context of climate change liability.

uncertainties within the causation chain between human GHG emissions and flooded island states as thwarting to furnish the respective proof of causation.

bb. Cumulative Causation

Further problems regarding state liability for damages caused by climate change arise in the context of cumulative causation. State responsibility is shaped for dealing with bilateral conflicts.[569] This complicates the matter of liability if a common good like the air or the sea is damaged.[570] As every state contributes to the causes of climate change, this raises the question of whether the *conditio sine qua non formula* applies individually for every state.[571] According to this formula, a contribution may only then be considered as causal if the consequences would not apply, if – hypothetically – the contribution would not have occurred.[572] In the case of air pollution it therefore has been argued that it is impossible to justify a liability as it is impossible to assign a certain emission to certain damage.[573] Closer based on the *conditio sine qua non fomula*: Even in the hypothetical scenario that a single state does all it can be expected of it to reduce its GHG emissions, this would not change the fact that the territories of endangered states will be flooded. Even if one of the major emitting countries were to undertake drastic measures to reduce its emissions, this would lead to an only marginal delay. This reasoning seems to indicate that due to manifold causes, it is impossible to ascertain liability for any climate change damages caused by states.

Some authors therefore argue that a limitation of the no harm rule would be necessary. With regard to CO2-concentrations in the atmosphere, they point out that this legal instrument should not provide any possibility of legal defence for the infringed party.[574] This view is held due to the problems caused by a cumulative causation, as well as the absence of any "planning element."[575] The latter term aims to point out the absence of coordination regarding emission rules within the international community. This is aggravated by problems with the attribution of air pollution that makes it, according to some authors, impossible to apply the no harm rule in cases of transboundary air pollution.[576]

---

569 See *Hobe*, p. 534.

570 See *Hobe*, p. 534.

571 Regarding the applicability of this formula in international law see *Castellanos-Jankiewicz*, p. 9 et seq.

572 See MüKo-*Oetker*, Vol. 2, § 249, marg. no. 103.

573 See *Schröder*, DVBl. 1985, 1173 (1175); *Epiney*, AVR 1995, (309) 354.

574 See *Wolfrum*, DVBl. 1984, 493 (496).

575 See *Wolfrum*, DVBl. 1984, 493 (496).

576 See *Schröder*, DVBl. 1986, 1173 (1175 et seqq.).

The lack of effective international cooperation however should not lead to complete disregard of this legal instrument. This would provide an incentive for parties potentially facing financial obligation to block any progress in this regard, which would be counterproductive for long-term efforts to address climate change. Above all, this understanding would conflict with a state's raison d'être of protecting territorial integrity[577] – a premise which experts emphasise.[578] However, these opinions can be interpreted in their historical context, in that many of these sources were written at a time when the severity of environmental damages caused by GHG and the consequences for certain states' territorial integrity could not yet be determined. In this context, cumulative causation must not be used as an excuse for states to simply not act – as an extension of this conclusion would mean that environmental law could not apply to climate change issues due to its complexity.[579] This result though clearly would not be consistent with the principles of international law.[580]

Overall, these problems regarding cumulative causation are not necessarily obstacles to establishing potential liability. Substantive and procedural issues emerging from a cumulative causation of potential opponents will be examined in more detail in § 4 E. and F.

The *conditio sine qua non fomula* can be applied to cumulative causation in the following way: If all states implemented mechanisms to reduce their GHG emissions to a reasonable level in line with the scientific level of knowledge, a rise in sea levels would not threaten certain endangered states in a way that they will lose their state territories. Therefore, the GHG emissions of all states are causal for the sea level rise.

Concluding, the criterion of causation within the no harm rule is met.

e. *Due Diligence*

There is general consensus that in order to trigger liability, a state must additionally have infringed an objective standard of care.[581] This element is referred to as "standard of care"[582], "wrongful conduct"[583] or "due diligence"[584]. The ARS

577 See *Epiney*, AVR 1995, (309) 333.
578 See *Wolfrum*, DVBl. 1984, 493 (494).
579 See *Verheyen*, p. 177.
580 See *Verheyen*, p. 177.
581 See *Verheyen*, p. 152.
582 *Sands*, p. 711.
583 *Handl*, OYIL 2007, 531 (544); *Tomuschat* in: Hestermeyer et al., 3 (15).
584 *Tomuschat* in: Hestermeyer et al., 3 (16).

use a similar notion termed 'wrongful act' in their title, as well as within their articles.[585] The following section uses "due diligence" to encompass all the aforementioned terms.[586]

This criterion is highly relevant to this study as it determines the rules of state practice. It is the centrepiece of international responsibility.[587] The following section will examine if a state acted without due diligence if it does not ensure that GHG emissions within its territory do not exceed critical limits.[588] The idea of due diligence reflects the condition also codified in the previously cited Art. 2 (b) ARS, i.e. the requirement of a breach of an international obligation in order to trigger liability. This agreement exists despite the fact that neither the *Trail Smelter Case* nor Principle 21 or the succeeding resolutions of the United Nations General Assembly[589] established or refered to such a requirement.[590] In the *Trail Smelter Case*, the lack of establishing clear standards of responsibility can be traced back to the fact that the parties accepted Canada's responsibility for proven damage.[591]

International obligations of states can either be based on customary law or on a treaty.[592] It will be shown in the following paragraphs that a "persistent gap in treaty law"[593] can be seen in international environmental law.

The most important international treaties that concern environmental duties are the UNFCCC and the Kyoto Protocol.[594] The UNFCCC embodies the basic framework for the international response to climate change, while the Kyoto Protocol "nests within the UNFCCC."[595]

The Kyoto Protocol is the first and thus far only legally binding treaty for reductions in GHG emissions.[596] Its original commitment period (2008-2012)[597] was amended during the Doha round in 2012 when the COP reaffirmed that the

585 For example, Artt. 1-3, 15-18, 28-31, 34-37 ARS.

586 In doing so, the argumentation of *Birnie et al.*, p. 215 et seq., that any term containing 'fault' or the like is in fact a tautology is followed.

587 See *Tomuschat* in: Hestermeyer et al., 3 (15); *Verheyen*, p. 169.

588 See *Grote Stoutenburg* in: Gerrard/Wannier, 57 (80).

589 Hereinafter, the United Nations General Assembly will be referred to as UNGA.

590 See *Verheyen*, p. 152.

591 See *Birnie et al.*, p. 216.

592 See *Birnie et al.*, p. 214.

593 *Werksman* in: Gerrard/Wannier, 409 (409).

594 See *Voigt*, 77 Nordic J. of Int. L. 2008, 1 (5).

595 *Wold et al.*, p. 149.

596 See *Brunnée* et al., in Lord et al., Policy Considerations, 50 (55) para. 4.13.

597 See Art. 3(1) Kyoto Protocol.

second commitment period will commence on 1 January 2013 and resolved that it will end on 31 December 2020.[598]

The commitments determined for the states listed in Annex I of the Kyoto Protocol were the answer to an international consensus that the current obligations for these states were inadequate.[599] This obligation is referred to as the hallmark of the Kyoto Protocol.[600] However, the hallmark does not bind the major emitting countries[601], either because they did not sign it (e.g. the USA) or they are not burdened with reduction obligations due to their status as developing countries (e.g. China, India and Brazil).[602] In addition, the Kyoto Protocol aimed at a worldwide emission reduction of 5% based on the emission level in 1990.[603] This however is only a fraction of the necessary amount of reduction.[604] It also does not apply to emissions from the aviation and shipping industries and does not account for changes in land use or forestry.[605]

Thus, for a variety of reasons, the Kyoto Protocol is not a useful international treaty for creating a binding level of due diligence for all states worldwide which would prevent the inundation of endangered states. It is described as a generally inadequate response to the enormous and complex problems related to climate change.[606] Critics pointed out that the striking feature of the climate regime (including the Kyoto Protocol) was that its participants consistently presented it as being based on global cooperation driven by science, whereby science routinely played second fiddle to economic and/or political considerations.[607] Consequently, various scientists recently considered the United Nations negotiations

---

598 See U.N. Doc. FCCC/KP/CMP/2012/13/Add.1, Decision 1/CMP.8, p. 3 para. 4.

599 See *Yamin/Depledge*, p. 565.

600 See *Gordon*, 78 U. Colo. L. Rev. 2007, 1559 (1585).

601 For a list of the top 20 polluters – including pollution caused by a change in land use and forestry – (in that order: USA, (Western Europe,) China, (Eastern Europe,) Russia, Brazil, India, Japan, Germany, India, United Kingdom, Australia, Mexico, France, Italy, Indonesia, Ukraine, Iran, Spain, South Africa, Poland, Thailand) see: http://www.grida.no/graphicslib/detail/top-20-greenhouse-gas-emitters_1072, last accessed 29 April 2014.

602 See *Voigt*, 77 Nordic J. of Int. L. 2008, 1 (5).

603 See Art. 3(1) Kyoto Protocol.

604 See *Gillespie*, 22 UCLA J. Envtl. L. & Pol'y 2003-2004, 107 (117); similar: *Brunnée* et al., in Lord et al., Policy Considerations, 50 (56) para. 4.13.

605 See *Brunnée* et al., in Lord et al., Policy Considerations, 50 (56) para. 4.13.

606 See *Gordon*, 78 U. Colo. L. Rev. 2007, 1559 (1560).

607 See *Yamin/Depledge*, p. 382.

on GHG reduction to have failed.[608] They regard the aim to prevent any temperature increase higher than 2°C as impossible and therefore call for enhanced regional efforts in conceptualising and implementing local adaption strategies in anticipation of a warmer climate.[609]

The key environmental framework, the UNFCCC, has been signed by 194 states and reiterates the no harm rule in its preamble.[610] It is considered to be the main treaty concerning anthropogenic climate change and it is applicable to most issues pertaining to climate change damage.[611] However, it has been criticised due to its lack of substance and a low degree of obligation.[612] Yet its objective could be expedient to shape the extent of due diligence:

> *"The ultimate objective of this Convention and any related legal instruments that the Conference of the Parties may adopt is to achieve, in accordance with the relevant provisions of the Convention, stabilisation of greenhouse gas concentrations in the atmosphere at a level that would prevent dangerous anthropogenic interference with the climate system. Such a level should be achieved within a time frame sufficient to allow ecosystems to adapt naturally to climate change, to ensure that food production is not threatened and to enable economic development to proceed in a sustainable manner."*[613]

Viewed in isolation, this provision is considered to be non-binding.[614] Some experts however have argued that this Article, together with the commitment of Art. 4(2) UNFCCC, is indeed a binding international obligation for all member states.[615] Thus the efforts to stabilise the GHG concentration at a level that prevents dangerous anthropogenic interference with the climate system can then be

---

608 See Axel Bojanowski, "Wirkungslose UNO-Konferenzen: Forscher fordern Ende der Weltklimagipfel," Spiegel Online Wissenschaft, 13 December 2012, available at: http://www.spiegel.de/wissenschaft/natur/gescheiterte-uno-konferenzen-forscher-wollen-klimagipfel-abschaffen-a-872633.html, last accessed 29 April 2014.

609 See Axel Bojanowski, "Wirkungslose UNO-Konferenzen: Forscher fordern Ende der Weltklimagipfel," Spiegel Online Wissenschaft, 13 December 2012, available at: http://www.spiegel.de/wissenschaft/natur/gescheiterte-uno-konferenzen-forscher-wollen-klimagipfel-abschaffen-a-872633.html, last accessed 29 April 2014.

610 See *Brunnée* et al., in Lord et al., Policy Considerations, 50 (53) para. 4.06.

611 See *Verheyen*, p. 144.

612 See *Vanderheiden*, p. 56.

613 Art. 2 UNFCCC.

614 See *Verheyen* in: Koch/Caspar, 20 (40).

615 See *Redgwell* in: Evans, 687 (703); *Verheyen*, pp. 55-67; *Voigt*, 77 Nordic J. of Int. L. 2008, 1 (5), similar: *Haritz*, p. 383, who argues that the need for compliance with both the Kyoto Protocol and the UNFCCC arises *inter alia* from the precautionary principle.

interpreted and operationalised on the basis of current scientific and legal standards.[616] Based on this understanding, certain GHG concentrations (e.g. 750 ppm and above) have to be considered as unacceptable, if the obligatory goal is to prevent global average temperatures from rising more than 2°C.[617]

This interpretation has been challenged with good reason, as the title 'objective' as well as the wording 'should' instead of 'shall' indicate a non-binding nature.[618] Moreover, the wording 'aim' (to reach the 1990 emission levels) in Art. 4(2)(b) UNFCCC suggests only a tentative target of a step-by-step implementation.[619] It is therefore more convincing to consider the cited UNFCCC provisions as non-binding. Nevertheless, the framework is of paramount symbolic importance[620] and therefore its interpretation can give guidance in determining what is to be considered as 'due diligence.'

Neither the Kyoto Protocol nor the UNFCCC contain binding provisions which trigger state liability to compensate states suffering from environmental damages due to climate change.[621] Furthermore, traditional state participation in such regimes which are based on consent, becomes increasingly difficult.[622] This diminishes the probability that binding due diligence standards on a contractual basis can be expected in the near future.

With regard to other views on standards of (obligatory) due diligence arising from customary international law, there are two major approaches in the literature which attempt to define criteria for due diligence. These approaches will be summarised in the following subsections. It bears noting that the academic discussion about this subject has been described as "deeply divided"[623]. The following discussion about due diligence is not to be confused with the discussion concerning the categories 'fault liability' and 'strict liability'[624]. Fault liability is based upon intentional or negligent conduct that constituted a wrongdoing that resulted in damage.[625] Conversely, strict liability (*prima facie* liability) does not

616 See *Voigt*, 77 Nordic J. of Int. L. 2008, 1 (5).
617 See *Verheyen*, pp. 55-67.
618 See *Tomuschat* in: Hestermeyer et al., 3 (18).
619 See *Tomuschat* in: Hestermeyer et al., 3 (19).
620 See *Vanderheiden*, p. 56.
621 Same result: See *Kehrer*, p. 219, who additionally lists UNCLOS in this context.
622 See *Peel*, p. 22.
623 *Birnie et al.*, p 217.
624 See *Haritz*, p. 152 et seqq., who provides a short overview of these two approaches to liability.
625 See *Haritz*, p. 153.

require fault or wrongfulness, i.e. the standard of care does not play any role.[626] There is a broad consensus that a strict liability (irrespective of whether the actors concerned have acted with due diligence) does not exist in general international law.[627]

The following discussion will focus on the measure for wrongful conduct. It outlines points of view which agree that wrongful conduct is necessary for liability, i.e. it presupposes fault liability. In accordance with the terminology used by *Lefeber*, the two major opinions can be divided into those who argue for a 'liability sine delicto' and those who promote a 'liability ex delicto' only.[628]

aa. Liability sine Delicto

Some authors argue that defining 'due diligence' does not presuppose an international treaty or a similar self-imposed commitment. The level of scientific knowledge determines the respective duties, which then in turn have to be considered as measures of due diligence. This is in line with what *Lefeber* termed "liability *sine delicto*"[629].

According to authors who argue from this position, acting with due diligence means compliance with existing climate change policies and the respective regulations which aim at reversing the trend of steadily increasing GHG emissions[630] - as agreed upon in the objective of the UNFCCC. "In essence, the duty is to act reasonably under the circumstances (i.e. not to create unreasonable risks), and the duty is owed to those who are foreseeably at risk from the defendant's behaviour."[631] According to this viewpoint, the increase in scientific understanding of the implications of climate change implies increased knowledge of duty, a duty which is being neglected through excessive emissions.[632]

Verheyen similarly establishes the standards of due diligence based on the following three elements: (i) opportunity to act or prevent, (ii) foreseeability of harm and (iii) proportionate measures.[633]

626 See *Haritz*, p. 153.

627 See *Verheyen*, p. 152; *Tomuschat* in: Hestermeyer et al., p. 16.

628 See *Lefeber*, p. 47-228, overview at p. 47-53.

629 *Lefeber*, p. 145 et seqq. (*sine delicto stricto sensu*), p. 189 et seqq. (*sine delicto lato sensu*).

630 See *Larson*, 21 Mich. J. Int'l L. 1999-2000, 495 (513 et seqq.); *Voigt*, 77 Nordic J. of Int. L. 2008, 1 (10).

631 *Herweijer/Muir Wood* in: WJA, 224 (230).

632 See *Herweijer/Muir Wood* in: WJA, 224 (231).

633 See *Verheyen*, pp. 177-184; also: *Voigt*, 77 Nordic J. of Int. L. 2008, 1 (10).

An opportunity to act, according to this approach, requires that a state does not act where it otherwise could have.[634] The assessment of this criterion has to be based on the findings of the IPCC-Report.[635] This requires every single state to do what it can – even if (in line with the precautionary principle[636]) full scientific certainty does not exist.[637] Effective mitigation measures in this context need to be assessed on the basis of best available technologies based on which states are required to substantially reduce their GHG.[638] The possibility for a state to reduce its own GHG hence is a sufficient opportunity to act.[639]

The second element of foreseeability only requires the state to be aware of the possibility that its behaviour causes damage.[640] The reference point for foreseeability is today's best scientific knowledge.[641] Climate change damages have, at the latest, been foreseeable since the 1st IPCC-Report in 1990.[642] The dangers emerging from climate change have been acknowledged by all states signing the UNFCCC in 1992.[643] This viewpoint also implies that emissions released before that time do not violate any international legal emission standard as there were none at that time.[644]

This approach is convincing for the most part. Yet it is a matter of doubt if in 1990 states could already foresee the consequences that have currently been predicted. The level of scientific knowledge and certainty is increasing constantly, thus it is challenging and somewhat arbitrary to establish a specific moment of enlightenment. It would be more convincing to require general foreseeability of the specific damage at a particular time. Foreseeing a specific damage at a particular time might be more difficult to prove, but it is a more thorough approach to determine a lack of diligence wit regard to a specific damage.

The determination of the third element - proportionate measures - requires a balance of interests. This balance takes into account the technical and economic

---

634 See *Voigt*, 77 Nordic J. of Int. L. 2008, 1 (10).
635 See *Voigt*, 77 Nordic J. of Int. L. 2008, 1 (10).
636 See above, § 4. B. 4. d. aa. (2).
637 See *Voigt*, 77 Nordic J. of Int. L. 2008, 1 (11).
638 See *Voigt*, 77 Nordic J. of Int. L. 2008, 1 (11).
639 See *Voigt*, 77 Nordic J. of Int. L. 2008, 1 (11).
640 See *Kehrer*, p. 167.
641 See *Voigt*, 77 Nordic J. of Int. L. 2008, 1 (12).
642 See *Voigt*, 77 Nordic J. of Int. L. 2008, 1 (12); similar: *Grote Stoutenburg* in: Gerrard/Wannier, 57 (82); *Haritz*, p. 372, who base their arguments on the precautionary principle, see above § 4 B. 4. d. aa. (2).
643 See *Voigt*, 77 Nordic J. of Int. L. 2008, 1 (10).
644 See *Grote Stoutenburg* in: Gerrard/Wannier, 57 (84).

abilities of the respective state, as well as the intensity of the anticipated harm.[645] The magnitude of anticipated harm can lead to the conclusion that the requirements regarding its probability can be lower.[646] *Verheyen* adds that "[t]he risk from climate change posed to States, in particular to small island States is so great (e.g. loss of territory) that States could reasonably be required to reduce emissions much more quickly than is politically intended at the moment."[647] Scientific studies could thus determine the level of necessary reductions in GHG emissions.[648] This would also reflect *inter alia* Principle 18 of the Stockholm Declaration:

> "*Science and technology, as part of their contribution to economic and social development, must be applied to the identification, avoidance and control of environmental risks and the solution of environmental problems and for the common good of mankind.*"

Authors exemplified a scientific approach based on the calculations of the German 'Scientific Advisory Council of the Federal Government Global Environmental Changes.'[649] According to this body, between 2010 and 2050, no more than 750 billion tons of CO2 may be emitted (and only small amounts afterwards) in order to ensure that temperatures do not rise more than 2°C by the end of this century.[650] The probability of achieving this forecast is declared to be 67%.[651] Due to the lack of a worldwide emission certificate system, it is proposed that a *per capita* emission cap could determine maximum emissions per country.[652] This German body is hardly in a position to define the international due diligence standards, but equivalent calculations could be based, for instance, on the data of the IPCC-Report. Acting with 'due diligence' could then be understood as compliance with the standards based on the IPCC's findings.

---

645 See *Verheyen*, p. 183 et seqq.; *Voigt*, 77 Nordic J. of Int. L. 2008, 1 (12 et seq.); also: *Epiney*, AVR 1995, (309) 345.

646 See *Verheyen*, p. 184.

647 *Verheyen*, p. 186, also: *Voigt*, 77 Nordic J. of Int. L. 2008, 1 (12 et seq.).

648 See *Oschmann/Rostankowski*, ZUR 2010, 59 (64), who are following this point of view.

649 See *Oschmann/Rostankowski*, ZUR 2010, 59 (64).

650 See Kassensturz für den Weltklimavertrag – Der Budgetansatz, Sondergutachten des Wissenschaftlichen Beirats der Bundesregierung Globale Umweltveränderungen, Berlin 2009, p. 15. Available at http://www.bmbf.de/pubRD/wbgu_sn2009.pdf, last accessed 29 April 2914. This report will hereinafter be referred to as *WBGU*, Der Budgetansatz.

651 See *WBGU*, Der Budgetansatz, p. 15.

652 See *WBGU*, Der Budgetansatz, p. 31.

The decision to not reduce the emissions of GHG sufficiently is a political one that is due in part to the short- to medium-term economic prosperity derived from the reallocation of resources for production without due diligence in regards to environmental damage.[653] Arguably, if the global community profits from the GHG emissions that are concomitant with economic prosperity, that said community should compensate endangered states for the costs with which they are faced.[654]

According to authors who support this approach, most states cannot be considered to have acted with due diligence in the present case.

bb. Liability ex Delicto

There exists another view which does not entirely contradict the concept of due diligence previously outlined *per se*. This view however denies that liability (thus far) can be triggered. According to this approach, solutions can only be found through mutual agreement, i.e. outside the framework of state responsibility.[655] *Lefeber* refers to this approach as "liability *ex delicto*."[656] In the complex fields of global warming and state responsibility, only the negotiations of states themselves can determine rules of liability[657]. Any "lawyer's trick" aiming at a "short-cut to the desired goal" without the "support at the grassroots" is condemned to failure.[658] In other words, customary international law is appropriate to preserve cooperative agreements.[659] However, it is not necessarily the most convenient way to develop them.[660] The reasoning behind this position is based on pragmatic considerations and can be summarised as follows:

First of all, GHG emissions are not prohibited by international law. Emissions are understood to be an unavoidable outcome of activities undertaken to satisfy humanity's needs and wants, from the automobile production to households' energy needs to prepare food.[661] As all states currently allow activities that contribute to GHG emissions and most of them regulate those emission levels, "some level of emission is clearly not wrongful."[662]

653 See *Larson*, 21 Mich. J. Int'l L. 1999-2000, 495 (514).
654 See *Larson*, 21 Mich. J. Int'l L. 1999-2000, 495 (514).
655 See Tomuschat, 3 (10).
656 *Lefeber*, p. 55 et seqq.
657 See *Nanda* in: WJU 2010, 42 (45); similar: *Kunig*, Jura 1998, 160 (163).
658 *Tomuschat* in: Hestermeyer et al., 3 (28 et seq.).
659 See *von Glahn/Taulbee*, p. 511.
660 See *von Glahn/Taulbee*, p. 511.
661 See *Tomuschat* in: Hestermeyer et al., 3 (15 et seq., 23).
662 *Werksman* in: Gerrard/Wannier, 409 (420).

With regard to various principles in international law, this does not necessarily mean that no liability can be triggered.[663] However, the long history of the ILC, as well as state practice regarding this subject are considered as evidence to the contrary:[664] After decades of struggling with the broad field of state liability[665], the ILC finally decided to address one issue at a time. In 1992, it began with the issue of preventing transboundary harm and subsequently addressed questions regarding remedial measures.[666] The ILC then drafted the rules on the 'Prevention of Transboundary Harm from Hazardous Activities.'[667] It is noteworthy that these rules do not address the question of reparation for past damage.[668] The ILC continued its work with the 'Draft principles on the allocation of loss in the case of transboundary harm arising out of transboundary activities' published in 2006.[669] As the general commentary on the part of the ILC testifies, this draft is considered to be non-binding.[670] This conclusion is furthermore supported by the use of the word 'should' instead of 'shall', as well as the avoidance of the word 'reparation.'[671] Furthermore, the ILC clarified in its comments that after careful consideration, it concluded that issues regarding global commons require separate treatment.[672] As a result of the lack of legal clarity in the ILC's draft principles, liability based on the no harm rule has also been described as "inadequate".[673]

Interpreted within its historical context, it is noted that the ILC takes the position that it is at the discretion of the states to establish a binding liability regime, apart from classical state liability cases and within new problem areas.[674] Ultimately, customary law is the result of state practice.[675] State practice is one of the pillars upon which international law (and the corresponding case law) is based.[676] This further complicates the argument for a state liability based on

663 See *Tomuschat* in: Hestermeyer et al., 3 (23).
664 See *Birnie et al.*, p. 217.
665 See *Tomuschat* in: Hestermeyer et al., 3 (23).
666 See ILC Report, U.N. Doc. A/56/10, at 144 et seq. para. 82 (2001).
667 See ILC Report, U.N. Doc. A/56/10, at 146 et seqq. Para 97 (2001).
668 See *Tomuschat* in: Hestermeyer et al., 3 (24).
669 See ILC Report, U.N. Doc. A/61/10 at 106, para. 66 (2006).
670 See General Commentary, ILC Report, U.N. Doc. A/61/10 at 113, para. 11 (2006).
671 See *Tomuschat* in: Hestermeyer et al., 3 (24).
672 See General Commentary, ILC Report, U.N. Doc. A/61/10 at 112, para. 7 (2006).
673 *Yamin/Depledge*, p. 69.
674 See *Tomuschat* in: Hestermeyer et al., 3 (25).
675 See *Hobe*, p. 191.
676 See Art. 38 (1) lit. b., c. ICJ Statute

customary law, especially in cases where state practice has no precedent for a liability framework for environmental damage, although there may have been considerable efforts in that regard. State liability without stipulated measures is therefore, according to this view, a non-effective tool to achieve the goals of international environmental law.[677] In fact, the only international regime which accounts for compensation in cases of transboundary harm is the Convention on Supplementary Compensation of Nuclear Damages.[678] However, this convention is limited in that it stipulates the primary liability of the owner or the operator, and states are only involved in the provision of insurance or supplementary compensation.[679] The only clear example for a direct and absolute liability of the state for damage is the 1972 Space Objects Liability Convention.[680]

States are obviously reluctant to bind themselves in a field where tremendous financial burdens are impending.[681] In the complex area of environmental damage caused by climate change, it is difficult to replace an international consent by deriving liability rules from customary law.[682] Therefore the only approach which offers a viable solution is the creation of a binding legal regime for climate change damage by way of treaty.[683] International environmental law is inadequate as it does not prohibit transboundary harm.[684] A certain conduct practiced by all states – such as GHG emissions – which is not rejected as unacceptable cannot possibly give rise to reparation claims.[685]

This conclusion is supported by general remarks on international law: As this field of law has a corporate character, its quality depends on the behaviour of the involved actors among each other.[686] It is recommended that international law should not be overstrained in an attempt to derive tailored solutions in individual cases, but to leave it to the state's discretion to advance international law.[687]

677 See *Birnie et al.*, p. 212.
678 See *Handl*, 37 Envtl Pol'y & L. 2007, 116 (121).
679 See *Birnie et al.*, p. 218.
680 See *Birnie et al.*, p. 218.
681 See *Handl*, 37 Envtl Pol'y & L. 2007, 116 (121). This corresponds to the recent discussion of the COP in Warsaw that has been summarised further above, see § 2. E. 4.
682 See *Handl*, OYIL 2007, 531 (544).
683 See *Tomuschat* in: Hestermeyer et al., 3 (6).
684 See *Birnie* et al., p. 217.
685 See *Tomuschat* in: Hestermeyer et al., 3 (26 et seq.).
686 See *Kunig*, Jura 1998, 160 (163).
687 See *Kunig*, Jura 1998, 160 (163).

This view is also supported by the '*Advisory Opinion on Responsibilities and Obligations in the Area*'[688], which the ITLOS published in February 2011. Addressing the question of filling liability gaps of UNCLOS through resorting to customary law, the ITLOS stated to be aware of the ILC's undertakings in order to establish liability rules for acts not prohibited under international law.[689] However, these efforts have not yet led to provisions entailing such liability.[690] These remarks can only be interpreted in a way that customary law does not fill the liability gap.

cc. No Applicability of International Law

A working paper for the United Nations Commission on Human Rights *inter alia* examined the legal challenges connected with the complete loss of some SIDS' state territories and argues for another approach.[691] As early as 2004, the author asked:

> *"Is this a matter of law at all? Is this not rather [...] an exceptional situation in which a practical global solution needs to be found? Would there not be more likelihood of delivering more for the affected communities if the problem were seen as a global responsibility, even if only a limited number of States undertook to admit them?"*[692]

The subsequent urgent call for a comprehensive proposal of an official of a body endued with the respective authority[693] was however left unanswered[694].

dd. Pulp Mills Case – A New Impact?

In 2010, the ICJ made remarks on due diligence in the *Pulp Mills Case* between Argentina and Uruguay. Both countries had signed the bilateral treaty '*Statute of the River Uruguay*', which contained the following Article 36:

> *"The Parties shall co-ordinate [...] the necessary measures to avoid any change in the ecological balance and to control pests and other harmful factors in the river and the areas affected by it."*

688 Hereinafter: ITLOS Advisory Opinion 2011; available at https://www.itlos.org/fileadmin/itlos/documents/cases/case_no_17/Adv_Op_010211_eng.pdf, last accessed 29 April 2014.

689 See ITLOS Advisory Opinion 2011, p. 61 para. 209.

690 See ITLOS Advisory Opinion 2011, p. 61 para. 209.

691 See U.N. Doc. E/CN.4/Sub.2/AC.4/2004/CRP.1, p. 9, para. 28.

692 U.N. Doc. E/CN.4/Sub.2/AC.4/2004/CRP.1, p. 9 para. 28.

693 See U.N. Doc. E/CN.4/Sub.2/AC.4/2004/CRP.1, p. 9 para. 31.

694 See U.N. Doc. A/HRC/10/61 (2009), p. 20, footnote 91.

The ICJ considered this provision to contain an obligation to "exercise due diligence in acting through the Commission for the necessary measures to preserve the ecological balance of the river."[695] This obligation to act with due diligence "entails not only the adoption of appropriate rules and measures, but also a certain level of vigilance in their enforcement and the exercise of administrative control applicable to public and private operators."[696]

The ICJ's judgement clearly stated that due diligence also comprises the duty to implement prevention measures and to ensure their effectiveness. It furthermore clarified that state responsibility cannot be negated through focusing solely on the duties of private actors.

This understanding of due diligence could also offer guidance for the no harm rule. However, it must be taken into account that the ICJ determined due diligence within a bilateral treaty. It cannot be considered as given that the same rules for due diligence apply for an element of a customary law principle. The due diligence the ICJ referred to clarified requirements to ensure the implementation of self-imposed duties. These duties are negotiated by the parties and are clear regarding their content. The same degree of due diligence cannot be expected for the international scope of measures addressing climate change. Not only are obligations in this field vaguer, but in contrast to a treaty, there are no enforceable primary obligations to take certain measures. The no harm rule is an independent secondary obligation that aims to protect other states' legally protected interests rather than ensuring the proper conduct of a treaty. Thus the respective cases of due diligence have different purposes and are not interchangeable.

The *Pulp Mills Case* therefore gives no clear indication with regard to the interpretation of 'due diligence' according to the no harm rule.

ee. Discussion

The suggestion to find a solution in a field other than law[697] undermines the singularity of the extraordinary scenario that this thesis is aiming to frame juristically. However, within the intervening ten years since the urgent call to have official consideration of this topic within the United Nations, i.e. as a responsibility of the UN legal office of the ILC,[698] there has been no notable progress. This indicates that it is highly unlikely that a solution 'outside the law' will be found. It seems more appropriate to consider the situation in the context of responsibility

---

695 *Pulp Mills Case*, p. 77 para. 187.
696 *Pulp Mills Case*, p. 79 para. 197.
697 See U.N. Doc. E/CN.4/Sub.2/AC.4/2004/CRP.1, p. 9 para. 28.
698 See U.N. Doc. E/CN.4/Sub.2/AC.4/2004/CRP.1, p. 9 para. 27.

being triggered by irresponsible behaviour which leads to a damage. This situation does not lead to a legal vacuum, as indicated by asking if this was a question of law at all.[699]

The 'liability *sine delicto*' approach has, above all, the advantage that it more or less clarifies desirable standards for state liability in the field of environmental international law. It reflects the binding nature of the customary no harm rule and encourages states to intensify and enhance their collaboration.

It would, however, be practically impossible for certain countries to comply with such rules of due diligence. This especially applies to the approach of implementing a *per capita* emission cap to determine maximum emissions per country.[700] The USA for example would then have to reduce their GHG emissions from about 20 tons *per capita* annually in 2010 to less than 1 ton p.a. in 2020.[701] One could take the view that this has been foreseeable since 1990 at the latest – so it is the respective country's fault that it is by now unable to comply with the due diligence standards while other states still can achieve such an aim. If, for example, Germany accomplishes its self-imposed objectives to reduce GHG emissions by 40% until 2020 (compared to emissions in 1990), it would act with due diligence in the sense of a scientific *per capita* approach, thus could not be held responsible for its GHG emissions according to the no harm rule.[702] This would be an approach that sets clear and objectively verifiable standards for actions that are to qualify as due diligence.

Yet substantial questions remain unanswered, for example: To what extent does the historical responsibility of states for former GHG emissions have to be considered? And, first and foremost, the approach of liablity *sine delicto* appears to be a backdoor implementation of a Kyoto Succession Protocol – an achievement at which the international community failed despite numerous environmental conferences for such purpose. Considering the amount of practical, legal, and ethical questions that remain unanwered, and considering the existing arguments as reasonable as they are contradictory, to whom is it to find the final answers which so far could not be stipulated?

The second, more pragmatic approach (liability *ex delicto*), however, is similarly unsatisfactorily. This approach in short amounts to the following: There is, without a doubt, transboundary harm being inflicted upon other sovereign

699 See U.N. Doc. E/CN.4/Sub.2/AC.4/2004/CRP.1, p. 9 para. 28.
700 See *Oschmann/Rostankowski*, ZUR 2010, 59 (64).
701 See *WBGU*, Der Budgetansatz, p. 31.
702 See *Oschmann/Rostankowski*, ZUR 2010, 59 (64).

states. This development was foreseeable for, and preventable by, other states.[703] Nevertheless, even in this scenario polluting countries cannot be held liable – at least as long as the activity itself is not explicitly illegal.[704] The reason for that is that no binding regime exists yet. In the field of climate change damage, the reluctance of potential claim opponents, i.e. predominantly the industrialised world, to establish such rules therefore results in a situation in which, according to this point of view, affected states cannot defend their territorial integrity and sovereignty against exterior pollution.

This approach might be unsatisfactory, but it probably mirrors the actual state of affairs. Real progress will only be possible when the wealthier nations decide to do something – which they unsurprisingly will most likely only do if it were for their own good.[705]

The ICJ or other institutions of international jurisdiction are hardly in the position to unilaterally decide upon such a key issue of international law, which the international community has been addressing for decades in conference upon conference without adequate results. Concrete legal consequences are only possible when the criterion 'due diligence' is defined in more specific detail.[706] International courts therefore have been cautious regarding general principles as a source of law in those cases where this would result in judicial lawmaking that is independent from the will of states.[707] As international law "derives its authority and much of its legitimacy through the explicit or implicit consent of states,"[708] international courts are "conservative in their interpretation and application of the law, particularly when the implications of their findings could affect all members of the international community."[709]

It might thus be naïve to expect international law to solve problems as complex as climate change without the respective political support.[710] This is especially true with a view to questions like, for example, the possible inclusion of the aspect of historical responsibility in a binding compensation regime. With

703 For an affirmation of the elements "environmental damage," "border crossing," "substantiality," and an expression of doubt regarding "causation," see Kehrer, p. 171.
704 See e.g. *Tomuschat* in: Hestermeyer et al., 3 (15 et seq.).
705 See *Gordon*, 78 U. Colo. L. Rev. 2007, 1559 (1564).
706 See *Werksman* in: Gerrard/Wannier, 409 (417).
707 See *Birnie et al.*, p. 220; *Spier* in: Faure/Peeters, 47 (48).
708 *Werksman* in: Gerrard/Wannier, 409 (411).
709 *Werksman* in: Gerrard/Wannier, 409 (411).
710 See *Birnie et al.*, p. 1.

regard to the potential of case law to enforce legal standards rather than to reflect a certain political situation, "the international legal system has always been pragmatic rather than principled."[711] Negotiations surrounding the evolution of environmental law illustrate the classic dilemma of politics: That of immediate satisfaction versus long-term costs.[712] These facts limit the capability of jurisdiction (and thus also of international law itself), as the resolution of environmental disputes by interstate claims is substantially dependent on the consent and good faith of the states concerned.[713] Judicial activism that is too politicised would likely face severe criticism, as the judiciary has not been democratically elected.[714]

Therefore, the pragmatic approach of liability *ex delicto*, which denies state liability for damage resulting from non-prohibited acts such as the emitting of GHG, better reflects the current status – and limits – of international law. Establishing general liability for direct compensation on the part of those responsible for climate change would have serious consequences; the implementation of such liability might potentially take years or decades.[715] In this context, the no harm rule *alone* is an inadequate basis for an endangered state's claim to a new state territory.

From the endangered states' legal perspective, the following remarks made by the ILC in 2006 with regard to state liability, however, were promising:

> "*In general terms,* [...] *the earlier reluctance to accept liability for damage to environment* per se, *without linking such damage to damage to persons or property*[...] *is gradually disappearing.*[...] *In the case of damage to natural resources or the environment there is a right of compensation or reimbursement for costs incurred by way of reasonable preventive, restoration or reinstatement measures.*"[716]

This, however, is only the beginning of a development that might lead to stricter liability in the future. The current international regime does not reflect what is essential or desirable, but what is now politically possible.[717] Authors strongly urge the international community in this context to develop a binding and clarifying

711 *Birnie et al.*, p. 213, citing Art. 33 UN-Charter.

712 See *von Glahn/Taulbee*, p. 528 et seq.

713 See *Birnie et al.*, p. 1.

714 See *Haritz*, p. 85.

715 See *Brunnée* et al., in Lord et al., 1 (5) para. 1.08.

716 ILC Report, U.N. Doc. A/61/10, p. 143-144 para. 8 (2006) with numerous further references.

717 See *Brunnée* et al., in Lord et al., 1 (6) para. 1.12.

legal regime addressing these issues.[718] When the first endangered state becomes uninhabitable, it is possible at that point for such a regime to have been established already. This would then most likely overrule the customary law primarily examined within this thesis. Regarding the progress of the last decades, quick progress however is questionable.

5. Interim Result

The no harm rule *alone* does not provide for a claim on the part of endangered states to a new state territory. The precautionary principle, understood as arguing for an alleviation of the standard of proof, is suitable to overcome remaining minor uncertainties with regard to issues of causality. However, there is no persuasive specification of clear standards of due diligence.

Nevertheless, a few issues need to be pointed out: All quoted authors discuss compensation for *any* transboundary damage caused by the emission of GHG. This thesis, however, focuses only on such cases of land loss that result in the uninhabitability of whole states. Several peculiarities distinguish this scenario from the more general issue of state liability for *any* environmental damage attributable to the emission of GHG. One of these peculiarities is the very practical fact that the relocation of several endangered states with fewer than 1 million citizens in total is a challenge involving severe but not system-threatening financial burdens for potential opponents. This applies especially in comparison to the financial burdens of the second adaption option, the immigration scenario.[719] The costs of the latter option would also be considerable – and would probably be paid by the international community as well, as a sunken endangered state will most likely not be able to afford such migration. Politically, this makes a special solution for endangered states more realistic. This solution would have to account for the different political and legal classifications of endangered states when compared to states suffering more generally from climate change damage.

Another crucial difference between endangered states and those states more generally damaged by climate change is the loss of territorial sovereignty in the case of the first and a mere infringement of territorial sovereignty in the case of the latter.[720] The (relative) damage for endangered states is far bigger, which could allow for special treatment of endangered states. This makes it necessary

---

718 See e.g. *Tomuschat* in: Hestermeyer et al., 3 (6); *Brunnée* et al., in Lord et al., 1 (6) para. 1.11.; more confident: *Handl*, OYIL 2007, 531 (546).

719 See *Jarvis*, 9 Seattle J. Soc. Just. 2010-2011, 447 (462).

720 For further differences see below § 4. C. 4. b. aa.

to consider other aspects of international law to comprehensively examine if endangered states can claim a new state territory.

C. The No Harm Rule in the Context of other International Law

1. Introduction

In order to avoid the isolated treatment of the no harm rule, international law shall in the following be further examined with closer consideration of other rules and principles argueing against or for a claim on the part of endangered states to be provided with a new state territory. "There are, of course, other standards, principles and sources of law that could inform the relevant standard of due diligence" in the context of climate change liability.[721] An *isolated* view of Principle 21 of the Stockholm Declaration and Principle 2 of the Rio Declaration (and thus of the no harm rule) is an "inconclusive guide to the precise contours of liability for environmental damage, [... the two principles] must be interpreted within the framework of customary rules on which both are based"[722].

Environmental (see under 2.) and general (see under 3.) principles and aspects of international law will therefore be examined in the following in order to take into account the diverse fields of international law touched upon in the case of endangered states.

Predominantly, the following examination will focus on the criterion 'due diligence' of the no harm rule. This criterion is, as just outlined, the only hurdle justifying the denial of an endangered state's claim to a new state territory. Moreover, "[t]he question of how much due diligence states must demonstrate is the area of the law of state responsibility, as it relates to climate change, that is least developed."[723]

This criterion, therefore, needs further consideration. The rules and principles which will be examined in the following could serve as interpretational guidelines for the criterion 'due diligence' in the case of state inundation. This elaboration could lead to an exemption to the general finding that – based on the no harm rule alone – GHG emissions giving rise to a claim to compensation cannot be assessed. In other words, a violation of (more or less) fundamental principles of international law could indicate that, in the case of total land loss, a

721 *Werksman* in: Gerrard/Wannier, 409 (423).

722 *Birnie et al.*, p. 218, emphasis added.

723 *Werksman* in: Gerrard/Wannier, 409 (419).

breach of the criterion 'due diligence' of the no harm rule can be affirmed. This would then trigger liability, e.g. by way of a claim to a new state territory.

2. General Rules and Principles in International *Environmental* Law

a. *Introduction*

The intention to ensure compensation for environmental damage has already been reflected in the 1982 World Charter for Nature[724] wherein the signatories declared that

> *"[a]ll persons, in accordance with their national legislation, shall have the opportunity to participate, individually or with others, in the formulation of decisions of direct concern to their environment, and shall have access to means of redress when their environment has suffered damage or degradation."*[725]

Yet ten years later, the language of Principle 13 of the Rio-Declaration, which stipulates that "*[S]tates shall develop national law*" for the purpose of compensation and "*shall also co-operate in [...a] more determined manner,*" sounds like cautious backpedaling despite simultaneously growing environmental concerns. This shift in emphasis reflects the unwillingness to establish rules of international law that might impose excessive costs.[726] This attitude is said to be a consequence of the Chernobyl accident in 1986, which did not lead to any compensation claims despite quite clear evidence for international liability.[727] However, the reluctance of the affected Northern European Countries can in that case also be explained by the political circumstances in those days.[728]

This reasoning enlightens the contradictory tendencies in international environmental law going back more than three decades.[729] Due to the steadily increasing awareness of the need to protect the global environment, states on the one hand have put a lot of effort in developing the field of environmental law.[730] Yet on the other hand, they are very reluctant to agree upon binding treaties, mainly for fear that these could result in tremendous financial strains.[731] Of

---

724 Available at http://www.un.org/documents/ga/res/37/a37r007.htm, last accessed 29 April 2014.

725 Art. 23 World Charter for Nature.

726 See *Sands*, p. 701.

727 See *Sands*, p. 701.

728 See *Voigt*, 77 Nordic J. of Int. L. 2008, 1 (3).

729 See *Beyerlin*, OYIL 2007, 425 (427).

730 See *Beyerlin*, OYIL 2007, 425 (427).

731 See *Beyerlin*, OYIL 2007, 425 (427); *Handl*, 37 Envtl Pol'y & L. 2007, 116 (121).

course, this does not mean that principles are irrelevant for the development of a practical solution. Instead, the differing interests of the parties involved have to be taken into consideration distinctly within the interpretation of the respective principles. Thus far, compensation has been uncommon.

With regard to the present leading question whether endangered states can claim a new state territory, some of these environmental principles shall be outlined and interpreted in the following to contribute to the findings provided by the no harm rule[732] and the precautionary principle[733]. Conclusions will be drawn from the principle of common but differentiated responsibilities (see under b.) as well as the principle of sustainable development (see under c.). Finally, a number of other principles will be touched upon more generally. They are less relevant, but still valuable sources for the overall understanding of the regime of rules and principles in international environmental law regarding the present question. This group of principles comprises the principle of *inter*generational equity as well as that of *intra*generational equity, along with the principles of co-operation, of preventive action, and of shared natural resources (see under d.).

b. Principle of Common but Differentiated Responsibilities

aa. Introduction

The first principle to be examined at this point is what is called the principle of common but differentiated responsibilities. It proves that international law does not always apply equally to all states.[734] This principle has been called "one of the most important and controversial principles shaping the climate change regime."[735] It is *inter alia* expressed in Principle 7 of the Rio Declaration, which states:

> *"In view of the different contributions to global environmental degradation, States have common but differentiated responsibilities. The developed countries acknowledge the responsibility that they bear in the international pursuit of sustainable development in view of the pressures their societies place on the global environment and of the technologies and financial resources they command."*

It is also one of the key principles of the UNFCCC,[736] where it is being referred to in the preamble as well as in Articles 3(1) and 4. It was derived from the

---

732 See above, § 4. B.

733 See above, § 4. B. 4. d. aa. (2).

734 See *Birnie et al.*, p. 132; *Sands*, p. 235.

735 *Wold et al.*, p. 161.

736 See *Brunnée* et al., in Lord et al., 50 (53) para. 4.07.

application of equity in general international law[737] and reflects the elements of solidarity and conditionality.[738] It mirrors the "idea that humankind as a whole has a moral duty to ensure the continued existence of natural conditions that permit its survival."[739]

bb. Content and History

The two main elements of the principle of common but differentiated responsibilities are mirrored in its name: Firstly, the protection of the environment at national, regional and international levels is a *common* responsibility of all states.[740] Secondly, in determining the degree of responsibility (and thus obligation), one has to take into account both the *differentiated* contributions to the level of GHG concentration in the atmosphere as well as the respective abilities of states to prevent, reduce, and control the threats emerging from climate change.[741] This differentiation applies especially with regard to particularly vulnerable countries such as small island states affected by flooding resulting from global warming.[742]

After having been established in theory, the principle was introduced into international treaties. It is, for example, reflected in the asymmetric obligation schemes of the Montreal Protocol on Substances That Deplete the Ozone Layer.[743]

As early as 1949, the idea of common (but not yet differentiated) responsibilities for shared resources not under a single state's sole jurisdiction was reflected in the preamble of the Convention for the Establishment of an Inter-American Tropical Tuna Commission.[744] Its most noteworthy implementation as yet was in the Kyoto Protocol, which imposed very different obligations to different groups of states based on this principle and which specifically took into consideration the historical contribution and different capabilities of the respective states.[745]

---

737 See *Sands*, p. 233.

738 See *Birnie et al.*, p. 133 et seqq.

739 *Tomuschat* in: Hestermeyer et al., 3 (8).

740 See *Peel* in: Axelrod, 48 (60); *Birnie et al.*, p. 133; *Sands*, p. 233.

741 See *Sands*, p. 233; *Peel* in: Axelrod, 48 (60).

742 See *Wold et al.*, p. 161.

743 See *Beyerlin*, OYIL 2007, 425 (442).

744 Available at www.iattc.org/pdffiles/iattc_convention_1949.pdf, last accessed 29 April 2014. For further examples of both bilateral and multilateral contractual implementations of one or both elements of the principle of common but differentiated responsibilities, see *Sands*, p. 234.

745 See *Nanda* in: WJU 2010, 42 (49). See the numerous references to Parties in Annex I of the Kyoto Protocol; see also the differing emission goals in Annex B.

The concept especially aims at improving the situation of developing countries, which are the ones most affected by climate change even though, historically, they contributed least.[746] Their special status is emphasised in numerous international treaties such as the 1974 CERDS or, again, the Rio Declaration,[747] which in this context stresses:

> "*The special situation and needs of developing countries, particularly the least developed and those most environmentally vulnerable, shall be given special priority.*"[748]

Developed countries, the main contributors to the emergence of climate change or to the hole in the ozone layer, should therefore bear the main burden of the respective consequences.[749] Despite universal acceptance of the abstract validity of this concept,[750] its concrete implementation seems to be a task of Herculean dimensions. "[T]he nature, content and extent of [common but differentiated responsibilities] in the climate regime [...] has been disputed since the ink dried on the [UN]FCCC."[751]

cc. Legal Status

There is consensus that the principle of common but differentiated responsibilities cannot be considered part of customary international law.[752] Thus, it might not be a suitable basis for an interstate claim due to global environmental damage.[753] Attitudes towards the more precise understanding of this concept remain ambivalent up to this point.[754] One noteworthy view within the spectrum of opinions is the position of the United States, who commented on Principle 7 of the Rio Declaration *inter alia* at the 2002 World Summit on Sustainable Development in Johannesburg in the following way:

> "*The United States does not accept any interpretation of principle 7 that would imply a recognition or acceptance by the United States of any international obligations or liabilities, or any diminution of the responsibilities of developing countries under international law.*"[755]

---

746 Similar: *Sands*, p. 234 et seq.
747 See further examples at *Sands*, p. 235.
748 Art. 6 Rio Declaration.
749 See *Birnie et al.*, p. 136.
750 See *Birnie et al.*, p. 133.
751 *Brunnée* et al., in Lord et al., 50 (53) para. 4.07.
752 See *Beyerlin*, OYIL 2007, 425 (442); *Sands*, p. 236; *Tomuschat* in: Hestermeyer et al., 3 (8).
753 See *Birnie et al.*, p. 135.
754 See *Beyerlin*, OYIL 2007, 425 (442).
755 U.N. Doc. A/Conf 199/20 (2002), p. 145, para. 20.

Nevertheless, it is also far from being mere soft law but can be considered a "framework principle."[756] The phrasing used in principle 7 – e.g. 'responsibility' instead of 'obligation' – suggests that it is meant to serve as guideline as well as interpretation aid in international law.[757] With regard to what *Sands* calls "special needs" of developing states, this understanding can result in different legal obligations.[758] According to some authors, the principle, when considered in the context of climate change, does not only present a conceptual framework but actually obligates developed states to lead the way and curtail GHG emissions. Only then is the developing world obligated to agree on any form of reduction commitments.[759]

dd. Implications for this Study

If this principle is understood to be providing a framework, the direction in which its underlying ideas argue has to be taken into consideration.[760] These underlying ideas were, *inter alia*, identified as solidarity, the application of equity in general international law, and taking into account the needs of developing states against the background of developed states' responsibility for climate change.[761]

SIDS are states that the principle of common but differentiated responsibilities is meant to protect. Their existence is threatened by the consequences already briefly summarised.[762] The special needs of these endangered states can be identified fairly easily: If they cannot keep their old state territory, they need a new one in order to continue to exist. The alternative adaption scenario to state relocation, an immigration scenario, would not reflect this need. The respective states would cease to exist in that case.

The protection of developing states is undisputedly the main objective of the principle of common but differentiated responsibilities. Furthermore, the principle states that the degree of responsibility of developed states is higher because

---

756 *Birnie et al.*, p. 135.

757 See *Beyerlin*, OYIL 2007, 425 (442), who argues that this legal institute is to be regarded as a 'principle' according to Dworkin's definition which Beyerlin describes at p. 433 et seqq. This distinction is also explained in the present thesis, see above § 4. A. 3. However, the present thesis does not follow the terminological distinction of "rule" and "principle," see above § 4. A. 3.

758 *Sands*, p. 235.

759 See *Wold et al.*, p. 162.

760 See *Birnie et al.*, p. 135.

761 On the ideas of solidarity and of the needs developing countries, see *Birnie et al.*, p. 133 et seqq. On the idea of the application of equity, see *Sands*, p. 233.

762 See above § 2. D.

they caused, and cause, climate change to a greater degree than developing states. Also, they are more capable of contributing to a solution. These findings, understood as guiding the leading question, argue for a stricter interpretation of 'due diligence' in the context of the no harm rule. Due diligence also encompasses awareness of the unequal responsibilities (and possibilities, e.g. to defend oneself or to combat climate change) amongst states. The principle of common but differentiated responsibilities argues for imposing higher standards of due diligence on wealthier states, and especially so when the protection of less developed states – as in the present case endangered states – is at stake.

However, the rather indeterminate and non-binding legal status of this principle has to be born in mind. Overall, the violation of due diligince has not been sufficiently established through the application of this principle, and thus neither has the violation of the no harm rule. It might rather be one argument out of several.

c. *Principle of Sustainable Development*

aa. Introduction

The principle of sustainable development is of utmost importance in international environmental law. "[I]f any single provision of the Rio Declaration can contribute to the normative development of international environmental law, this is likely to be it."[763] It emerges from the very important aspect of state sovereignty and goes on to develop independently.[764] Since the 1992 Earth Summit, the principle of sustainable development has emerged as powerful legal concept the acceptance of which increases as the overarching framework for the endeavours of the international community.[765]

The principle comprises various substantive elements which are set out in Principles 3 through 8 of the Rio Declaration.[766] None of the concepts mentioned in these principles were new at that point, but the Rio Declaration brought them together in a more systematic form than had been achieved up to then.[767] In addition, procedural elements of the principle are found in Principles 10 and 17

763 *Sands*, p. 237.

764 See *Wold et al.*, p. 158.

765 See *Yamin/Depledge*, p. 59.

766 According to *Epiney/Scheyli*, p. 89, these subprinciples comprise, *inter alia*, the principle of intergenerational equity (see below § 4. C. 2. d. bb.) and the precautionary principle (see above § 4. B. 4. d. aa. (2)). See *Birnie et al.*, p. 116.

767 See *Birnie et al.*, p. 116.

of the Rio Declaration.[768] Not all of these elements of the Rio Declaration are relevant for the present study. For the purpose of clarification, this section shall begin with the examination of Principle 4 of the Rio Declaration, which is also called the "integration principle."[769] It reads as follows:

> *"In order to achieve sustainable development, environmental protection shall constitute an integral part of the development process and cannot be considered in isolation from it."*

Authors refer to this (main) element of sustainable development as "[i]ntegration of environmental protection and economic development."[770]

Another definition of sustainable development – which is considered to be the most famous one –[771] was presented by the Brundtland Commission in 1987:

> *"Sustainable development is development that meets the needs of the present without compromising the ability of future generations to meet their own needs. It contains within it two key concepts:*
>
> - *the concept of 'needs', in particular the essential needs of the world's poor, to which overriding priority should be given; and*
> - *the idea of limitations imposed by the state of technology and social organization on the environment's ability to meet present and future needs."*[772]

A generally accepted definition of sustainable development does not exist.[773] Its designation is likewise indeterminate: The principle is also referred to as "concept of sustainable development"[774] or "right to sustainable development"[775]. Subsequently to the Earth Summit in 1992, the United Nations, furthermore established the 'Commission on Sustainable Development' to "ensure an effective follow-up of the United Nations Conference on Environment and Development (UNCED), also known as Earth Summit."[776]

---

768 See *Birnie et al.*, p. 116.

769 *Peel* in: Axelrod, 48 (60). Selected subprinciples assigned to sustainable development (principle of intergenerational equity, principle of intragenerational equity) will be addressed further below, see § 4. C. 2. d. bb. – cc.

770 *Birnie et al.*, p. 116.

771 See *Beyerlin*, OYIL 2007, 425 (443).

772 U.N. Doc. A/42/427, Annex, Part 1, Chapter 2, para. 1.

773 See *Hobe*, p. 521.

774 E.g. *Birnie et al.*, p. 123.

775 *Yamin/Depledge*, p. 72 et seq.

776 Self-description of the Commission on Sustainable Development, available at http://sustainabledevelopment.un.org/csd.html, last accessed 29 April 2014.

bb. Content and History

The principle of sustainable development is described as a guideline giving important impulses and political guidance for all parties acting in the field of international environmental protection and development.[777] Its purpose is the establishment of a balance of interest, which does not mean that the right of states to economic development is necessarily trumped by environmental protection or the obligation to protect human rights.[778] Instead, international case law has thus far concentrated on the balancing of criteria such as the necessity or the degree of interference.[779] This shows that few rights are ever absolute or unqualified.[780] There is as of yet no clarity what exactly sustainable development means.[781] However, for the first time, this concept makes a state's management of its own domestic environment a matter of international concern in a systematic way.[782]

In the *Gabčikovo-Nagymaros Case* from 1997, the ICJ made very significant judicial remarks with regard to the present question in the context of sustainable development:

> "*Throughout the ages, mankind has, for economic and other reasons, constantly interfered with nature. In the past, this was often done without consideration of the effects upon the environment. Owing to new scientific insights and to a growing awareness of the risks for mankind – for present and future generations – of pursuit of such interventions at an unconsidered and unabated pace, new norms and standards have been developed, set forth in a great number of instruments during the last two decades. Such new norms have to be taken into consideration, and such new standards given proper weight, not only when States contemplate new activities but also when continuing with activities begun in the past. This need to reconcile economic development with protection of the environment is aptly expressed in the concept of sustainable development.*"[783]

The background of the *Gabčikovo-Nagymaros Case* was a treaty obligation between Hungary and the legal predecessor of Slovenia from 1977 to embank the river Danube for the purpose of power production.[784] After having started to work on the project in 1978, Hungary decided in 1989 to suspend the work due

---

777 See *Beyerlin*, OYIL 2007, 425 (443).
778 See *Birnie et al.*, p. 115.
779 See *Birnie et al.*, p. 115.
780 See *Birnie et al.*, p. 115.
781 See *Gillespie*, 22 UCLA J. Envtl. L. & Pol'y 2003-2004, 107 (126); *Birnie et al.*, p. 125, *Beyerlin*, OYIL 2007, 425 (443); *Peel* in Axelrod, 48 (59).
782 See *Birnie et al.*, p. 124.
783 *Gabčikovo-Nagymaros Case*, p. 78 para. 140.
784 See *Gabčikovo-Nagymaros Case*, p. 17 para. 15.

to intense ecological criticism.[785] In these proceedings, the ICJ decided that there is a remarkable impact of the principle of sustainable development despite clear contractual obligations to embank the river Danube:

> *"For the purposes of the present case, this means that the Parties together should look afresh at the effects on the environment of the operation of the Gabčikovo power plant. In particular they must find a satisfactory solution for the volume of water to be released into the old bed of the Danube and into the side-arms on both sides of the river."*[786]

Two aspects of this decision are particularly significant for this thesis. First, the ICJ considered the necessity of including the aspects of environmental protection and economic development an applicable criterion also in cases of the continuation of activities that had been begun in the past.[787] Secondly, the ICJ ruled to "look afresh" at the effects, as "[i]t is not for the Court to determine what shall be the final result of these negotiations to be conducted by the Parties."[788] This is a good example for a solution intended to further the objective of sustainable development in accordance with the Rio Declaration without at the same time deciding upon the question of what exactly is to be considered sustainable and what is not.[789] It is upon the states to decide on this question. The present issue of state liability might also contain aspects belonging to the category of politics.[790] Yet this state discretion is not an insurmountable obstacle to any judicial assessment, as the *Gabčikovo-Nagymaros Case* shows.

cc. Legal Status

Again, international lawyers do not entirely agree on the legal quality of the principle of sustainable development. With regard to the wide scope of the principle and its content's indeterminacy, it has been considered as being of only limited operational value.[791] Others infer from the *Gabčikovo-Nagymaros Case* that the ICJ, by invoking the concept of sustainable development, indicates its own legal function.[792] As the ICJ did not provide further details as to the practical consequences, the Separate Opinion of the ICJ's then Vice

---

785 See *Gabčikovo-Nagymaros Case*, p. 25 para. 21 et seq.
786 *Gabčikovo-Nagymaros Case*, p. 78 para. 140.
787 See *Gabčikovo-Nagymaros Case*, p. 78 para. 140; *Birnie et al.*, p. 115.
788 *Gabčikovo-Nagymaros Case*, p. 78 para. 141.
789 See *Birnie et al.*, p. 127.
790 This issue will be addressed in more detail further below, see § 4. C. 5.
791 See *Hobe*, p. 522.
792 *Sands*, p. 208.

President *Judge Weeramantry* is often quoted for further guidance.[793] *Judge Weeramantry*, under the caption "Sustainable Development as a Principle of International Law," firstly stresses that "development can only be prosecuted in harmony with the reasonable demands of environmental protection."[794] He then concludes:

> "*It is thus the correct formulation of the right to development that that right does not exist in the absolute sense, but is relative always to its tolerance by the environment. The right to development as thus refined is clearly part of modern international law. It is compendiously referred to as sustainable development.*"[795]

Overall, there is a wide and general recognition of the concept.[796] It rests on a basis of worldwide acceptance, not only among developing countries.[797] Its components come from well-established areas of international law such as human rights, state responsibility, environmental law, economic and industrial law, equity, territorial sovereignty, abuse of rights, and good neighbourliness, among others.[798] With regard to the history of mankind's environmental considerations, it is not merely a principle of modern international law but one of the most ancient ideas of mankind, which also plays an important part in the service of international law.[799]

Lowe has elaborated more intensively on the 'legal function' which authors assign to the principle, also *inter alia* with references to the Separate Opinion of *Judge Weeramantry*.[800] First, he makes the rather disparaging observation that the concept of sustainable development has its place amongst other concepts like democracy, human rights, and the sovereign equality of states which are rooted in theoretical obscurity and confusion, suffering from a reluctance to test theoretical principles for their practical utility.[801] He then, however, stresses that there is more to the concept without attributing to it the necessity to consider it

---

793 See *Sands*, p. 208, footnote 141.
794 *Gabčikovo-Nagymaros Case*, Separate Opinion of Judge Weeramantry, 88 (92). Available at http://www.icj-cij.org/docket/files/92/7383.pdf, last accessed 29 April 2014.
795 *Gabčikovo-Nagymaros Case*, Separate Opinion of Judge Weeramantry, 88 (92).
796 See *Gabčikovo-Nagymaros Case*, Separate Opinion of Judge Weeramantry, 88 (93).
797 See *Gabčikovo-Nagymaros Case*, Separate Opinion of Judge Weeramantry, 88 (94).
798 See *Gabčikovo-Nagymaros Case*, Separate Opinion of Judge Weeramantry, 88 (95).
799 See *Gabčikovo-Nagymaros Case*, Separate Opinion of Judge Weeramantry, 88 (110 et seq.).
800 See *Lowe* in: Boyle/Freestone, 19 (31).
801 See *Lowe* in: Boyle/Freestone, 19 (30 et seq.).

a primary rule of international law.[802] Its relevance rather lies in its normative force when considered in international judgements.[803] In this context, he makes the following statement that is highly relevant to the present study:

> *"Sustainable development can properly claim a normative status as an element of the process of judicial reasoning. It is a meta-principle, acting upon other legal rules and principles – a legal concept exercising a kind of interstitial normativity, pushing and pulling the boundaries of true primary norms when they threaten to overlap or conflict with each other."*[804]

In contrast to *Lowe*, other authors go even further and stress the suitability of the concept to be a potential source for (subsequent) legal norms, as the modification of primary norms through juridical interpretation generates new (modified) norms.[805] In other words, the interpretation of a norm based on a principle shapes this norm. In this way, the principle of sustainable development affects binding law. These statements further confirm the approach of this thesis to look at the overall framework and to interpret the central no harm rule and its criterion 'due diligence' in the context of other principles.

The arbitral tribunal in the *Iron Rhine Case* considered the duties determined in Principle 4 to be a principle of general international law applying not only in the case of autonomous activities, but also in that of activities aimed at the implementation of specific treaties.[806] This ruling is another example of the normative force of the principle of sustainable development.

Other authors contradict the legal relevance of the concept: Despite its appeal, the meaning of the phrase 'sustainable development' has become increasingly lost in a labyrinth of political and philosophical considerations; hence a derivation of a concrete claim from a concept as vague as this one is doomed to failure.[807] The specific normative implications of the principle's main elements are far from certain.[808]

Overall, however, there is a fairly broad consensus – even amongst the judiciary elements, which includes the ICJ – that at least some normativity can be attributed to the concept of sustainable development, especially as a guide for interpretation in the case of international lawsuits.

---

802 See *Lowe* in: Boyle/Freestone, 19 (31).
803 See *Lowe* in: Boyle/Freestone, 19 (31).
804 *Lowe* in: Boyle/Freestone, 19 (31), followed by *Birnie et al.*, p. 127.
805 See *Beyerlin*, OYIL 2007, 425 (445).
806 See *Iron Rhine Case*, p. 29 para. 59.
807 See *Gillespie*, 22 UCLA J. Envtl. L. & Pol'y 2003-2004, 107 (125).
808 See *Gillespie*, 22 UCLA J. Envtl. L. & Pol'y 2003-2004, 107 (126).

dd. Implications for this Study

"[I]t is difficult to see an international court reviewing national action and concluding that it falls short of a standard of 'sustainable development', save possibly in an extreme case."[809] This opinion is persuasive. The lack of exact rules as well as of unambiguously obligatory commitments does not leave room for a wide application of this principle. However, the present study is examining a situation which most certainly could be designated to be the (possible) exemption to those 'extreme cases.'

Moreover, as indicated above, the ICJ in the *Gabčikovo-Nagymaros Case* showed a way to decide upon certain aspects of a question while leaving the elaboration of the details to the states' discretion. It decided upon the 'if' without answering 'how' – an imaginable solution also for the issue of whether or not endangered states can claim a new state territory.[810] Moreover, this case law confirms that states have the duty to consider aspects of environmental protection not only when an activity begins but also in the course of its continuation.[811] This idea can be transferred also to the emission of GHG.

With regard to sustainable development, an infringement of this concept in the worldwide scope of GHG emissions has to be assessed before anything else. A more or less well-balanced consideration of economic and ecological interests could under no circumstances result in the failure, despite better knowledge, to set up a plan to reduce the emission of GHG, eventually resulting in the dissolution of whole state territories. This conclusion is supported by the findings of the *Stern Review*, according to which the costs of adaption will be 5 to 20 times higher than the costs of mitigation would be.[812] This finding proves that a reduction of GHG emissions is even highly recommendable from an (only) economic (long-term) point of view.

It is thus obvious that the current level of GHG emissions do not comply with the concept of sustainable development.

What does this imply for endangered states? As already quoted, this concept is a meta-principle in international law, which "pushes and pulls the boundaries of true primary norms,"[813] with a certain degree of normativity. Its additional infringement therefore further strengthens the impression that states did not act

809 *Birnie et al.*, p. 126.

810 This approach will be addressed in the context of this thesis further below, see § 4. C. 5.

811 See *Gabčikovo-Nagymaros Case*, p. 78 para. 140; *Birnie et al.*, p. 115.

812 See *Stern Review*, Summary of Conclusions, p. vi.

813 *Lowe* in: Boyle/Freestone, 19 (31).

with 'due diligence' in the course of the no harm rule. Also, the "overriding priority" which, according to the definition of the Brundtland Commission, should be given in particular to the essential needs of the world's poor,[814] argues for a stricter interpretation of this criterion in the case of endangered states.

The *Gabčikovo-Nagymaros Case* is proof of a certain degree of commitment, which emerges from this principle. Similarly to the principle of common but differentiated responsibilities, the principle of sustainable development alone does not give sufficient reason to consider the criterion 'due diligence' not met. However, it is suitable as one argument among many concerning this matter.

d. Other Principles

aa. Introduction

International environmental law has amongst its principles some which are of minor importance for the present study. Nevertheless, they should be examined as they still might provide useful additional information. Only their core essence shall be portrayed briefly. The question of whether or not the findings lead to an amended result regarding the 'due diligence' criterion of the no harm rule will be addressed if and when appropriate.

bb. Principle of Intergenerational Equity

The principle of intergenerational equity is considered a subcategory of sustainable development.[815] It is *inter alia* codified in Principle 3 of the Rio Declaration, which reads as follows:

> "*The right to development must be fulfilled so as to equitably meet developmental and environmental needs of present and future generations.*"[816]

Principle 1 of the Stockholm Declaration similarly states that

> "*Man […] bears a solemn responsibility to protect and improve the environment for present* and future generations."[817]

Numerous binding and non-binding treaties in international environmental law indicate that present interests should not be served exclusively, but that any

---

814 See U.N. Doc. A/42/427, Annex, Part 1, Chapter 2, para. 1.

815 See *Sands*, p. 209 et seq., *Lowe* in: Boyle/Freestone, 19 (26 et seqq.); *Birnie et al.*, p. 119 et seqq.

816 The principle is also codified in other international treaties such as Art. 3(1) UNFCCC.

817 Emphasis added.

action and decision must also aim at protecting the environment for, and of, future generations.[818] "For the first time in the history of humankind, human beings have the capacity to alter irreversibly the environment of the planet earth as a result of the global cumulative effect of human activities."[819] Thus, it is apposite to apply the principle of intergenerational equity to the phenomenon of global warming.[820]

The core of this idea is the necessity to preserve options also for future generations, including access to resources and a certain quality of the natural environment.[821] This core idea is also promoted by the above-cited Brundlandt Commission's definition of sustainable development, which calls for a meeting of "the needs of the present without compromising the ability of future generations to meet their own needs."[822] It marks a shift in treatment of intertemporal issues: Whereas international law traditionally used to relate the present only to the past (e.g. territorial claims), it has increasingly been relating the present to the future.[823] This is *inter alia* due to the long half-life of GHG.[824]

The principle has recently attracted some attention, when in September 2012 two Canadian girls at the age of 13 and 15 prompted the United Nations Committee on the Rights of the Child to question Canada on climate change.[825] One of the girls is being quoted as follows: "My inherent right to life, and my right to culture as an Indigenous person, are being jeopardised not only by climate change but by my country's lack of environmental standards and policies."[826]

Once more, *Judge Weeramantry* made remarks on the legal status of this concept in his dissenting opinion on the ICJ's Advisory Opinion on the Legality of the Threat or Use of Nuclear Weapons. This was the first case in which

818 See *Ohlhoff*, p. 189 et seq. with numerous examples for such treaties.

819 *Redgwell* in: Churchill/Freestone, 41 (41).

820 See *Redgwell* in: Churchill/Freestone, 41 (51).

821 See *Wold et al.*, p. 165; *Birnie et al.*, p. 126.

822 U.N. Doc. A/42/427, Annex, Part 1, Chapter 2, para. 1.

823 See *Weiss* in: Vig/Axelrod, 98 (106).

824 See *Wold et al.*, p. 165.

825 See "Teen girls prompt United Nations Committee on the Rights of the Child to question Canada on climate change," available at http://www.davidsuzuki.org/media/news/2012/09/teen-girls-prompt-united-nations-committee-on-the-rights-of-the-child-to-questio/, last accessed 29 April 2014.

826 "Teen girls prompt United Nations Committee on the Rights of the Child to question Canada on climate change," available at http://www.davidsuzuki.org/media/news/2012/09/teen-girls-prompt-united-nations-committee-on-the-rights-of-the-child-to-questio/, last accessed 29 April 2014.

intergenerational equity had been introduced.[827] Referring explicitly to the concept of intergenerational equity, he characterised (as early as 1996) the right of future generations as "woven […] into international law through major treaties, through juristic opinion and through general principles of law recognized by civilized nations."[828]

Many authors are less clear regarding this principle's legal status. They prefer, for example, not to answer the question of whether it can be considered part of customary law also in a non-treaty context.[829] Others refer to various treaties such as the London Dumping Convention, the Climate Change Convention and the International Whaling Convention, which prove that already today the interests of future generations are incorporated into international treaty law.[830] However, specific rights, such as a representation of future generations in legal proceedings before international courts, have not yet emerged from this principle.[831] The principle therefore is described as having no concrete normativity, making it a chimera whose relevance in case law has not exceeded the level of a rhetorical device.[832]

According to another view, the principle has limited practical legal consequences.[833]

Jacobs argues very differently. She examines a potential claim Tuvalu had threatened to bring before the ICJ against the USA in 2002 because of their GHG emissions, arguing that those might lead to the loss of Tuvalu's islands, thus its state territory.[834] In the course of this, *Jacobs* recommends that Tuvalu should argue that the following generations of the Tuvalu nation will never have the opportunity to experience island life.[835] Despite the fact that a state's "capitalist endeavours" remain central to that state's sovereignty, *Jacobs* argues, a ruling of the ICJ to require the USA to reduce GHG emissions would be correct.[836] She views "global warming [as] a concern which trumps the pursuit of economic

827 See *Jacobs*, 14 Pac. Rim L. & Pol'y J. 2005, 103 (123).
828 *Advisory Opinion on Nuclear Weapons*, Dissenting Opinion of Judge Weeramantry, 429 (455).
829 See *Beyerlin*, OYIL 2007, 425 (446).
830 See *Birnie et al.*, p. 121.
831 See *Birnie et al.*, p. 121.
832 See *Lowe* in: Boyle/Freestone, 19 (27).
833 See *Sands*, p. 210.
834 See *Jacobs*, 14 Pac. Rim L. & Pol'y J. 2005, 103 (103).
835 See *Jacobs*, 14 Pac. Rim L. & Pol'y J. 2005, 103 (125).
836 See *Jacobs*, 14 Pac. Rim L. & Pol'y J. 2005, 103 (125).

success," and especially so "when the end result of the opposite ruling would be the extinction of a sovereign nation."[837]

Others consider the possibility of expanding our concepts of judicial standing for future generations for the purposes of this principle.[838] Intergenerational aspects can also have vital procedural effects insofar as they imply an interpretation that expands bilateral arrangements by incorporating multilateral purposes, which address common concerns.[839]

For the present study, this has the following consequences: All actors of the international community undoubtedly should bear in mind the consequences of any action for future generations. This does not sufficiently happen with regard to the expected impacts of climate change. The loss of state territory will make the respective (former) state's environmental resources completely inaccessible for its citizens.

The concept of intergenerational equity, however, focuses on continuing access to *any* resource and *any* environment rather than on establishing a guarantee for the conservation of the contemporary *status quo* for next generations. The aim of this principle – namely to meet developmental and environmental needs of present and future generations and to preserve access to resources and a certain quality of the natural environment – cannot mean that the exact same resources are to be preserved, e.g. a specific state territory. The principle rather ensures that similar opportunities exist for the following generations in terms of resources and the environment. There is no indication that the principle also intends to guarantee the very same state or the very same environment being preserved. *Jacobs*' approach thus expands the principle's application to endangered states' territories, bearing the principle's very low level of normativity in mind.

The principle of intergenerational equity therefore does not provide additional help for the purpose of deciding the present question.

cc. Principle of Intragenerational Equity

The principle of intragenerational equity is a further sub-principle of that of sustainable development.[840] It does not focus on intertemporal responsibility but addresses inequity within the existing economic system.[841] It is not mentioned by name in the Rio Declaration, but several of its provisions (especially those

---

837 *Jacobs*, 14 Pac. Rim L. & Pol'y J. 2005, 103 (125).

838 See *Wold et al.*, p. 165.

839 See *Ohlhoff*, p. 193.

840 See *Birnie et al.*, p. 116.

841 See *Birnie et al.*, p. 122.

recognising the special needs of developing countries) imply the principle's relevance in contemporary international environmental law.[842] This approach has very much in common with the principle of common but differentiated responsibilities already discussed in this thesis.[843] In fact, the latter is even considered to be a subcategory of intragenerational equity (together with financial assistance and capacity-building for developing countries).[844]

The principle of intragenerational equity has severe limitations when used as a basis for judicial decision-making.[845] It does not provide any precise criteria on how to maintain the proper balance between environmental protection and development and what, exactly, the 'proper balance' is.[846] This is, however, as the question of this thesis shows, not necessary, either. A principle can still serve as a guideline in a case before a court or tribunal even if it is ambiguous in some of its aspects.

The principle in its substance, however, does not exceed the principle of common but differentiated responsibilities in any regard. It is much less discussed or explicitly incorporated into international treaties.

Therefore, no additional conclusions for the present thesis can be drawn with regard to the principle of intragenerational equity which would exceed the inferences based on the principle of common but differentiated responsibilities.

dd. Principle of Co-Operation

The principle of co-operation emerged from the principle of good-neighbourliness laid down in Article 74 UN-Charter in relation to social, economic, and commercial matters.[847] One of its elements is incorporated into Principle 27 of the Rio Declaration,[848] which reads as follows:

> "*States and people shall cooperate in good faith and in a spirit of partnership in the fulfilment of the principles embodied in this Declaration and in the further development of international law in the field of sustainable development.*"

The principle's importance and its practical significance are reflected by its affirmation in nearly all international environmental agreements on the bilateral,

842 See *Birnie et al.*, p. 122.
843 See above § 4. C. 2. b.
844 See *Birnie et al.*, p. 122.
845 See *Lowe* in: Boyle/Freestone, 19 (29).
846 See *Lowe* in: Boyle/Freestone, 19 (29).
847 See *Sands*, p. 203.
848 See *Sands*, p. 203.

regional, and global levels.[849] The obligation to cooperate is even more important in general international law.[850] It is incorporated most prominently in Art. 1(3) UN-Charter where it is described as one of the key objectives of the United Nations: "The Purposes of the United Nations are: [...] 3. To achieve international co-operation in solving international problems of an economic, social, cultural, or humanitarian character." One author describes the principle of co-operation "without hesitation" as one of the three constitutive pillars of the post-war international order, the UN-Charter.[851] It is, according to him, the "alpha and omega of United Nations law, but also of general international law."[852]

It is, however, an obligation of conduct and not of result.[853] Regarding the environmental damage likely to threaten endangered states' statehood, the reason for underlying global warming is a poor outcome of climate change negotiations leading to insufficient progress. Yet, global warming can certainly not be attributed solely to a quantitative lack of environmental negotiations. If the obligation to cooperate comprised nothing but the process of negotiating itself, it would have to be considered satisfied. There is, however, more to the principle. Negotiations aim at results and certainly are not ends in themselves. Therefore, states are obligated to cooperate in good faith to find solutions compatible for all parties concerned.[854]

Framing this principle in a way that stresses the obligation to negotiate in good faith, in addition to the negotiation itself, could be significant with regard to some states' refusal to enter into binding commitments to reduce the emission of GHG. Some major emitting states are not interested at all in a worldwide commitment to seriously reduce emissions and thus block international climate change negotiations.[855] This behaviour does not show good faith; thus it might violate the principle to co-operate. Based on this and other infringed-upon principles, it could, therefore, be argued that due diligence is lacking. One author deems it "possible that this failure of good faith is occurring, especially when viewed from the perspective of the SIDS given the limited time frame in which climate change must be confronted."[856]

849 See *Sands*, p. 203 et seq. with references to respective examples.
850 See *Dupuy*, EJIL 2000, 19 (22).
851 See *Dupuy*, EJIL 2000, 19 (22).
852 *Dupuy*, EJIL 2000, 19 (23).
853 See *Dupuy*, EJIL 2000, 19 (24).
854 See *Dupuy*, EJIL 2000, 19 (24); see also Principle 27 of the Rio Declaration.
855 Similar: *Lefeber*, p. 53.
856 *Gillespie*, 22 UCLA J. Envtl. L. & Pol'y 2003-2004, 107 (129).

With regard to the situation of endangered states, the Office of the U.N. High Commissioner for Human Rights[857] stated the following:

> *"The inundation and disappearance of small island States would have implications for [various rights]. The disappearance of a State for climate change-related reasons would give rise to a range of legal questions [...]. While there is no clear precedence to follow, it is clear that insofar as climate change poses a threat to the right of peoples to self-determination, States have a duty to take positive action, individually and jointly, to address and avert this threat."*[858]

This statement is clearly arguing for a duty to cooperate effectively with regard to the precise scenario this thesis is examining. The specific obligations deriving from the principle of co-operation, however, are not outlined clearly, especially in international case law.[859] It cannot be assumed, therefore, that an international court would consider this principle infringed upon by certain states. This could only be the case if the court found that states did not co-operate in good faith. Together with other principles, such a finding could argue for compensation in favour of endangered states. An individual state's lack of good faith while co-operating could, however, be very difficult to prove. Thus, this principle only provides limited implications in the context of this thesis.

ee. Principle of Preventive Action

The principle of preventive action is closely related to principle 21 (the no harm rule),[860] especially with regard to demands for due diligence.[861] The avoidance of damage, if at all possible, requires states to take action at an early stage.[862] Activities that cause or may cause damage to the environment in violation of the standards established under the rules of international law are prohibited by this principle.[863] In comparison to the precautionary principle, the principle of preventive action is older and more general as it does not focus on cases of scientific uncertainty.[864] It is incorporated in the Rio Declaration only indirectly, i.e.

---

857 Hereinafter, the Office of the U.N. High Commissioner for Human Rights will be referred to as OHCHR.

858 U.N. Doc. A/HRC/10/61 (2009), p. 14 et seq., para. 41.

859 See *Sands*, p. 204 et seq.

860 For a detailed examination of the no harm rule see above § 4. B. 4.

861 See *Sands*, p. 200.

862 See *Sands*, p. 201 with references to the *Gabčikovo-Nagymaros Case*.

863 See *Sands*, p. 201.

864 See the descriptions of *Sands*, p. 200 (principle of preventive action) and p. 217 et seq. (precautionary principle).

between the lines of Principle 11, demanding from states to enact "*effective* environmental legislation."[865] The numerous international commitments incorporating the principle of preventive action, however, are proof of wide support for it.[866]

Moreover, international case law clarified the principle's status in international law: In the *Iron Rhine Case*, the arbitral tribunal concluded in 2005 that "[t]oday, in international environmental law, a growing emphasis is being put on the duty of prevention."[867] This "duty [to prevent harm] has now become a principle of general international law. This principle applies [also] in autonomous activities."[868] This classification has been confirmed more recently by the ICJ in the *Pulp Mills Case*[869]: "The Court points out that the principle of prevention, as a customary rule, has its origins in the due diligence that is required of a State in its territory."[870] After references to its *Corfu Channel Case*, the ICJ very clearly points out that a "State is thus obliged to use all the means at its disposal in order to avoid activities which take place in its territory, or in any area under its jurisdiction, causing significant damage to the environment of another State."[871]

The principle of preventive action may take on a number of forms one of which is the application of liability rules.[872]

For the present study, these findings amount to the following: The principle of preventive action, as a well-implemented legal instrument of customary international environmental law, requires states to avoid harming other states. In contrast to the no harm rule, the principle – as its name indicates – focuses on prevention rather than compensation. Similar to the principle of intragenerational equity,[873] its preventive approach raises awareness of the future consequences of both actions and – especially – lack thereof.

Again, the contemporary progress of the international community as well as the progress which is to be expected in the nearer future do not support the conclusion that the requirements of the principle of preventive action are currently met by the international community, respectively most of its members.

865 *Sands*, p. 202, emphasis added.
866 See *Sands*, p. 202 et seq., who provides a comprehensive list of examples.
867 *Iron Rhine Case*, p. 90 para. 222.
868 *Iron Rhine Case*, p. 29 para. 59.
869 See *Sands*, p. 200.
870 *Pulp Mills Case*, p. 55 para.101.
871 *Pulp Mills Case*, p. 56 para.101.
872 See *Sands*, p. 202.
873 See above § 4. C. 2. d. cc.

This finding is a considerable additional argument making the case for a breach of 'due diligence.' The unequivocal ICJ statement in the *Pulp Mills Case* especially undermines this finding. Also, by focusing on prevention, the principle puts the failure to act on the same level as positive action. It thus does not make a difference if states pollute the environment themselves or if they fail to set up rules that prevent private actors in the area of their jurisdiction from polluting the environment. The duty to prevent harm corresponds to the prohibition of causing harm.

In summary, the principle of preventive action is a suitable (but not insurmountable) argument to reason that states did (and do) not act with due diligence regarding their GHG emissions.

ff. Principle of Shared Natural Resources

The principle of shared national resources is basically pursuing the idea to fairly divide the utilisation of those natural resources used jointly by more than one state.[874] It is in part quite closely related to the no harm rule,[875] i.e. reflecting a balance of interest between two or more states' territorial sovereignty.[876] Also, its origin can be traced back to the principle of good-neighbourliness.[877]

The ILC addressed this topic in five Reports on Shared Natural Resources so far, the first one having been published in 2003[878] and the latest one in 2008,[879] resulting in draft articles on the law of transboundary aquifers.[880] These articles refer to many principles already discussed in the present thesis. Article 6, for example, is a concretisation of the no harm rule;[881] Article 15 can be traced back to

874 See *Beyerlin* in: FS Doehring, 37 (59).

875 See U.N. Doc. A/CN.4/533/(2003), para. 11, p. 5.

876 See *Handl*, 26 Nat. Resources J. 1986, 405 (412).

877 See *Beyerlin* in: FS Doehring, 37 (60).

878 See "Shared Natural Resources: First Report on Outlines," U.N. Doc. A/CN.4/533/ (2003), available at http://www.internationalwaterlaw.org/bibliography/UN/UNILC/Groundwater/Yamada%201st%20Report-Addendum.pdf, last accessed 29 April 2014.

879 See "Fifth Report on Shared Natural Resources: Transboundary Aquifers," U.N. Doc. A/CN.4/591 (2008), available at http://www.internationalwaterlaw.org/bibliography/UN/UNILC/Groundwater/Yamada%205th%20Report.pdf, last accessed 29 April 2014.

880 See U.N. Doc. A/CN.4/591 (2008), p. 17 et seqq.

881 See "Article 6: Obligation not to cause significant harm to other aquifer States," U.N. Doc. A/CN.4/591 (2008), p. 19. The no harm rule has been discussed above, see § 4. B. 4.

the principle of co-operation.[882] These draft articles focus on the resource 'water' only.[883] Nevertheless, they are further proof of the entangled nature of principles in international law, partly depending on each other, partly overlapping to a great extent. While not delivering further significant findings content-wise, this set of rules based on the principle of shared natural resources further demonstrates the necessity to consider the overall picture of international law to find adequate solutions to questions like the present one.

The legal nature of this principle is discussed controversially, as well, but it cannot be denied that the notion has found general approval in state practice.[884] This leads to substantive criteria similar to the no harm rule.[885]

For the present study, this principle leads to several findings: The idea of shared utilisation of natural resources in general justifies the limitation of a state's territorial sovereignty. Certainly this does not lead to a collective ownership of those shared resources.[886] However, the whole ecosystem of the world is a natural resource shared by all of mankind, and international law urges to be considerate in doing so.[887] Some authors consider any kind of GHG emissions permitted as long as it is not expressly prohibited.[888] The principle of shared natural resources clarifies that the utilisation or pollution of a shared resource (in this case the atmosphere) entails the duty to be considerate in doing so. Thus, GHG are not emitted in a legal vacuum.

With regard to the indeterminate legal status of this principle, its implications for the criterion 'due diligence' yet are rather minor.

3. Rules, Principles and other Aspects in *General* International Law

a. Introduction

The examination of international environmental law rendered a number of results. It is an evolving field of international law with very few clear and binding

---

882 See "Article 15: Scientific and technical cooperation with developing states," U.N. Doc. A/CN.4/591 (2008), p. 22. The principle of co-operation has been discussed above, see § 4. C. 2. d. dd.

883 *Eckstein*, 18 Colo. J. Int'l Envtl L. & Pol'y 2007, 537 et seqq. comments the articles.

884 See *Handl*, 26 Nat. Resources J. 1986, 405 (410 et seq.).

885 *Handl*, 26 Nat. Resources J. 1986, 405 (413 et seqq.) examines the criteria very similar to those of the no harm rule.

886 See *Eckstein*, 18 Colo. J. Int'l Envtl L. & Pol'y 2007, 537 (553) with references to the discussion within the Sixth Committee, which stressed this point, *inter alia*.

887 Resemblant: *Gabčikovo-Nagymaros Case*, p. 78 para. 140.

888 See e.g. *Tomuschat* in: Hestermeyer et al., 3 (15 et seq.).

treaty obligations despite there having been considerable negotiation efforts over recent decades. Due to this lack of concrete results, this field of law tends to be shaped and determined by principles. Although they are discussed controversially, overall principles are increasingly accepted, also by the ICJ, as (in parts) having evolved into customary international law and thus being binding according to Art. 38 ICJ Statute. The content and criteria of these principles remain rather vague in most cases; the same applies to their legal status. Moreover, they sometimes overlap to a certain extent. This makes it more difficult to draw clear conclusions for the present study. This ambiguity is also caused in part by the nature of these principles, which is not to set up clear rules but rather to serve as guidelines for arguments. This meant that it was necessary to examine a broader scope of environmental principles in order to find the answer to the present question of an endangered state's claim to a new state territory. The starting point for this elaboration is the no harm rule. Other environmental principles serve as guidelines to interpret the no harm rule (more precisely: Its criterion 'due diligence') in due consideration of the practical and legal peculiarities of the present case.

But the scenario of losing a whole state territory, leading to the threat of losing statehood and losing cultural identity and cultural heritage, cannot be answered solely on the basis of the environmental aspects of international law. Environmental harm affects territorial sovereignty, thus principles from general international law[889] are considered as legal underpinnings of the protection of the environment.[890]

Due to the above reasons, this subchapter will broaden the angle and consider the ways in which other scopes of international law might provide further arguments that help answer the present question.

Many authors (and other actors in international law) have taken instructive, sometimes creative approaches to drawing conclusions regarding liability for environmental harm in general, or climate change liability in particular. This starts with a consideration of human rights (see under b.) or, regarding the loss of state territory, the right to self-determination (see under c.). Fundamental state rights/a state's right to exist will be discussed (see under d.), and further topics will be discussed more briefly (see under e.), some of which have already been touched upon while examining the principles of international environmental law. These concepts are: The principle of sovereign equality and territorial

889 For a comprehensive introduction into the general principles of international law see *Friedmann*, 57 Am. J. Int'l L. 1963, p. 279 et seqq.

890 See *Brownlie*, p. 276.

integrity, the principle of unjust enrichment, as well as some more general considerations of international law, starting with the purpose of modern international law aiming at ensuring peace and stability throughout the world, and the historical development of international law.

b. Human Rights[891]

aa. Introduction

In 2007, *Apisai Ielemia*, then Prime Minister of Tuvalu, called upon the members of the international community:

> *"Tuvalu joined the United Nations on 5 September 2000, firmly believing in the Organisation's noble pillars of development, security and human rights. We are now calling on the United Nations to uphold these pillars and ensure that our nation survives. While some believe that resettlement is the best solution, this clearly is not our preference. Tuvalu is a nation with a unique language and culture. Resettlement would destroy the very fabric of our nationhood and culture."*[892]

The human rights framework complements the UNFCCC by underlining that international cooperation is not merely a matter of the obligations of a State towards other States, but also of the obligations towards individuals.[893] For this reason it is useful to examine potential breaches of human rights also in the context of states' due diligence when emitting GHG.

Whereas most human rights treaties do not expressly mention environmental considerations, failure to protect the environment adequately may nonetheless give rise to individual human rights violations.[894] This applies especially with respect to climate change, which already today undermines the realisation of a broad range of internationally protected human rights.[895] Any forced relocation by virtue of global warming leading to rising sea levels and inundation of land implies challenges for sovereignty, statehood and nationality.[896] The

891 This chapter is considering international human rights law only. There are also regional variations of human rights law, e.g. the European Convention on Human Rights or the African Charter on Human and Peoples' Rights (see *Addo*, p. 287 et seqq.), which are however of no significant relevance in the context of this thesis.

892 *Apisai Ielemia*: "A Threat to our Human Rights: Tuvalu's Perspective on Climate Change," published 1 June 2007, available at http://unchronicle.un.org/article/threat-our-human-rights-tuvalu-s-perspective-climate-change/last accessed 29 April 2014.

893 See U.N. Doc. A/HRC/10/61 (2009), p. 28, para. 87.

894 See *Sands*, p. 797.

895 See *Humphreys* in: id., 1 (1).

896 See *Weinbaum*, 20 Pac. Rim L. & Pol'y J. 2011, 429 (444).

human rights implications of climate change are obvious[897] and will be outlined within this subchapter. Over the last few decades there has therefore been a move towards integrating environmental considerations into the human rights discourse.[898] Especially with regard to climate change the damage of which is expected to affect individuals as well as whole sectors of society, there is an increasing discussion about the link between those two topics and a consequent liability.[899]

The ongoing discussion is summarised within this subchapter, which is to be understood as a subject further contributing to an understanding of what is to be required to act with due diligence when emitting GHG.

bb. History

The Universal Declaration of Human Rights[900] was adopted by the General Assembly on 10 December 1948[901], three years after the end of World War II and the subsequent signing of the UN-Charter. The establishment of the United Nations itself as well as its Charter was a turning point and value change in the development, not only within the international community in general, but also concerning human rights law in particular.[902] After the UN-Charter itself had marked the beginnings of modern international human rights law[903], the UNDHR was the first international instrument that elaborated detailed human rights standards which are applicable on a global level.[904] Together with the 'International Covenant on Civil and Political Rights'[905] and the 'International Covenant on Economic, Social and Cultural Rights'[906] (both adopted in 1966) it represents the

897 See *Brunnée et al. in*: Lord et al., 23 (38); *Barnett* in: Humphreys, 257 (267).
898 See *Sands*, p. 797.
899 See *Brunnée et al.* in: Lord et al., 23 (38).
900 Hereinafter, the Universal Declaration of Human Rights will be referred to as UNDHR, available at http://www.un.org/en/documents/udhr/index.shtml, last accessed 29 April 2014.
901 See UNGA-Res. 217 (III) (1948).
902 See *Addo*, p. 151.
903 See *Brownlie*, p. 555.
904 See *Sands*, p. 777.
905 Hereinafter, the International Covenant on Civil and Political Rights will be referred to as ICCPR, available at http://www.ohchr.org/en/professionalinterest/pages/ccpr.aspx, last accessed 29 April 2014.
906 Hereinafter the International Covenant on Economic, Social and Cultural Rights will be referred to as ICESCR, available at http://www.ohchr.org/EN/ProfessionalInterest/Pages/CESCR.aspx, last accessed 29 April 2014.

key instruments of human rights at the international level.[907] None of these legal regimes however explicitly awards any environmental rights.[908]

A landmark that accelerated the debate about the interlinkage between climate change and human rights was the resolution on human rights and climate change[909], which the Human Rights Council[910] passed in March 2008.[911] In this the HRC recognised that "human beings are at the centre of concerns for sustainable development and that the right to development must be fulfilled so as to equitably meet the development and environmental needs of present and future generations."[912] Following this the first international body to examine the relationship between climate change and human rights was the OHCHR, which in its report concluded the following:[913]

> *"Climate change has various effects which affect human rights, such as extreme whether events, increased food insecurity and risk of hunger, increased water stress, stress on health status, sea level rise and flooding."*[914]

These effects befall endangered states without exception.

Small Island States had already tried to raise further awareness by framing their concerns regarding their continued existence in terms of human rights in November 2007 when they adopted the 'Male' Declaration on the Human Dimension of Global Climate Change.'[915] In this document SIDS pointed out that the environment provides the infrastructure for human civilisation whereas life depends on the uninterrupted functioning of natural systems.[916] They expressed their concern regarding the implications of climate change for the full enjoyment of human rights and thus requested an enhanced effort at mitigation.[917]

Another approach to addressing the human rights implications of the endangered states' loss of their territory had already been made in 2004, when the Working Group on Indigenous People (as part of the Commission on Human

---

907 See *Brunnée et al.* in: Lord et al., 23 (39).
908 See *Brunnée et al.* in: Lord et al., 23 (39).
909 See *Humphreys* in: id., 1 (3).
910 The Human Rights Council will hereinafter be referred to as HRC.
911 See U.N. Doc. A/HCR/7/L.21/Rev.1 (2008).
912 U.N. Doc. A/HCR/7/L.21/Rev.1 (2008), p. 2.
913 See *Knox*, 33 Harv. Envtl. L. Rev. 2009, 477 (477).
914 U.N. Doc. A/HRC/10/61 (2009), Annex, p. 31 et seq., table "Selected Human Rights Standards and Guidelines Relevant to Effects of Climate Change," first column.
915 See *Wold et al.*, p. 435.
916 See Male' Declaration on the Human Dimension of Global Climate Change, p. 1.
917 See Male' Declaration on the Human Dimension of Global Climate Change, p. 2 et seq.

Rights) released its working paper headed 'The Human Rights Situation of Indigenous Peoples in States and Territories Threatened with Extinction for Environmental Reasons.'[918] The author therein lists numerous legal problems and questions emerging from this scenario[919], yet does little to provide any answers.[920] Consequently the concluding statement asking to urgently assign a UN authority to address this question with comprehensive proposals[921] did not lead to any noteworthy reaction or development.[922]

cc. Content and Legal Nature

Little by little, human rights are changing from being a political ambition to being a legal reality.[923] They have ceased to be a mere matter of national authorities exclusively.[924] However, despite widespread general political and social endorsement, there is no consensus on the nature and character of international human rights law.[925]

The various human rights are divided into three categories.[926] The first generation comprises civil and political rights, the subsequent second generation includes economic, social and cultural rights and the latest and third generation contains matters such as the right to food, to peace or to a decent environment.[927] The latter category is commonly considered to comprise elements which are not yet parts of existing (binding) law, but "emerging" rights.[928] The right to life is the only human right which counts as *jus cogens*.[929]

Human rights are intended to protect against state interference.[930] Generally, they are a legal instrument that protects people within a certain state's jurisdiction from this very state.[931] Furthermore, traditionally they neither protect against natural causes, nor do they protect individuals from the international

---

918 U.N. Doc. E/CN.4/Sub.2/AC.4/2004/CRP.1.

919 One of these legal problems, maintaining or losing statehood, will be discussed further below, see § 5. B.

920 See U.N. Doc. E/CN.4/Sub.2/AC.4/2004/CRP.1, p. 3 et seqq. para. 8-13.

921 See U.N. Doc. E/CN.4/Sub.2/AC.4/2004/CRP.1, p. 9 para. 31.

922 See U.N. Doc. A/HRC/10/61 (2009), p. 20, footnote 91.

923 See *Addo*, p. 151.

924 See *Addo*, p. 151.

925 See *Addo*, p. 19.

926 See *Brownlie*, p. 567.

927 See *Brownlie*, p. 567.

928 See *Brownlie*, p. 567.

929 See *Grote Stoutenburg* in: Gerrard/Wannier, 57 (78).

930 See *Tomuschat* in: Hestermeyer et al., 3 (22).

931 See U.N. Doc. E/CN.4/Sub.2/AC.4/2004/CRP.1, p. 9 para. 28.

community.[932] This functional limitation is, however, not without exception, as will be shown in the following.

Case law related to human rights, especially with regard to liability in cases of infringements, is expected to become increasingly important.[933] In its 2004 Advisory Opinion on the 'Legal Consequences of the Construction of a Wall in the Occupied Palestinian Territory,' the ICJ commented on the opinion of Israel, which doubted that human rights law is applicable in the occupied Palestinian territory.[934] Israel had argued that human rights treaties were established only to protect citizens from their own government in times of peace.[935] The Court made it clear that governments are principally also bound by human rights outside their own state territory.[936] Furthermore, the Court considered that the applicability of human rights does not to cease in cases of armed conflicts[937] - another finding that highlights the broad range of the applicability of human rights.

This statement has been interpreted in a way that human rights, according to the ICJ, always remain in the background and can be used as guidelines for the interpretation of special regimes[938], a legal nature which has much in common with principles in international law. It is furthermore entirely consistent with case law and the conception of human rights to conclude that they would also be applicable across boundaries in environmental cases.[939] These are cases where damage arises which is caused by climate change, a phenomenon that is rooted in transboundary air pollution. Any state thus has to respect the human rights not only of its own citizens, but also those of other states' citizens.

dd. Relevant Human Rights

It is impossible to deny the threats to the very lives of endangered states' citizens caused by flooding.[940] Discussions about the human rights implications of

932 See *Tomuschat* in: Hestermeyer et al., 3 (22).
933 See *Brunnée et al.* in: Lord et al., 23 (40).
934 See *ICJ Advisory Opinion on Wall in the Occupied Palestinian Territory*, 136 (171), para. 86.
935 See *ICJ Advisory Opinion on Wall in the Occupied Palestinian Territory*, 136 (177), para. 102.
936 See *ICJ Advisory Opinion on Wall in the Occupied Palestinian Territory*, 136 (179), para. 109.
937 See *ICJ Advisory Opinion on Wall in the Occupied Palestinian Territory*, 136 (178), para. 106.
938 See *Tomuschat* in: Hestermeyer et al., 3 (23).
939 See *Birnie et al.*, p. 300.
940 See *Tomuschat* in: Hestermeyer et al., 3 (22).

climate change have increased in the recent decade. However, those discussions are not conducted in a very detailed manner, for example by examining single provisions based on a dogmatic approach. They rather focus on enumerating the affected human rights[941] and emphasising their transboundary applicability[942], also in environmental cases[943].

This thesis therefore will also desist from an elaboration of each provision that might be of importance. It is more revealing to identify those human rights whose infringement might be conclusive for the question if states acted with 'due diligence' in terms of the no harm rule.

A threat to various human rights is being discussed, amongst them: The rights to health and life, rights to adequate food, safe drinking water, shelter and property, right to the highest attainable standard of health and right to adequate housing, rights associated with culture as well as livelihood, with migration and resettlement as well as with personal security in the event of conflict.[944] Climate change also affects the human rights to privacy, family life and property.[945] However, some of these human rights might also be ensured if endangered states' citizens would have to migrate elsewhere. The constraint to leave a country does not necessarily lead to lower protection of certain human rights.

That said, there are some human rights, which are more clearly affected in the case of the impending extinction of states. Article 15 UNDHR is the most relevant provision in this regard. It guarantees everybody a right to a nationality. In particular this provision has been invoked to enhance the legal status of SIDS citizens.[946] *Apisai Ielemia* (then Prime Minister of Tuvalu) clarified in his statement from 2007 that "the climate change impact is an unprecedented threat to our nationhood. It is an infringement of our fundamental rights to nationality and statehood, as constituted under the Universal Declaration of Human Rights and other international conventions."[947] Any relocation enforced by climate change

---

941 See *Humphreys* in: id., 1 (1).

942 See ICJ Reports 2004, 136 (179), para. 109.

943 See *Birnie et al.*, p. 300.

944 See e. g. U.N. Doc. A/HRC/10/61 (2009), Annex, p. 31 et seq., table "Selected Human Rights Standards and Guidelines Relevant to Effects of Climate Change," second column; *Humphreys* in: id., 1 (1).

945 See *Aminzadeh*, 30 Hastings Int'l & Comp. L. Rev. 2007, 231 (246) (right to privacy and family life); *id.* (248) (right to property).

946 See *Weinbaum*, 20 Pac. Rim L. & Pol'y J. 2011, 429 (444); *Gillespie*, 22 UCLA J. Envtl. L. & Pol'y 2003-2004, 107 (122).

947 *Apisai Ielemia*: "A Threat to our Human Rights: Tuvalu's Perspective on Climate Change" (1 June 2007) available at: http://unchronicle.un.org/article/

and consequent inundation of a state territory implicates challenges for sovereignty, statehood and nationality.[948] GHG emissions that lead to the loss of whole state territories are the severest infringement of Article 15 UNDHR – in case such a loss would result also in the loss of statehood, leading to the respective citizens' loss of their nationality. Furthermore, one could argue that such a loss of statehood would indirectly affect *all* human rights because citizens depend on their respective state for the protection of these rights.[949]

Beyond, there are various human rights provisions aiming at ensuring the protection of social and/or cultural aspects of life. For example, the International Covenant on Econimic, Social and Cultural Rights, being one of the three pillars of human rights[950], prominently bears the crucial importance of social and cultural aspects of human rights in its name. The UNDHR also emphasises this importance *inter alia* in its Art. 22, which states:

> *"Everyone, as a member of society, has the right to social security and is entitled to realisation, through national effort and international co-operation and in accordance with the organisation and resources of each State, of the economic, social and cultural rights indispensable for his dignity and the free development of his personality."*

Most nations – and all endangered states – are social and cultural entities, bound together by their customs, their values and their histories. "Climate change will result in considerable spiritual and cultural loss."[951] Together with the right to a nationality, these social and cultural aspects of human rights are the most important ones in the context of this study.

ee. Implications for this Study

International lawyers are – as is frequently the case – divided regarding the potential contribution of human rights law addressing compensation for liability related to climate change. For example, ideas revolving around human rights discourses are considered philosophically alluring, yet they remark that "it needs to be clearly recognised that these will not solve the problem of adequately confronting climate change."[952] Hence, only a state-to-state strategy can effectively address climate change as any other approach would not reflect the current

threat-our-human-rights-tuvalu-s-perspective-climate-change/, last accessed 29 April 2014.

948 See *Weinbaum*, 20 Pac. Rim L. & Pol'y J. 2011, 429 (444).

949 Similar: U.N. Doc. A/HRC/10/61 (2009), p. 14 et seq., para 41.

950 See *Brunnée et al.* in: Lord et al., 23 (39).

951 *Burkett* in: Gerrard/Wannier, 89 (103).

952 *Gillespie*, 22 UCLA J. Envtl. L. & Pol'y 2003-2004, 107 (123).

international system based on the Westphalian Peace.[953] This applies despite the undisputed merit of human rights approaches.[954]

The point is made, that the human rights-based frameworks, in general, are not yet sufficiently developed to be practical for the particular adaptation context faced by worst-case scenario island nations.[955] More precisely, however, "the human rights framework cannot stand *alone* in helping to secure compensation for SIDS like Tuvalu."[956] Therefore, "multiple approaches to addressing climate change and providing redress for climate change victims should be viewed as complementary."[957] This point of view corresponds with the purpose of this thesis to draw lessons from a broad range of international (general and environmental) law in order to provide an answer to the present question.

In combination with international environmental law, human rights law has the potential to play a robust role in responding to the adverse impacts of climate change.[958] The discussion whether human rights (p.r.n. in conjunction with other principles, e.g. the no harm rule) could be a legal basis within the field of climate change liability is one which is hotly debated. There is a considerable tendency to take the view, that human right case law, as well as liability for breaches of human rights, is becoming increasingly important.[959] The prevailing view amongst experts is that climate change is a violation of human rights – some even refer to it as the most serious violation ever.[960] The resulting need for the evacuation of endangered states gives rise to a variety of human rights issues.[961]

SIDS basically have a fair standard of human rights.[962] This means, that – unlike the situation in other countries – it is not sufficient to enhance human rights at the level of the state.[963] In their case, what is required instead, is reducing GHG worldwide emissions *per se*, in order to avoid human rights violations.[964] Endangered states' citizens who move voluntarily or forcibly across an international

953 See *Gillespie*, 22 UCLA J. Envtl. L. & Pol'y 2003-2004, 107 (124).
954 See *Gillespie*, 22 UCLA J. Envtl. L. & Pol'y 2003-2004, 107 (125).
955 See *Weinbaum*, 20 Pac. Rim L. & Pol'y J. 2011, 429 (438).
956 *Weinbaum*, 20 Pac. Rim L. & Pol'y J. 2011, 429 (443), emphasis added.
957 *Weinbaum*, 20 Pac. Rim L. & Pol'y J. 2011, 429 (447); similar: *Aminzadeh*, 30 Hastings Int'l & Comp. L. Rev. 2007, 231 (265).
958 See *Nanda* in: WJU 2010, 42 (55).
959 See *Brunnée et al.* in: Lord et al., 23 (40).
960 See *Spier* in: Faure/Peeters, 47 (47).
961 See U.N. Doc. E/CN.4/Sub.2/2005/28, p. 2 para. 5.
962 See *Barnett* in: Humphreys, 257 (265).
963 See *Barnett* in: Humphreys, 257 (266).
964 See *Barnett* in: Humphreys, 257 (267).

border due to environmental factors would be entitled to general human rights guarantees in a receiving state; however they would often not have a right of entry to that state.[965]

It is highly unlikely that GHG emissions will be sufficiently reduced to avoid these threats. This means that in all likelihood human rights violations will not be averted (and indeed are already happening) in the case of endangered states. This, due to the interpretational function of human rights, suggests insufficient due diligence with regard to the environmental (and human rights related) damage caused by GHG emissions.

The OHCHR report, which commented precisely on the situation of endangered states, only contributes little in terms of this question by stating "[h]uman rights law does not provide clear answers as to the status of populations who have been displaced from sinking island States."[966] However, in the following sentence the author argues for a long-term political solution to this scenario with regard to the human rights of the people being affected by such a disaster.[967] The report furthermore clarifies that "[t]he inundation and disappearance of small island States would have implications for [...] the full range of human rights for which individuals depend on the State for their protection."[968] Therefore, "[s]tates have a duty to take positive action, individually and jointly, to address and avert this threat. Equally, States have an obligation to take action to avert climate change impacts which threaten the cultural and social identity of indigenous peoples."[969]

This statement does not only show the basic relevance of human rights regarding the legal consequences of the loss of a state territory, it also stresses the duty and the obligation of states. This could be a conclusive argument for determining a degree of 'due diligence' (as an element of the no harm rule) which does not necessarily have to be based on contractual consent between all states (as the liability *ex delicto* approach demands[970]), but which can also be determined by the insufficient performance of countermeasures to certain threats – at least in very obvious or extreme cases like the present one.

The immediately affected human rights can be ascribed to first and second generation rights, i.e. they have a more intense binding effect.[971]

965 See U.N. Doc. A/HRC/10/61 (2009), p. 20 et seq. para. 58.
966 U.N. Doc. A/HRC/10/61 (2009), p. 20 para. 60.
967 See U.N. Doc. A/HRC/10/61 (2009), p. 20 et seq. para. 60.
968 U.N. Doc. A/HRC/10/61 (2009), p. 14 et seq., para 41.
969 U.N. Doc. A/HRC/10/61 (2009), p. 14 et seq., para 41.
970 See above § 4. B. 4. e. bb.
971 See *Brownlie*, p. 567.

Human rights of endangered states' citizens are being infringed by GHG emissions. The crucial question, namely whether this finding leads to a clear liability for climate change damage, cannot (yet) be answered unambiguously. There is much to be said for the intermediary approach of denying a liability based on human rights considerations, yet to argue for using human rights as a further guideline while interpreting international law.[972] Doing so, in the context of the present thesis and in conjunction with the no harm rule, would rather argue for a breach of due diligence and thus in favour of a potential claim of endangered states.

It is not only the financial interests of endangered states that are being affected. The possible fate of not only the respective state, but also of the respective cultural and social entity is at stake. Climate change caused by GHG emissions thus affects the identity of the respective citizens. Human rights aimed at protecting culture, livelihood and nationality (*inter alia*) aim at granting identity. A state relocation (e.g. based on a claim) would still have a severe impact on cultural communities and their identities. At the very least, however, this adaptation scenario would keep together a community which encountered this fate as a social entity, while at the same time preserving its legal status. In the context of human rights, these are two key advantages of a state relocation strategy compared with a migration scenario.

States have a duty to address and avert the threats posed by climate change, which adversely affect the SIDS' citizens human rights.[973] This duty is also codified in the relevant treaties. For example, the preamble of the UNDHR contains the pledge of member states "to achieve, in co-operation with the United Nations, the promotion of universal respect for and observance of human rights and fundamental freedoms."[974] There is little evidence indicating that states will succeed in fulfilling this responsibility in the case of endangered states.

This could support an argument in favour of a claim in conjunction with the no harm rule. As outlined further above, the no harm rule alone does not suffice as basis for a claim.[975] However, the present case does not only affect environmental damage, but also concerns human rights. This suggests one should not reduce

---

972 See *Tomuschat* in: Hestermeyer et al., 3 (23).

973 See U.N. Doc. A/HRC/10/61 (2009), UN High Commissioner for Human Rights on the Relationship between Climate Change and Human Rights, p. 14 et seq., para 41.

974 Art. 1 (3) of the International Covenant on Economic, Social, and Cultural Rights contains a further commitment by signatory states to the promotion of the realisation of human rights.

975 See above §. 4. B. 5.

the no harm rule criterion 'due diligence' to environmental considerations solely. Other considerations, such as human rights implications, should also be taken into account. In extreme cases, when the human rights to nationality, social and cultural identity are at stake, this might justify assessing an insufficient degree of due diligence, even without self-imposed (contractual) commitments.

c. *Right of Self-Determination*

aa. Introduction

According to Art. 1(1) ICESCR,

> *"[a]ll peoples have the right of self-determination. By virtue of that right they freely determine their political status and freely pursue their economic, social and cultural development."*

The right to self-determination, also referred to as "principle of self-determination"[976], has been described as possibly the most dynamic and controversial principle of modern international law.[977] It is a fundamental principle of international law.[978] In general, this right applies equally to all peoples, also those who already live in independent states.[979] Furthermore, it is codified in Art. 1(2) UN-Charter as one of the main purposes of the United Nations. This provision beyond interlinks the right to self-determination with the principle of equality.[980] These very prominent references raise the question if this right also guards an already existing state against its extinction due to global warming.[981]

bb. Content and History

The right to self-determination is interlinked with human rights – respectively is referred to as one of the fundamental human rights itself.[982] Its realisation is an essential condition for the effective enjoyment of individual human rights.[983] It is rooted in the idea of enlightenment, understood as precondition for a people to decide upon its fate autonomously.[984] The first occasion where the underlying

---

976 *Brownlie*, p. 580.
977 See *Thürer*, AöR 1984, 113 (113).
978 See U.N. Doc. A/HRC/10/61 (2009), p. 14 para. 39.
979 See *Heintze* in: Ipsen, para. 28, marginal no. 4.
980 See *Heintze* in: Ipsen, para. 28, marginal no. 4.
981 See *Kehrer*, p. 125.
982 See *Kaczorowska*, p. 598.
983 See U.N. Doc. A/HRC/10/61 (2009), p. 14 para. 39.
984 See *Thürer*, AöR 1984, 113 (115).

idea appeared, was the U.S.-American Declaration of Independence from 1776, stating a lack of consent of the governed.[985] The first appearance of the concept itself was shortly before the settlements at the Versailles Peace Conference after World War I.[986]

Originally, the concept (in the post-war era) was primarily called upon in the context of decolonisation.[987] There are only 6 non-European countries that have never been colonies (Thailand, Iran, Turkey, Liberia, Afghanistan and Japan).[988] The principle emphasised the responsibility of the occupying (European) states, in order to enable a colonised people to determine themselves independently.[989]

Historically, the right to self-determination is to be understood as an entitlement against a certain state, aiming to achieve independence.[990] International law usually treats state borders as untouchable, aiming at ensuring territorial sovereignty, protecting states from exterior influences in internal matters, thus overall intends to maintain state stability.[991] This purpose to further stabilise a state traditionally is – quite different from the endangered states' situation – a strong argument against the enforcement of a certain people's right to self-determination.[992]

Two major legal functions of this concept need to be stressed. First, it serves as interpretational guideline for the work of the United Nations organs as well as for international cooperation.[993] Second, the principle is a bedrock for the development of emerging international law itself, inspiring and legitimating progress in this field of law.[994]

It is furthermore necessary to determine who is entitled to the right to self-determination. The concept is to be understood as "the right of cohesive national groups ('peoples') to choose for themselves a form of political organisation and their relation to other groups."[995] The right to self-determination is a collective

---

985 See *Thürer*, AöR 1984, 113 (115).
986 See *von Glahn/Taulbee*, p. 180.
987 See *von Glahn/Taulbee*, p. 180.
988 See *Kaczorowska*, p. 588.
989 See *Thürer*, AöR 1984, 113 (117).
990 See *Hampson* in: H.-J. Heintze, 60 (63 et seq.).
991 See *Hampson* in: H.-J. Heintze, 60 (66).
992 See *Blay*, 18 N.Y.U. J. Int'l L. & Pol., 1985-1986, 441 et seqq., examines the traditional conflict of these two principles.
993 See *Thürer*, AöR 1984, 113 (132 et seq.).
994 See *Thürer*, AöR 1984, 113 (133).
995 *Brownlie*, p. 580.

right held by peoples rather than individuals.[996] International law does not comprise any binding provision on what is to be considered as a people, thus 'people' is an indeterminate legal concept that has to be interpreted in the context of the respective case.[997] There is, however, no difficulty regarding this qualification of endangered states' peoples. The basic element of a people is the awareness as well as the political will to be one people.[998] There is no doubt that this condition is met in the endangered states' cases.

cc. Legal Nature

The interpretations of the legal nature of the right to self-determination and its content differ.[999] Before World War II, the principle was generally considered to have no legal content.[1000] This changed considerably in the post-war era when the principle was not only mentioned in Artt. 1(2), 55 UN-Charter, but when United Nations organs in particular established the contemporary understanding of this right to be part of the law of the United Nations.[1001]

In December 1952, the General Assembly in its resolution on the rights of peoples and nations to self-determination *recommended* that "the State Members of the United Nations shall uphold the principle of self-determination of all peoples and nations."[1002] This approach became more relevant in the context of colonial countries[1003] when the General Assembly in 1960 adopted the 'Declaration on the Granting of Independence to Colonial Countries and Peoples'[1004]. This document does not speak of a recommendation, but considers the right to self-determination to be a part of obligations stemming from the UN-Charter.[1005]

In his Advisory Opinion concerning the *Western Sahara Case*, the ICJ in 1970 confirmed "the validity of the principle of self-determination".[1006] The court

996 See U.N. Doc. A/HRC/10/61 (2009), p. 14 para. 39.
997 See *Heintze* in: Ipsen, para. 28, marginal no. 5.
998 See *Heintze* in: Ipsen, para. 28, marginal no. 5.
999 See *Thürer*, AöR 1984, 113 (113); *Kaczorowska*, p. 611.
1000 See *Brownlie*, p. 580 with further references to the rare legal sources from prior to 1945 regarding this principle. *Thürer*, AöR 1984, 113 (114 et seqq.) summarises the historical development of the concept.
1001 See *Brownlie*, p. 580.
1002 UNGA-Res. 637 VII (1952).
1003 See *Brownlie*, p. 581.
1004 See UNGA-Res. 1514 XV (1960).
1005 See *Brownlie*, p. 581 with further references.
1006 *Western Sahara Case*, 12 (33) para. 59.

based this statement *inter alia* on the UNGA-Resolution 2625 (XXV)[1007] (also from 1970), which in its annex contains the 'Declaration on Principles of International Law concerning Friendly Relations and Co-operation amongst States in Accordance with the Charter of the United Nations'[1008]. This declaration includes the following remarks:

> *"Every State has the duty to promote, through joint and separate action, realisation of the principle of equal rights and self-determination of peoples in accordance with the provisions of the Charter, and to render assistance to the United Nations in carrying out the responsibilities entrusted to it by the Charter regarding the implementation of the principle [...]."*[1009]

This understanding was recalled very expressively in the ICJ's more recent Advisory Opinion on 'Legal Consequences of the Construction of a Wall in the Occupied Palestinian Territory' from 2004, where the ICJ stated that "[t]he Court indeed made it clear that the right of peoples to self-determination is today a right *erga omnes*."[1010]

Authors assign a legal status to the right to self-determination in different ways. For example, one argument is that the right to self-determination does not lead to a certain people's right to nation building, but that they are entitled to autonomy.[1011] Others emphasise that the right to self-determination is not to be understood as a right to secession[1012] and must not be enforced by violence.[1013]

With only few exceptions the concept of self-determination has been limited to cases of decolonisation in international practice.[1014] However, each case is different, which makes it impossible to deduce any clear rules from international case law.[1015]

The concept is considered to be a binding part of international law at the latest since the two covenants on human rights (ICCPR and ICESCR) entered into

---

1007 See *Western Sahara Case*, 12 (33) para. 58.

1008 Hereinafter, the Declaration on Principles of International Law concerning Friendly Relations and Co-operation amongst States in Accordance with the Charter of the United Nations will be referred to as UN Friendly Relations Declaration.

1009 UNGA-Res. 2625 XXV (1970), 121 (123 et seq.).

1010 *ICJ Advisory Opinion on Wall in the Occupied Palestinian Territory*, 136 (172), para. 88.

1011 See *Hampson* in: H.-J. Heintze, 60 (72).

1012 See *Thürer*, AöR 1984, 113 (129 et seq.).

1013 See *Thürer*, AöR 1984, 113 (130 et seqq.).

1014 See *Kaczorowska*, p. 611.

1015 See *Kaczorowska*, p. 611.

force in 1976.[1016] In this context, the ICJ is being invoked, which in its judgement concerning the *East Timor Case* in 1995 made very clear that "the right of peoples to self-determination, as it evolved from the Charter and from United Nations practice, has an *erga omnes* character, [...] has been recognised by the United Nations Charter and in the jurisprudence of the Court [...] [and] it is one of the essential principles of contemporary international law."[1017] This understanding is also expressed in the OHCHR Report on the relationship between climate change and human rights from 2009, calling the right to self-determination a fundamental principle of international law.[1018] Today this principle "has acquired the highest possible status in the rudimentary hierarchy of international law."[1019]

dd. Implications for this Study

If sea level rise causes the loss of a state's territorial basis, this impairs the citizens' right to self-determination, i.e. their ability to determine their political, economic, social and cultural future.[1020]

The just quoted OHCHR Report from 2009 likewise confirms that "[s]ea level rise and extreme weather events related to climate change are threatening the habitability and, in the longer term, the territorial existence of a number of low-lying island States."[1021] This will have implications for the right to self-determination[1022], whereby (despite a lack of clear precedents)

> *"it is clear that insofar as climate change poses a threat to the right of peoples to self-determination, States have a duty to take positive action, individually and jointly, to address and avert this threat. Equally, States have an obligation to take action to avert climate change impacts which threaten the cultural and social identity of indigenous peoples."*[1023]

It is currently not to be expected that states will adequately address and avert this threat, either individually or jointly. They will thus very likely breach their obligation to implement sufficient measures, which would preserve the current mode of self-determination in endangered states. In the light of the findings from examining the no harm rule[1024], this could contribute to the argument that

---

1016 See *Schweisfurth*, chap. 9, marginal no. 341.
1017 *East Timor Case*, 90 (102), para. 29.
1018 See U.N. Doc. A/HRC/10/61 (2009), p. 14, para. 39.
1019 *Grote Stoutenburg* in: Gerrard/Wannier, 57 (76).
1020 See *Grote Stoutenburg* in: Gerrard/Wannier, 57 (76 et seq.).
1021 U.N. Doc. A/HRC/10/61 (2009), p. 14, para. 40.
1022 See U.N. Doc. A/HRC/10/61 (2009), p. 14, para. 40.
1023 U.N. Doc. A/HRC/10/61 (2009), p. 14 et seq., para. 41.
1024 See above §. 4. B. 4.

'due diligence' is not met when environmental harm is so intense that it divests a people of its right to self-determination. This could justify compensation based on the no harm rule. *In rem* restitution (thus a relocation strategy including the distribution of a new state territory) would be the only option to compensate a certain people's loss of the possibility of self-determination.

One approach (as early as 1984) furthermore understands the right to self-determination as interpretation guideline also whilst further developing international law.[1025] This viewpoint highlights the importance of sense and purpose of this legal concept to contribute to a peaceful world, and thus stability, and also to contribute to enlightenment, democracy and independence.[1026]

In this context it is important to highlight this principle's traditionally contradicting interest to preserve states from internal conflicts between rivalling social or cultural communities, which throughout history likely lead to massacres and other atrocities[1027]. Authors consequently so far tend to focus on the question wheter a certain people have a right to found (i.e. not to keep) a state based on the right to self-determination.[1028] The principle usually is contrary to the territorial integrity of the respective people's state.[1029] These dangers and issues do not exist in the case of endangered states.

The relation between the aim of international law to protect state stability and the right to self-determination is highly relevant for the application of this latter legal concept to endangered states. This thesis does not consider the more common case of founding a new state based on the principle of self-determination, but it considers the question whether this concept supports the preservation of an existing sovereign state. In this context, state stability has to be ascribed to the very main purpose of international law itself: The will to achieve and maintain peace and security in the world, which is also codified in the preamble of the UN-Charter.[1030] This leads to an understanding of the right to self-determination as "philosophical manifestation" of the founders of the United Nations, being a guiding principle for international institutions while exercising their duties.[1031]

1025 See *Thürer*, AöR 1984, 113 (132 et seq.).

1026 See *Thürer*, AöR 1984, 113 (115).

1027 See *Hampson* in: H.-J. Heintze, 60 (72).

1028 See the description of the different scenarios being considered at *Hampson* in: H.-J. Heintze, 60 (60 et seq.).

1029 *Blay*, 18 N.Y.U. J. Int'l L. & Pol., 1985-1986, 441 et seqq., examines the traditional conflict of these two principles.

1030 See *Thürer*, AöR 1984, 113 (118). This purpose of international law will be addressed in more detail further below, see § 4. C. 3. e. dd.

1031 See *Thürer*, AöR 1984, 113 (119).

Endangered states' citizens are in danger of losing their self-determination. This circumstance is due to other states' GHG emissions. This finding substantially supports the argument to consider this behaviour of other states as insufficient in terms of due diligence. The established nature of this principle underscores this reasoning. This counts especially since the most traditional counterargument[1032] against the exercise of this right does not apply in this case: This thesis does not consider a group of people who want to achieve independence against the will of their respective (current) state authority which is to be respected as sovereign subject of international law. On the contrary, the principle in the case of endangered states would be an argument in favour of saving these sovereign states (and the respective cultural and social entities) from extinction. The interest of the respective endangered state and its citizens are congruent.

GHG emissions that infringe the right to self-determination of endangered states' peoples are not conducted with due diligence.

d. Fundamental State Rights/State's Right to Exist

aa. Introduction

The existence of so-called fundamental state rights (also referred to as "basic principles"[1033]) has already been discussed since the 18th century.[1034] The term 'fundamental state rights' can be confusing, as usually fundamental rights describe the relation between a state and its respective citizens, where the state is (with very limited exceptions) the opponent.[1035] Moreover, as compared with national law, there is no such hierarchy of norms in international law, which is comparable to the relation between ordinary law and constitutional law.[1036] The term might therefore indeed be imprecise, but it rather aims at highlighting the irreversible nature of this legal instrument.[1037]

Authors have addressed the question whether fundamental state rights might give rise to a state's right to exist[1038], which makes these rights worth examining in the context of this thesis.

1032 For a detailed examination of the traditional conflict between the right to self-determination and a state's territorial sovereignty see *Blay*, 18 N.Y.U. J. Int'l L. & Pol., 1985-1986, p. 441 et seqq.

1033 See *Kunig*, Jura 1998, 160 (161, footnote 15).

1034 See *Berber*, Vol. I, § 22, p. 178.

1035 See *Kunig*, Jura 1998, 160 (161).

1036 See *Kunig*, Jura 1998, 160 (161).

1037 See *Berber*, Vol. I, § 22, p. 179.

1038 See e.g. *Kehrer*, p. 97 et seqq.; *Kunig*, Jura 1998, (160) 160 et seqq.

bb. Content and History

According to *Berber*, who was one of the leading authors with regard to fundamental state rights in the last century,[1039] the concept of fundamental state rights reached its climax in the 19th century, but also had considerable influence in the 20th century.[1040] Its underlying ideas have been incorporated in the UN Friendly Relations Declaration.[1041] The principles in this declaration however differ significantly with regard to their respective legal nature, which means that referring to 'fundamental state rights' in the context of this declaration is not really adequate.[1042]

According to one viewpoint, fundamental state rights arise from the very existence of states within a framework that governs their relations among each other as well as the order of the entirety of states.[1043] They comprise the following five traditional rights: Self-preservation, independence, equality, deference and association.[1044] In particular the first three of these rights (self-preservation, independence and equality) are relevant for endangered states in the present case. After a brief summary of international case law (e.g. the *Corfu Channel Case*), it is argued that the ICJ applied legal principles which were not (yet) fully established customary law, which also shifts fundamental state rights closer towards formally acknowledged extrapositive international law.[1045]

The right to self-preservation traditionally comprises capacities of states to defend their rights and interests towards other states in exceptional situations.[1046] Immediately, such a right of defence is of little avail in the context of inundation: This right indeed aims at defending territorial integrity against exterior state influences.[1047] However, no endangered state can defend its territory against a rise in the sea level, neither by force nor peacefully. Their vital interests are undisputed[1048], though not practically protected.

The purpose of fundamental state rights is to counteract the fact that, within state practice as basis for the system of international law, there is a tendency to

1039 See *Kehrer*, p. 100.
1040 See *Berber*, Vol. I, § 22, p. 178 with illustrative examples.
1041 See *Berber*, Vol. I, § 22, p. 178; *Kehrer*, p. 102.
1042 See *Kunig*, Jura 1998, 160 (161).
1043 See *Scupin* in: Strupp/Schlochauer, Vol. I, p. 723.
1044 See *Scupin* in: Strupp/Schlochauer, Vol. I, p. 723.
1045 See *Scupin* in: Strupp/Schlochauer, Vol. I, p. 732.
1046 See *Partsch* in: Strupp/Schlochauer, Vol. III, p. 255.
1047 See *Partsch* in: Strupp/Schlochauer, Vol. III, p. 256.
1048 See *Partsch* in: Strupp/Schlochauer, Vol. III, p. 410 et seq. concerning states vital interests.

benefit the powerful players at the expense of weaker parties.[1049] This thought however quickly leads to the controversial dispute of juridical positivism vs. natural law[1050], a question too complex, too little revealing and of too little relevance in the context of this study to be addressed in detail. It is important, however, in this context to stress that the existence of fundamental state rights and/or a state's right to exist does not presuppose any natural law approach.[1051] Even international lawyers who favour the positivistic approach accept the superior right of self-preservation as basis for interstate cooperation.[1052]

The concept of fundamental state rights does thus not presuppose a choice between natural or positivistic law but it needs to be differentiated between norms *generated* by interstate consent and those norms, which were preconditioned in this context.[1053] Fundamental state rights are rooted in the elementary concept of mutual esteem of other states' honour, territorial integrity and political independence, whereas international law further shapes these respective notions.[1054]

cc. Legal Nature

It is a very complex question whether certain fundamental state rights can be derived as *ius cogens* immediately from the very structure of the framework of international law itself.[1055] In order to argue for such an approach, the following noteworthy UN General Secretary's remarks in his 'Survey of international law' dated 23 April 1971 is being quoted[1056]:

> *"The doctrines of the sovereignty and equality of States have provided the bases of international law since the emergence of a society of independently governed States. These elements have formed the starting point for the development of various fundamental principles of international law relating to the conduct of States and, in particular, of the rule forbidding interference in the affairs of other States. The basic rights and duties of States derived from these principles may thus be said to consist, in essence, of the exercise of sovereignty by individual States and the respect these States owe in turn to the exercise of sovereignty by others, within an international community governed by international law."*[1057]

1049 See *Kunig*, Jura 1998, 160 (161), see also *Berber*, Vol. I, § 22, p. 178.

1050 See *Kunig*, Jura 1998, 160 (161).

1051 According to *Verdross/Simma*, § 77, authors mistakenly created a relation between these two questions.

1052 See *Scupin* in: Strupp/Schlochauer, Vol. I, p. 724.

1053 See *Verdross/Simma*, § 75.

1054 See *Verdross/Simma*, § 77.

1055 See *Kunig*, Jura 1998, 160 (161).

1056 See *Verdross/Simma*, § 77.

1057 U.N. Doc. A/CN.4/245, p. 9 para. 23.

Based on the fundamental idea of sovereign equality, these rights thus do not need any contractual basis, but are the oldest, most important and "holiest" part of unwritten international law.[1058] They are no delusions based on natural law, but norms arising from the concept of the international community.[1059] The term 'fundamental state rights' describes those principles of the respective contemporary international law which emerge as inherency from its character as logical necessity.[1060] E.g., Art. 51 UN-Charter speaks of "the inherent right of individual or collective self-defence."[1061]

This legal reasoning however does not necessarily need to be called upon, as existing treaties already comprise a great extent of those rights, which are being referred to as fundamental state rights.[1062] For example, the principle of sovereign equality is also codified *inter alia* in Art. 2 No. 1 UN-Charter, the right of self-preservation can be derived (indirectly) from the already quoted Art. 51 UN-Charter.[1063]

This leads to the following findings: First of all, fundamental state rights are not overruled by *leges speciales*. They comprise an undisputed right to self-preservation. They furthermore do not explicitly comprise an absolute right to exist. Such a right can however be derived from the concept of fundamental state rights.[1064] Other forms of states' extinction (e.g. via annexation) in the past are not to be considered as counterargument for this finding, as this only describes the factual and not the legal level:[1065] Annexation is illegal, although international law so far has no tools to counter these facts.[1066] However, this does not make the annexation (which must be considered an infringement of Art. 2 No. 4 UN-Charter) legal.[1067]

The right to exist, though, overall underlies more concrete principles and rights; it cannot be considered a primary norm itself, as it is too abstract to derive

1058 See *von Liszt*, § 13, p. 115 et seq.
1059 See *von Liszt*, § 13, p. 116.
1060 See *Berber*, Vol. I, § 22, p. 179.
1061 See *Berber*, Vol. I, § 22, p. 179 et seq.
1062 See *Kunig*, Jura 1998, 160 (161).
1063 According to *Kunig*, Jura 1998, 160 (161). This provision, however, does not explicitly speak of such a right, but rather clarifies the right to self-defence in case of an armed conflict.
1064 See *Kehrer*, p. 114.
1065 See *Kehrer*, p. 114.
1066 See *Kehrer*, p. 112.
1067 See *Kehrer*, p. 112.

specific legal consequences in individual cases.[1068] It must rather be considered an autonomous legal imperative, albeit without concrete legal consequences in case of an infringement.[1069] This supports the conclusion to also have recourse to this legal instrument as a tool for further interpretation, at least in cases of severe infringements like the present one.

dd. Implications for this Study

Kehrer examines fundamental state rights with regard to endangered states and a possible right to exist. She points out that only states as subjects of international law can be entitled by a potential right to exist that might be derived from fundamental state rights.[1070] Such protection applies to the preservation of the legal status as 'state.'[1071] Furthermore, she elaborates the question whether these rights might be inapplicable due to *leges speciales*, e.g. the right to self-determination or rights arising from the territorial integrity of respective states.[1072] This she denies persuasively, arguing that these other concepts are only meant to protect certain elements of a state, while a potential right to exist aims at protection of statehood itself.[1073]

Endangered states face a concrete threat of extinction due to other states' behaviour and omissions. This is, (*inter alia*) in the light of fundamental state rights, the most central and severe offence in international law.[1074]

The (largely undisputed) fundamental right of self-preservation is connected to the (more controversial) concept of international emergency law.[1075] At the bottom line this is nothing but a balance of interest between a state's right to exist and the international community's interest in peace and stability.[1076] This is very similar in the present case – with the modification that a potential claim of endangered states to a new state territory would not necessarily lead to negative implications for international peace and stability. This is especially true when compared with the second option, namely an immigration scenario. A claim would only affect the international community's interests in respect of assets

1068 See *Kehrer*, p. 114 et seq.
1069 See *Kehrer*, p. 115.
1070 See *Kehrer*, p. 100.
1071 See *Kehrer*, p. 98.
1072 See *Kehrer*, p. 98 et seq.
1073 See *Kehrer*, p. 98 et seqq.
1074 See *Scupin* in: Strupp/Schlochauer, Vol. I, p. 724.
1075 See *Partsch* in: Strupp/Schlochauer, Vol. III, p. 258.
1076 See *Partsch* in: Strupp/Schlochauer, Vol. III, p. 258 et seq.

and, in parts, a certain countries' territorial sovereignty.[1077] However, no comment is made on any explicit legal protection of a state's right to exist.[1078]

Others who examine the situation of SIDS do not only (briefly) try to deduce a state's right to exist from fundamental state rights and other principles of international law, such as territorial integrity, sovereign equality or the right to self-determination.[1079] It is also being argued *e contrario*: If a such a right was not part of international law, this would mean that, for example, a military attack by one state on another state would undisputedly be illegal, whereas an (attributable) flooding of another state would have no legal consequences.[1080] This appears to be a regulatory gap.[1081] There is no convincing explanation as to why a military assault on a state's territorial integrity should be illegal, whereas a state's extinction by other means does not lead to comparable conclusions.[1082] However, according to this opinion, international law is not yet capable of guaranteeing the protection of states, as history has proven that even certain hostile assaults on state sovereignty have been remedied by recognition in state practice despite their clear unlawfulness.[1083]

To conclude, fundamental state rights, understood as interpretational guideline, form a further argument to reach the conclusion that GHG emissions are not practiced with due diligence. Despite the foreseeability of sea level rise, states take no sufficient measures, which could prevent the inundation of endangered states. In the long run this will lead to an (involuntary) relinquishing of all fundamental state rights. These rights are considered to arise immediately from the concept of the international community.[1084] Any noncompliance with these rights (in the present case in the form of GHG emissions which lead to the extinction of states) has no immediate legal consequences in terms of an explicit and enforceable right to exist. However, such noncompliance is a further

---

1077 In which case the country should be compensated for a (preferably and probably necessarily voluntary) abandonment of a part of its territorial sovereignty, see below § 4. C. 5.

1078 See *Kehrer*, p. 109, who summarises Partsch and thereby observes this fact.

1079 See *Kehrer*, p. 118 et seqq. Most of these approaches are also considered at other points in this thesis, though in a different context. Therefore, *Kehrer's* argumentation will not be discussed in detail at this point.

1080 See *Kehrer*, p. 126 et seq.

1081 See *Kehrer*, p. 127.

1082 See *Kehrer*, p. 126 et seq.

1083 See *Kehrer*, p. 112 et seq.

1084 See *von Liszt*, § 13, p. 116.

argument to conclude that this behaviour of states does not sufficiently comply with requirements in terms of due diligence.

This finding is particularly relevant in the case of endangered states where whole states are at stake. The interference in other cases (i.e. states which suffer from climate change damage but are not threatened by extinction) is less intensive as these states can still enjoy their fundamental state rights so long as they are states. This might lead to a different conclusion in those less grave cases with regard to an insufficient degree of 'due diligence' in the context of the no harm rule.

e. *Other General Principles and Aspects in International Law*

aa. Introduction

The following subchapters consider various principles and other topics, which are worth being selectively highlighted in the context of this thesis. Some of these concepts have already been mentioned when considering other principles, but they are worth being emphasised in their own right, as most of them class among the core principles and cornerstones upon which contemporary international law is built. Also, purpose and development of international law deserve some attention in this context.

bb. Principles of Sovereign Equality and Territorial Integrity

A fairly crucial aspect in the context of this thesis is the principle of sovereign equality. It is one of the very core principles in international law[1085], codified in Art. 2 No. 1 UN-Charter, which explicitly states that

> *"[t]he Organisation is based on the principle of the sovereign equality of all its Members."*

Territorial sovereignty and territorial integrity are subparts of a state's internal sovereignty[1086] and "either emerge as a consequence or an attribute of sovereignty itself, or they are granted to the state by the rules of international law."[1087] Ultimately, any references to these concepts thus are aspects of sovereignty.

These principles have already been referred to within this thesis while examining the no harm rule[1088], a concretisation of the principle of sovereign equality.[1089] Nevertheless, due to their vital importance for the understanding of the basic framework of contemporary international law, a few further remarks are

---

1085 See *Jacobs*, 14 Pac. Rim L. & Pol'y J. 2005, 103 (120).

1086 See *Epping/Gloria* in: Ipsen, para. 23, marginal no. 66 et seq.

1087 *Shaw*, NYIL 13, 61 (77).

1088 See above § 4. B. 4. e. aa.

1089 See *Jacobs*, 14 Pac. Rim L. & Pol'y J. 2005, 103 (120).

made in this subchapter with regard to the implications for endangered states' sovereignty in a scenario of the loss of their state territory.

The notion 'sovereign equality' first appeared in October 1943 in the 'Declaration on General Security' and superseded its predecessor 'equality of nations' with the purpose of clarifying the legal rather than factual nature of this equality as the term 'sovereign' implies a hierarchy, which the term 'equality' denies.[1090] It has so far not played a vital role in international case law – a fact that might be explained by the unspecific nature of the concept, which is criticised for making little sense.[1091] Nevertheless, it is instructive in the context of this thesis as it highlights a development in international law: By choosing the term that emphasises the noun 'equality' (in contrast to 'principle of equal sovereignty', for example) two objectives were pursued.[1092] First, there was the intention to avoid any legal superiority of any one state over another, and second, it sought to strengthen the community discipline within all (UN-member-)states.[1093]

The relevance of sovereignty must not be underestimated. Authors speak of its "pre-eminence" in international law.[1094] Therefore, "any discussion of international law must begin with the context of state sovereignty."[1095]

The principle of sovereign equality is a display of substantive equity.[1096] This remark is being interpreted as fair balance between the different states' interests and needs.[1097] With regard to endangered states, this balance must be applied in a way that states have to avoid other states' extinction.[1098] This indicates an implicit right to exist.[1099] Such a right could be considered the bottom line of sovereign equality.[1100]

Jacobs examines a potential claim of Tuvalu against the United States, however not regarding a total land loss, but compensation for 'normal' damage resulting

1090 See *Fassbender/Bleckmann* in Simma, 2nd ed., Art. 2 No. 1 marginal no. 22.
1091 See *Fassbender/Bleckmann* in Simma, 2nd ed., Art. 2 No. 1 marginal no. 45.
1092 See *Fassbender/Bleckmann* in Simma, 2nd ed., Art. 2 No. 1 marginal no. 45 et seq. with further references.
1093 See *Fassbender/Bleckmann* in Simma, 2nd ed., Art. 2 No. 1 marginal no. 45 et seq. with further references.
1094 See *Wold et al.*, p. 152.
1095 *Wold et al.*, p. 152.
1096 See *Bleckmann* in Simma, 1st ed., Art. 2 No. 1 marginal no. 46.
1097 See *Kehrer*, p. 123.
1098 See *Kehrer*, p. 123.
1099 See *Kehrer*, p. 123.
1100 See *Kehrer*, p. 123.

from changed climate.[1101] She considers a state's sovereign right over its own natural resources (being a section of sovereign equality) as one of the two general principles of customary international environmental law Tuvalu could assert for the purpose of suing polluting states.[1102] The only obstacle she identifies for Tuvalu in this context is (different from the opinion held in this thesis[1103]) the proof of causation.[1104]

Kehrer, examining a possible right to exist, initially argues in favour of the existence of such a right based on sovereign equality[1105], but does not describe it as "primary norm" – a finding that leads to no responsibility of emitting states and no compensation for inundated states.[1106] This argumentation is inconsistent, especially with regard to the crucial interest of states to further exist. Despite not being a primary norm, this approach still can argue in one way or another and thereby give guidance as interpretational aid.

More extensive comments were made on the principle of sovereign equality in the light of states' contradicting interests and rights and state responsibility.[1107] The principle of sovereign equality is being considered in the context of the no harm rule with the following result: International law understood as right to co-exist incorporates sovereign equality (and territorial integrity), a principle which aims at the protection of each state against any adverse effects for one's own state territory caused by other states.[1108] This protection is the only way to ensure each state's right to exist undisturbed and unimpaired.[1109] The sovereignty of each single state thus ends where another state is adversely affected.[1110] This tenet is not absolute – but any acceptable interference in another state's sovereignty or territorial integrity is only an exception.[1111] Common negative environmental influences between states are a mere consequence of the industrial revolution, a historical development that exceptionally allows the infringement of a prohibition.[1112] In this context, the necessity is being stressed that international

1101 See *Jacobs*, 14 Pac. Rim L. & Pol'y J. 2005, 103 et seqq.
1102 See *Jacobs*, 14 Pac. Rim L. & Pol'y J. 2005, 103 (119).
1103 See above § 4. B. 4. d. aa. (3).
1104 See *Jacobs*, 14 Pac. Rim L. & Pol'y J. 2005, 103 (120 et seq.).
1105 See *Kehrer*, p. 123.
1106 See *Kehrer*, p. 127.
1107 See *Epiney*, AVR 1995, 309 et seqq.
1108 See *Epiney*, AVR 1995, 309 (320).
1109 See *Epiney*, AVR 1995, 309 (320).
1110 See *Epiney*, AVR 1995, 309 (321).
1111 See *Epiney*, AVR 1995, 309 (322).
1112 See *Epiney*, AVR 1995, 309 (322).

environmental law has to find sensible solutions when faced with new challenges and developments.[1113] These can only be addressed adequately with an awareness of a certain legal principle's bedrock and its ground of validity.[1114]

The international community faces severe and new challenges without precedents. On the one hand, states that are (more) responsible for global warming have an interest in legitimately emitting GHG (and thus not to pay for the consequences of these emissions). This interest can be derived from their territorial sovereignty. Endangered states on the other hand have an interest in their continued existence. This thesis does not only consider the common situation where the no harm rule is applicable, i.e. (mere) adverse impacts on a state's territorial integrity due to environmental harm caused by another state. Rather, it considers a scenario of total land loss, affecting a state's territorial integrity to such an extent that it might lose its sovereignty completely and permanently.

In this context, the concept of sovereign equality is violated by the excessive GHG emissions of other states. If international law cannot provide legal protection for the statehood of endangered states, this would affect both 'sovereignty' and 'equality.' The sovereignty of endangered states would disappear. Furthermore, it would contradict the concept of equality if a state could be (indirectly) extinguished by fellow states without consequences. The intensity of this violation suggests that states did (and do) not act with due diligence within the meaning of the no harm rule. As the principle of sovereign equality is one of the core principles of contemporary international law, a severe violation thereof is a strong argument for compensation.

cc. Unjust Enrichment

An unconventional approach to compensating SIDS was made by *Weinbaum* in 2011.[1115] She first summarises the contemporary and future effects of climate change on SIDS, for which she uses the small island nation Tuvalu as example.[1116] Subsequently, she briefly explains that current mitigation and adaption strategies alone cannot address these threats appropriately.[1117] The two major approaches to justify a potential compensation claim, tort law (based e.g. on the no harm rule[1118])

1113 See *Epiney*, AVR 1995, 309 (323).

1114 See *Epiney*, AVR 1995, 309 (323).

1115 See *Weinbaum*, 20 Pac. Rim L. & Pol'y J. 2011, 429 et seqq.

1116 See *Weinbaum*, 20 Pac. Rim L. & Pol'y J. 2011, 429 (430 et seqq).

1117 See *Weinbaum*, 20 Pac. Rim L. & Pol'y J. 2011, 429 (436 et seqq).

1118 For a detailed examination of this principle of environmental international law see above § 4. B. 4.

and the human rights frameworks, in her opinion do not meet the immediate needs of SIDS' climate change victims.[1119] She therefore argues for the principle of unjust enrichment as most reasonable cause of action for a SIDS' compensation.[1120]

The principle of unjust enrichment is one of the general principles in international law, applicable as an independent basis of liability on both state and international levels.[1121] As early as 1963, *Friedmann* wrote that this principle is incorporated in all modern civil law codifications[1122] and can be applied (with limitations) in international law[1123]. As it has been applied in various cases of the ICJ and is therefore broadly recognised in state practice as well as case law, it can be characterised as a general principle of international law under Article 38(1)(c) ICJ Statute.[1124]

Based on the principle of unjust enrichment, a claimant can be entitled, where a defendant has been enriched at the plaintiff's expense.[1125] The underlying idea of this legal instrument is that without a legal cause, nobody should enrich himself at the expense of another.[1126]

The following three elements are necessary for a successful claim based on this principle: Firstly enrichment must accrue to the defendant, secondly the enrichment must occur at the plaintiff's expense and thirdly the enrichment must be unjust.[1127]

Considering the first criterion 'enrichment,' the definition may be broadly construed.[1128] It is merely necessary to identify something positive, e.g. an accretion of wealth is sufficient.[1129] The second criterion, compared to other legal instruments, comprises the peculiarity that there is no need for the plaintiff to prove some sort of guilt of the defendant.[1130] This allows a claim despite an

1119 See *Weinbaum,* 20 Pac. Rim L. & Pol'y J. 2011, 429 (438 et seqq.). Weinbaum's arguments are referred to in the respective subchapter of this thesis, see above § 4. B. 4. e. aa. (concerning tort law) and § 4. C. 3. b. ee. (concerning a human rights approach).

1120 See *Weinbaum,* 20 Pac. Rim L. & Pol'y J. 2011, 429 (447 et seqq.).

1121 See *Weinbaum,* 20 Pac. Rim L. & Pol'y J. 2011, 429 (448).

1122 See *Friedmann,* 57 Am. J. Int'l L. 1963, 279 (295).

1123 See *Friedmann,* 57 Am. J. Int'l L. 1963, 279 (298).

1124 See *Weinbaum,* 20 Pac. Rim L. & Pol'y J. 2011, 429 (447).

1125 See *Weinbaum,* 20 Pac. Rim L. & Pol'y J. 2011, 429 (447).

1126 See *Friedmann,* 57 Am. J. Int'l L. 1963, 279 (296).

1127 See *Fagan,* 76 N.Y.U. L. Rev. 2001, 626 (640) with further references.

1128 See *Weinbaum,* 20 Pac. Rim L. & Pol'y J. 2011, 429 (449).

1129 See *Fagan,* 76 N.Y.U. L. Rev. 2001, 626 (642) with further references.

1130 See *Wenger,* 40 U.S.F.L. Rev. 2006, 279 (301).

attenuated relationship among the parties.[1131] The third element, an unjustness of the enrichment, is generally met when the enrichment has been achieved mischievously or inequitably.[1132] According to another approach, the absence of a legal cause is required.[1133]

Weinbaum calls the principle of unjust enrichment a "gap-filling device" being "particularly relevant to SIDS."[1134] GHG emissions lead to benefits for emitter countries on the one hand, while on the other hand they result in negative results for other states[1135], a typical benefit at another parties cost.

According to *Weinbaum*, using the example of Tuvalu, all criteria are met in the present case: Industries that contribute to GHG emissions have led to economic development and an accumulation of wealth[1136]; a finding that especially applies to developed countries. Emitting countries hence are enriched. Furthermore, this enrichment occurs at the expense of the plaintiff, as SIDS' state territories are adversely affected to an extent that islands' nations must seriously consider permanent relocation of their entire people to ensure their survival.[1137]

The third criterion *Weinbaum* also considers as satisfied in the Tuvaluan context.[1138] She imprecisely refers to an "unfair" instead of an "unjust" enrichment and reasons "[w]hile citizens of the United States and Australia enjoy a relatively high quality of life as a result of each country's emissions, Tuvaluans must contemplate submerged lands and the loss of their status as a nation", which she considers "strikingly unfair"[1139].

With regard to a *general* climate change liability (i.e. for any state's damage that can be ascribed to anthropologically caused global warming) derived from principles in international law, the prevailing opinion is more convincing than *Weinbaum's* approach. According to this view, this liability generally has to be addressed adequately on a tort law based approach, whereas current international

1131 See *Weinbaum*, 20 Pac. Rim L. & Pol'y J. 2011, 429 (451).
1132 See *Fagan*, 76 N.Y.U. L. Rev. 2001, 626 (647), who provides case law examples in footnote no. 104.
1133 See *Friedmann*, 57 Am. J. Int'l L. 1963, 279 (296).
1134 *Weinbaum*, 20 Pac. Rim L. & Pol'y J. 2011, 429 (448).
1135 See *Weinbaum*, 20 Pac. Rim L. & Pol'y J. 2011, 429 (448).
1136 See *Weinbaum*, 20 Pac. Rim L. & Pol'y J. 2011, 429 (450).
1137 See *Weinbaum*, 20 Pac. Rim L. & Pol'y J. 2011, 429 (450).
1138 See *Weinbaum*, 20 Pac. Rim L. & Pol'y J. 2011, 429 (451).
1139 *Weinbaum*, 20 Pac. Rim L. & Pol'y J. 2011, 429 (451).

law does not yet seem to be sufficiently developed for any general liability.[1140] *Weinbaum* shifts the principle of unjust enrichment closer to full damages – an approach quite contrary to the cardinal distinction of these two concepts in all the relevant civil and common-law systems[1141]. Also, compared to the relation between private parties, international relations are highly complex, based on a history of economic-political development, which means one should only use this principle with caution.[1142]

Her comments on the third criterion (unjustness) are rather emotional and less juridical. A legal cause for the enrichment could be seen, for example, in the emitting state's sovereign right to exploit its own resources. This however could not possibly entitle states to cause other states' inundation. Accordingly, *Weinbaum's* result regarding this element has to be concurred with.

In conclusion, a gap-filling device such as unjust enrichment does not seem to be necessary. This legal instrument appears to be overstretched in the context of climate change liability, especially considering its common legal consequence, which is to surrender the respective enrichment.

Nevertheless, there is an important thought underlying this approach, which is relevant in the context of this thesis. *Weinbaum* points out the benefits of GHG emissions, leading to economic growth and thus wealth. GHG emissions do not only cause a rising sea level, but they also (so far) lead to a rising standard of living. This thought also underpins the principle of common but differentiated responsibilities[1143], but the context of unjust enrichment more clearly highlights the nexus between benefits on one side, achieved at the expense of other parties without legal justification.

It is not possible to convincingly argue a claim to a new state territory, which is solely based on the legal principle of unjust enrichment. Also it is of no avail to use this principle to interpret the no harm rule's criterion 'due diligence.' The only instructive thought in the context of this thesis that has been identified is the link between the economic damage on the one hand and the benefit in terms of wealth on the other hand.

In summary it can be said, therefore, that the principle of unjust enrichment does not really provide any additional arguments for or against a breach of the no harm rule's 'due diligence' in the context of this study.

1140 See above § 4. B. 4. e. bb.

1141 See *Friedmann*, 57 Am. J. Int'l L. 1963, 279 (297).

1142 See *Friedmann*, 57 Am. J. Int'l L. 1963, 279 (296).

1143 See above § 4. C. 2. b.

dd. Purpose of International Law: Peace and Security

To comprehensively examine the present question, it is instructive to also consider the purpose of contemporary international law.

The UN-Charter is the bedrock of modern international law. The collapse of the world order caused by World War II raised the inevitable question of a new legal world order for the post-war era.[1144] Joint action by the more powerful states against threats to stability of the international order was the primary concern while reframing the international order.[1145] "The [Charter's] obvious starting point is the master aim of the Founders: To create a lasting arrangement for peace and security."[1146]

The Preamble of the UN-Charter is very noteworthy in this context. Abridged, it prominently states the following:

> *"WE THE PEOPLES OF THE UNITED NATIONS DETERMINED to save succeeding generations from the scourge of war, which twice in our lifetime has brought untold sorrow to mankind, and to reaffirm faith in* [...] ***equal rights*** [...] ***of nations large and small,***
>
> *AND FOR THESE ENDS*
>
> *to practice tolerance and* ***live together in peace*** *with one another as good neighbours, and to unite our strength* ***to maintain international peace and security*** [...]
>
> *HAVE RESOLVED TO COMBINE OUR EFFORTS TO ACCOMPLISH THESE AIMS."*[1147]

This further elucidates the most important intent of international law: The creation and preservation of peace and security throughout the world.[1148] According to Art. 24 UN-Charter, the primary responsibility for the maintenance of international peace and security rests with the Security Council. This arrangement however only aims to achieve the ability to act quickly and effectively.[1149] Thus this provision does not exonerate other players in international law to promote and work towards peace and security, as the language "primary responsibility" and the context "to ensure prompt and effective action" in Art. 24 UN-Charter prove. There is a responsibility of each state, the United Nations and states represented on the governance structure of the United Nations for peace and stability.[1150]

1144 See *Grewe/Khan* in Simma, 2nd ed., Drafting History, marginal no. 1.

1145 See *Schachter*, 89 Am. Soc'y Int'l L. Proc. 1995, 45 (46).

1146 *Schachter*, 89 Am. Soc'y Int'l L. Proc. 1995, 45 (46).

1147 Emphasis added.

1148 See *Verdross/Simma*, § 92.

1149 See *Geiger* in Simma, 2nd ed., Art. 23, marginal no. 1.

1150 See *Roeben* in: Bogdandy/Wolfrum, 99 (135 et seqq., 153). Roeben primarily refers to cases of armed conflicts or severe crimes (e.g. genocide and ethnic cleansing). His general remarks, nevertheless, are also applicable in the present context.

The substantial function of international law can only be answered by looking at the respective challenges the world faces now and in the near future.[1151] In this context the cardinal peacekeeping function has to be kept in mind as well as three further challenges: Compensation between regions of different social and economic standards, international environment protection and international protection of the individual.[1152] However, it is not only these challenges, which have to be focussed upon while interpreting international law, but also the interaction between politics and international law.[1153] In this context, international law must not be overstretched: "Law is a technique to preserve cooperation agreements but is not necessarily the technique best suited to develop them."[1154]

The cardinal need for security and stability in international law is reflected by the concept of sovereignty.[1155] Territorial sovereignty "is the answer provided by international law as regards the needs for security, stability *and identity* felt by a particular group within a certain area."[1156]

This link not only between the purpose of international law (i.e. peace and security) and territorial sovereignty, but also between security and stability (thus peace) and the importance of granting (regional) identity is important in the context of this study. Mankind has organised itself in territorial entities (states) which are essential for the identity of any human being in our current world order. This identity is important for peace and stability throughout the world. Therefore, to further support the key purpose of international law, it is expedient to preserve regional identity, thus to preserve territorial sovereignty, hence to preserve statehood.

Moreover, the extended enumeration of contemporary challenges for the world[1157] all can be related to endangered states: Compensation between regions of different social and economic standards (as discussed in the context of common but differentiated responsibilities[1158]), international environment protection (e.g. promoted by the principle of sustainable development[1159], the precautionary

1151 See *Ipsen* in: id., para. 3, marginal no. 14.
1152 See *Ipsen* in: id., para. 3, marginal no. 14.
1153 See *Ipsen* in: id., para. 3, marginal no. 1 et seqq.
1154 *von Glahn/Taulbee*, p. 511.
1155 See *Shaw*, NYIL 13, 61 (78).
1156 *Shaw*, NYIL 13, 61 (79), emphasis added.
1157 See *Ipsen* in: id., para. 3, marginal no. 14.
1158 See above § 4. C. 2. b.
1159 See above § 4. C. 2. c.

principle[1160] and the no harm rule[1161]) and international protection of the individual (as elucidated within the subchapters about human rights[1162] and the right to self-determination[1163]).

This leads to two key findings in this subchapter: First, the situation of endangered states combines most of the severest challenges the international community currently faces. In this context it is important to stress the explicit equal status of "nations large and small" in the preamble of the UN-Charter. Second, the answer which international law (applied by states, international institutions and international jurisdiction) will provide for these states will therefore be an indicator for the effectiveness of international efforts to face those challenges and to consider the values and aims the international framework is build upon.

The purpose of international law – as well as the challenges the international community is facing now and in the near future – strongly supports an argument for the preservation of the statehood of endangered states. However, these considerations do not concern a legal principle but can rather serve as the basis for a teleological approach to interpreting other principles, in the present case the no harm rule. Acting with 'due diligence' in this way can also require adequately responding to severe contemporary challenges whilst corresponding to the purpose of international law. Endangered states are small nations, which cannot protect themselves autonomously. The failure to protect them against extinction – respectively causing their extinction – does not comply with the purposes of international law and thus is a further indicator for a lack of due diligence.

ee. Development of International Law

As mentioned above, international law is quickly evolving[1164] – especially its environmental scope[1165]. New and emerging precepts in international law are slowly being incorporated into a new generation of international law.[1166] This subchapter combines some thoughts to contribute to a more precise assessment of whether international law is (already) capable to concede endangered states a claim to a new state territory, a delicate approach with regard to the overall complexity global warming is imposing on the international community.

1160 See above § 4. B. 4. d. aa. (2).
1161 See above § 4. B. 4.
1162 See above § 4. C. 3. b.
1163 See above § 4. C. 3. c.
1164 See *Weiss* in: Vig/Axelrod, 98 (99); similar: *Spier* in: Faure/Peeters, 47 (47).
1165 See *Brunnée* et al., in Lord et al., 1 (1) para. 1.02.
1166 See *Pring/Pring* in: FS Nanda, 482 (483).

First, a fairly recent statement with regard to that development:

> *"From the perspective of tort law [...] the theory and practice of pleading and proving a civil wrong caused by one or more defendants' 'climate change' conduct, sufficient to trigger entitlement to money damages or injunctive relief, or both, is seriously problematic at present. Given the creativity and persistence of tort lawyers, however, it is likely that within the next several decades of the twenty-first century, [...] climate change torts will be recognised in individual cases that apply traditional tort causes of actions and evolving new tort causes of action."*[1167]

Environmental tort law will keep taking on increasingly greater significance.[1168] There is a rising discrepancy between the obvious need of effective environmental protection and the reluctance of states to act.[1169]

Recently, the same topic was discussed on a national level (i.e. under private law), comparing the successful mass fraud claims against the tobacco industry in the USA with potential claims against the hydrocarbon industry, as both actively perpetuated misinformation for their respective economic benefit.[1170] Comments on the successful campaigning of the hydrocarbon industry to systematically spread misinformation[1171] provide a further indication for the contrast between the current state of climate change science and the hesitant reaction of international politics and international law.

The importance of responsibility in international law increases.[1172] International responsibility is "an institution of international law" which indicates its evolution.[1173] Whereas the primary function of international law previously has been to serve sovereigns pursuing their national interests, the institutionalisation of responsibility evidences a shift towards serving the pursuit of common objectives and community interests.[1174]

What are other characteristics of the development of (general and environmental) international law – within the last century, especially in the post-war

1167 *Blomquist*, 46 Va. U. L. Rev. 2011-2012, 1053 (1055). Bloomquist primarily refers to domestic lawsuits, yet uses them as a reference to examine the development of international law.

1168 See *Hartmann*, p. 180.

1169 See *Hartmann*, p. 180 et seq.

1170 See *Dubats*, 7 Nw.J. L. & Soc. Pol'y 2012, 511 (511). The reasoning of *Dubats* has been summarized further above, see § 2. B. 4.

1171 See *Dubats*, 7 Nw.J. L. & Soc. Pol'y 2012, 511 (518 et seqq.).

1172 See *Roeben* in: Bogdandy/Wolfrum, 99 (156 et seqq.).

1173 See *Roeben* in: Bogdandy/Wolfrum, 99 (157).

1174 See *Roeben* in: Bogdandy/Wolfrum, 99 (157).

era? This question is *inter alia* answered by pointing out the increased humanitarian focus.[1175] This begins with the 'Martens Clause' from 1899 and 1907 (applicable in war as part of *ius in bello*), which for the first time built a bridge between natural law and positivism by incorporating a moral and ethical telos into international law.[1176] Further conclusions can be drawn from the *Corfu Channel Case* (1949)[1177], in which the ICJ made it clear, that elementary considerations of humanity are applicable in times of war and even more exacting in times of peace.[1178] This constant humanitarian development had its most recent cornerstone in the 'Responsibility to Protect,' a concept adopted by the UN General Assembly in 2005[1179] which, as *ultima ratio*, not only enables, but obliges the international community to act if a certain state does not meet its responsibilities.[1180]

'Responsibility to Protect' was first used as legal basis for the mission in Libya.[1181] This proves its practical relevance. It is designed only "to protect populations from genocide, war crimes, ethnic cleansing and crimes against humanity"[1182], thus not from climate change or the loss of their homeland. Nevertheless, this concept marks a double shift in international law, which is also important in the context of this thesis: First, the rights of the individual are not only theoretically protected, but an infringement can have very concrete consequences, including an armed conflict as *ultima ratio*. This also further strengthens the remarks made above with respect to the rising relevance of individual rights[1183] (human rights[1184] and the right to self-determination[1185]). Second, 'Responsibility to Protect' marks a noteworthy power shift away from states towards the international community. This step reflects the development that the world faces more and more global problems, which most adequately can be addressed

1175 See *Rensmann*, ZaöRV 2008, 111 et seqq.
1176 See *Rensmann*, ZaöRV 2008, 111 (113).
1177 See *Rensmann*, ZaöRV 2008, 111 (113).
1178 See *Corfu Channel Case*, 4 (22).
1179 See UNGA-Res. A/RES/60/1.
1180 For a detailed elaboration, see *Zifcak* in: Evans, 504 (504 et seqq.).
1181 See Die Zeit: "Dieser Krieg war gerecht," ['This war was just'] (27 October 2011, No. 44).
1182 UNGA-Res. A/RES/60/1, p. 30 para. 137.
1183 *Weiss* in: Vig/Axelrod, 98 (101), also emphasises the increased importance of the individual in international law.
1184 See above § 4. C. 3. b.
1185 See above § 4. C. 3. c.

on a global basis.[1186] This increase of power, of course, also leads to an increased responsibility at a global level.

'Responsibility to Protect' thus is one of the international law's answers provided while being faced with changed circumstances. It is a global solution to facilitate humanitarian interventions in order to prevent the commission of mass atrocity crimes.[1187] In this context, it is worth reiterating that the respective discourse in international law is shaped by the respective prevailing circumstances.[1188]

Global warming is one of the key prevailing issues for the international community - and for international lawyers. Within the United Nations, climate change is part of the so-called "new threats"[1189] - a term that indicates the necessity of new solutions. The United Nations Development Report states "[c]limate change is the defining human development issue of our generation."[1190] Another author (rejecting a - general - state liability for climate change damage[1191]) puts it this way: "Never before has humankind had to face up to a threat that involves not only every member of the international community, States and international organisations alike, but also every individual human being. [...] *Nostra res agitur.* [It is ours to act.]."[1192] It is furthermore being argued that the fundamental shift climate change causes in international law leads to "a new legal and political epoch: The postclimate era."[1193]

Unusually severe changes for international law in the decades ahead are being predicted.[1194] This viewpoint is *inter alia* being reasoned by the effects of new information technologies and their combination with globalisation to then (also with regard to the environmental scope) predict a strengthening of international law.[1195] Lessons from political theory tell us that viable communities need shared values to feel that they are linked to each other.[1196]

1186 *Weiss* in: Vig/Axelrod, 98 (99), also points out the necessity to enhance global cooperation in order to address global problems effectively.

1187 See *Zifcak* in: Evans, 504 (504).

1188 See *Kunig*, Jura 1998, 160 (163).

1189 See e.g. protocol of the 6587th meeting of the Security-Council, 20 July 2011, U.N. Doc. S/PV.6587, pp. 7, 13, 15, 18.

1190 UNDP - Human Development Report 2007-8, Fighting Climate Change: Human Solidarity in a Divided World, p. 1.

1191 See *Tomuschat* in: Hestermeyer et al., 3 (26 et seq.).

1192 *Tomuschat* in: Hestermeyer et al., 3 (4).

1193 *Burkett* in: Gerrard/Wannier, 89 (92).

1194 See *Weiss* in: Vig/Axelrod, 98 (105).

1195 See *Weiss* in: Vig/Axelrod, 98 (105 et seq.).

1196 See *Weiss* in: Vig/Axelrod, 98 (105).

Considered separately, none of these findings forms a sufficient argument to hence enforce the development of international law by anticipating an expected future development of stricter obligations and liability. However, the contrast between the constant progress of climate change on one hand and the stagnant pace of development of international law to find clear and binding responses is remarkable.

Overall, in terms of the endangered states' situation, the findings of this subchapter rather suggest an argument promoting solutions not only in the field of currently rather stagnating international politics, but also in the field of international law. This approach also follows the trend of international law to increasingly focus on common objectives and community interests instead of serving sovereign states to pursue their respective national interest[1197]. In conclusion, the development trends in international law as well as the extent of severe impacts of climate change help to substantiate an argument against the point of view that by no means can there be any liability for climate change damage as long as the states themselves do not agree upon a liability framework (*liability ex delicto*).[1198]

4. Conclusions

a. Introduction

Environmental as well as general international law has now been examined comprehensively in the context of a possible endangered states' claim to a new state territory based on the no harm rule. Of course, every single principle that has been referred to opens a new chapter for far more detailed discussion of its respective content, history and legal status. The purpose of this examination however was to outline the framework of contemporary international law with an eye towards the endangered states' expected loss of land. In this way, an answer to the present question can be provided that is based on a bigger picture. Climate change is a threat that should be tackled from as many (not only legal) angles as possible, including general international law, human rights and environmental law.[1199] The no harm rule is the appropriate starting point for such an elaboration, while other principles generally serve as interpretational guidelines and help to legally assess the peculiarities of the present case.

1197 See *Roeben* in: Bogdandy/Wolfrum, 99 (157).

1198 This opinion has been discussed further above in the context of an isolated application of the no harm rule, see § 4.B. 4. e. bb.

1199 See *Spier* in: Faure/Peeters, 47 (47), who adds private law and criminal law to this list.

This subchapter summarises the arguments with regard to the no harm rule criterion 'due diligence.' If states did not act with due diligence, this would lead to a claim for compensation, possibly in the form of a new state territory. Endangered states could hence benefit from a relocation strategy that would ensure their perspective of becoming a state again after the loss of their respective state territory.[1200] If no such claim exists, the endangered states would be dependent on a volunteering state to provide them with a new territory on a contractual basis. In this way, endangered states could potentially preserve their statehood. Alternatively the international community would have to formulate an immigration strategy, while it would be unclear if the whole respective people could be kept together as social and cultural entity or if these peoples would need to be split into groups and allocated to different states. Also, it is possible that the citizens of endangered states would then have to migrate disorderly without any formulated immigration strategy.

Politically, the latter scenario presumably is the most likely if a claim does not exist. The international community will in any event face severe challenges. For example, a total number of 250 Million climate refugees is expected within this century.[1201] The world will likely have more urgent problems than to give away territory to preserve endangered states' statehood or to at least guarantee to keep island peoples together as social and cultural entities. These aspects should be kept in mind while arguing for or against a claim of endangered states to better assess the practical consequences – which are the basis for a legal judgement that ultimately intends to establish a fair balance of interests.

Arguments and counterarguments for this claim will now be examined, whereby it is inevitable to summarise (and thus to reiterate) findings and statements made so far within this thesis. Subsequently, the obvious question will be addressed, namely what scope the claim actually has. In other words, the legal and political aspects of a potential state relocation will be disentangled.

b. *Does International Law Provide a Claim?*

Endangered states are getting swept up in the limelight of international attention. Their situation combines most of the severest contemporary challenges for the international community[1202]: Compensation between regions of different social

---

1200 This raises the question of what kind of legal entity an endangered state without a state territory would be. This question will be addressed further below, see § 5. B.

1201 See *Human Tide*, p. 6.

1202 *Ipsen* in: id., para. 3, marginal no. 14 lists these following most severe contemporary challenges.

and economic standards (endangered states are amongst the weakest economic players in the world and often are dependent on international support), international environment protection (no other state faces an existence-threatening development of the global climate) and international protection of the individual (the citizens of endangered states might lose their nationality as well as their cultural and social base and thus defining parts of their identity).

"To the extent that seas will continue to encroach on islands as a result of climate change, the key concern becomes what is the best way for the international community to facilitate the transition."[1203] World history does not provide any precedents for the inundation of a sovereign state.[1204] Also, a global challenge like climate change is unique in our history.

The first step has to be an examination of the legal framework, of international law, to identify arguments for or against a certain approach. In the course of this, international law must not be regarded fragmentary but the context and the overall picture of the various principles have to be elaborated.[1205] Two major functions of principles meanwhile have to be kept in mind: First, they serve as interpretational guidelines for the work of the United Nations organs as well as international cooperation.[1206] Second, principles are a bedrock for the development of emerging international law itself, inspiring and legitimating the progress in this field of law.[1207]

This subchapter will comprise arguments derived from international law for and against a claim of endangered states to a new state territory. It is however also important to keep in mind the political dimension of this topic for the purpose of not overstretching the potential of international law.[1208] Therefore, following the legal examination, a few political considerations will be highlighted before deciding upon they key question of this paragraph.

aa. Arguments for a Relocation Strategy Based on a Claim

For endangered states, a tort-based approach is the most appropriate starting point to reflect the third party negligence that causes the severe threat that

---

1203 *Burkett* in: Gerrard/Wannier, 89 (105).

1204 Similar: U.N. Doc. A/HRC/10/61 (2009), p. 14 et seq., para. 41.

1205 See *Birnie et al.*, p. 125; *Weinbaum*, 20 Pac. Rim L. & Pol'y J. 2011, 429 (447).

1206 See *Thürer*, AöR 1984, 113 (132 et seq.).

1207 See *Thürer*, AöR 1984, 113 (133).

1208 *von Glahn/Taulbee*, p. 511, warn not to overstretch international law because law might not be the best tool to develop agreements. The division of political and legal aspects will be addressed in more detail further below, see § 4. C. 5.

endangered states will likely sink into the water in the long run. The most obvious basis for a claim is the no harm rule, an acknowledged legal instrument of customary international law. The examination of this principle[1209] shows that basically, the criteria for a liability are met. There are only two key constraints. First, looking towards the threat of overwhelming financial burdens for the so-called first world (but also for less developed states like China, Brazil or India), a degree of due diligence that leads to a general liability for *any* climate change damage is simply unrealistic. Such an approach would contradict state practice and overstretch the potential of international law. Second, some authors doubt that causation can be proven – an opinion that, in the view of the author of this thesis, is obsolete by now[1210].

But even for those who doubt whether causation could be proven, the precautionary principle's content[1211] has to be considered. According to this principle, the lack of full scientific proof must not be misused as an excuse, especially when there are severe consequences impending. Regarding the threats of climate change, this principle has to be seen in the context of the *Stern Review*: Effective prevention are estimated to only cost 4-20% compared to a scenario of no action.[1212] These findings call for urgent action. Beyond, they also call for an alleviation of the standard of proof regarding causation between GHG emissions and climate change damage[1213] – at least when the extinction of whole states is impending. The precautionary principle thus eliminates remaining minor doubts with regard to 'causation' as element of the no harm rule.

This means that there is only one criterion of the no harm rule which is an obstacle for a liability: The proof that states which conducted excessive GHG emissions did not act with due diligence. Based on the no harm rule *alone*, it would not be possible to furnish this proof.[1214] However, many other principles and aspects of general and environmental international law indicate that this state behaviour does not indicate a sufficient degree of due diligence.

The principle of preventive action[1215] for example militates for a breach of due diligence. As the ICJ stated in the *Pulp Mills Case*, it "has its origins in the due diligence that is required of a State in its territory."[1216] "A State is thus obliged to

1209 See above § 4. B. 4.
1210 See above § 4. B. 4. d. aa. (3).
1211 See above § 4. B. 4. e. aa. (2).
1212 See *Stern Review*, Summary of Conclusions, p. vi.
1213 Similar: *Jacobs*, 14 Pac. Rim L. & Pol'y J. 2005, 103 (127).
1214 See above § 4. B. 5.
1215 See above § 4. C. 2. d. ee.
1216 *Pulp Mills Case*, p. 55 para.101.

use all the means at its disposal in order to avoid activities which take place in its territory, or in any area under its jurisdiction, causing significant damage to the environment of another State."[1217] The principle of preventive action is a suitable argument to reason that states did (and do) not act with due diligence regarding their GHG emissions.

The principle of sustainable development[1218] also argues in favour of endangered states: It particularly stresses the essential needs of the world's poor, to which overriding priority should be given[1219]. Its purpose to establish a balance of interests also argues for a claim based on which endangered states would have the (only) perspective to save their statehood. Moreover, the ICJ referred to this principle in the *Gabčikovo-Nagymaros Case* and considered the need to integrate environmental protection and economic development also applicable when continuing activities which begun in the past[1220] – a finding that stresses the historical responsibility of emitting states.

The discussion about a state's right to exist, derived *inter alia* from fundamental state rights[1221], highlights the importance to protect and preserve statehood itself.[1222] States are the determining legal entities in international law.[1223] The discussed right to exist stresses this unique status of states, which can, in the case of endangered states, only be preserved effectively by a claim to a new state territory. However, due to the unclear legal status of this legal principle, it only has minor relevance for the interpretation of 'due diligence.'

The principle of common but differentiated responsibilities[1224] is more significant in that regard. This concept especially aims at enhancing the situation of developing countries. It also highlights the primary responsibilities of wealthier states. In case of an irretrievable loss of a whole state territory, only a claim to a new state territory could appropriately ensure the purpose of this "framework principle"[1225] which *inter alia* reflects solidarity[1226]. Solidarity with other states

---

1217 *Pulp Mills Case*, p. 56 para.101.
1218 See above § 4. C. 2. c.
1219 See Report of the World Commission on Environment and Development: Our Common Future, U.N. Doc. A/42/427, Annex, Part 1, Chapter 2, para. 1.
1220 See *Gabčikovo-Nagymaros Case*, p. 78 para. 140; *Birnie et al.*, p. 115.
1221 See above § 4. C. 3. d.
1222 See *Kehrer*, p. 98 et seqq.
1223 See *Epping* in: Ipsen, para. 5, marginal no. 1.
1224 See above § 4. C. 2. b.
1225 *Birnie et al.*, p. 135.
1226 See *Birnie et al.*, p. 133 et seqq.

leastwise implies their preservation in case of a threat for their further existence that is due to other state's behaviours.

The examination of the no harm rule is furthermore complemented by its origin: The principle of sovereign equality[1227]. This key principle of contemporary international law has various purposes: First, any legal superiority of any one state over another was meant to be avoided and second, the community discipline within all (UN-member-)states was meant to be strengthened.[1228] The principle aims at the protection of each state against any adverse affects for one's own state territory caused by other states.[1229] The sovereignty of each single state ends where another state is adversely affected.[1230] There cannot be an interpretation of this principle that allows states to cause the inundation of other equal and sovereign states without consequences. This strongly argues for a lack of due diligence in the context of GHG emissions.

Individual rights add further pieces to the puzzle of the international framework: Human rights[1231] are obviously affected by climate change.[1232] Human rights jurisprudence as well as liability for breaches of human rights are becoming increasingly important.[1233] Any forced relocation by virtue of global warming leading to rising sea levels and inundation of land implicates severe challenges for sovereignty, statehood and nationality.[1234] The right to a nationality (Art. 15 UNDHR) as well as social and cultural rights are indispensable for peoples' dignity and the free development of their personality (Art. 22 UNDHR). The prospective loss of these substantial human rights which is due to other states' emissions indicates a lack of due diligence.

Even more concrete both legally and contentwise is the people's right to self-determination[1235]. This undisputed right is at stake due to excessive GHG emissions. The most established counter-argument against this principle does not apply to our case: The right to self-determination usually conflicts with the

---

1227 See above § 4. C. 3. e. bb.

1228 See *Fassbender/Bleckmann* in Simma, 2nd ed., Art. 2 No. 1 marginal no. 45 et seq. with further references.

1229 See *Epiney*, AVR 1995, 309 (320).

1230 See *Epiney*, AVR 1995, 309 (321).

1231 See above § 4. C. 3. b.

1232 See *Brunnée et al. in*: Lord et al., 23 (38); *Barnett* in: Humphreys, 257 (267).

1233 See *Brunnée et al.* in: Lord et al., 23 (40).

1234 See *Weinbaum*, 20 Pac. Rim L. & Pol'y J. 2011, 429 (444).

1235 See above § 4. C. 3. c.

territorial integrity of the respective people's state.[1236] In the case of endangered states, these two interests are concurrent. The state aims to further exist, its people want the state to further exist as legal entity to determine themselves. This strongly argues for a lack of due diligence.

It is also important to consider the purposes of international law. The UN-Charter, starting point of new post-war world order[1237], stresses in its preamble many principles and other issues which were discussed within this thesis: The responsibility towards succeeding generations, fundamental human rights, equal rights of nations large and small, the promotion of co-operation in good faith, good and peaceful neighbourliness and, last but not least, a unification of strength to maintain peace and security. Territorial sovereignty, understood as "the answer provided by international law as regards the needs for security, stability *and identity* felt by a particular group within a certain area"[1238] purposes to ensure the cardinal need for security and stability[1239]. An author who generally favours the *liability ex delicto* approach in this context calls it "quite plausible that liability may have as its origin other legal principles, in particular principles of fairness, equity and equality."[1240] Acting with due diligence in general requires to not counteract these purposes but to support them. This cannot be assessed in the case of excessive GHG emissions.

The development of international law also rather supports a claim of endangered states. Authors note that international law has become stricter and predict that this progress will continue[1241], also with regard to the evolution of climate change torts.[1242] Also, the humanitarian focus of international law has become increasingly important, fairly recently in the form of 'Responsibility to Protect.'[1243] International law has shifted towards an enhanced protection of the individual. The protection of the individual means, in the case of endangered states, to better reflect the citizens' human rights and their right to self-determination. The

1236 *Blay*, 18 N.Y.U. J. Int'l L. & Pol., 1985-1986, 441 et seqq., examines the traditional conflict of these two principles.

1237 See *Schachter*, 89 Am. Soc'y Int'l L. Proc. 1995, 45 (46).

1238 *Shaw*, NYIL 13, 61 (79), emphasis added.

1239 See *Shaw*, NYIL 13, 61 (78).

1240 *Tomuschat* in: Hestermeyer et al., 3 (10).

1241 See *Weiss* in: Vig/Axelrod, 98 (105 et seq.).

1242 See *Blomquist*, 46 Va. U. L. Rev. 2011-2012, 1053 (1055). Bloomquist primarily refers to domestic lawsuits, yet uses them as a reference to examine the development of international law.

1243 See *Rensmann*, ZaöRV 2008, 111 et seqq.

most appropriate approach for this purpose is a claim that preserves their state. In other words, this requires to also include individual rights when interpreting the no harm rule criterion 'due diligence.' Also, the increased institutionalisation of responsibility in international law proves a shift towards serving the pursuit of common objectives and community interests.[1244] This development marks a power shift away from states towards the international community.

International environmental law as a whole has "evolved at a time when the heterogeneity of the international community has rapidly intensified and when, simultaneously, the economic problems and development needs and aspirations of the less-developed states have become more prominent."[1245] The effectiveness of the environmental protection provided by international law depends on the whole range of competing social, economic and political considerations.[1246] This development makes it easier to argue for a claim that is not based on a treaty, but on legal principles whose relevance is constantly rising.

Overall, these considerations argue to assess a lack of 'due diligence' and thus to acknowledge an endangered states' claim to a new state territory. This claim would be based on the no harm rule interpreted by the framework of principles of international law (and other considerations) taking into account the legal and political peculiarities of the present case.

bb. Arguments for a Global Immigration Scenario

Arguments against a claim for endangered states – which necessarily would imply a global immigration scenario – are considerably sparser, but nevertheless very substantial.

The key issue is not to overstretch international law by trying to derive suitable solutions for individual cases that could be described as 'fair' or 'just.'[1247] This is not only legally questionable.[1248] It also does not correspond to state practice. A lack of state practice is the major restraint to consider environmental principles as binding parts of customary law.[1249] Despite considerable negotiation efforts in the past, states could thus far not agree upon a binding liability regime for climate change damage. Any "lawyer's trick" aiming at a "shortcut to the desired

1244 See *Roeben* in: Bogdandy/Wolfrum, 99 (157).
1245 *Birnie et al.*, p. 11.
1246 See *Birnie et al.*, p. 12.
1247 See *Kunig*, Jura 1998, 160 (163).
1248 See *Kunig*, Jura 1998, 160 (163) calls this approach dogmatically questionable.
1249 See *Schweisfurth*, p. 604, marginal no. 10.

goal" without the "support at the grassroots" therefore is considered to be condemned to failure.[1250]

Excessive costs impend in the context of climate change liability.[1251] States traditionally are unwilling to establish rules of international law that might impose serious financial burdens.[1252] A *general* liability for climate change damage would lead to tremendous negative effects – a "truly crushing liability" and an "economic disaster" would impend.[1253] Therefore, in the complex field of global warming and state responsibility, only negotiations of states themselves can determine rules of liability.[1254] It is difficult to replace international consent by deriving clear liability rules from customary law.[1255]

Negotiations surrounding the evolution of environmental law illustrate the politics' classic dilemma of immediate satisfaction versus long-term costs.[1256] Also, the ILC's approach to address issues of state liability step by step argues in favour of not counteracting this strategy by deriving claims from customary law at one's convenience.[1257] Furthermore, it seems not correct to sanction an action (GHG emissions), which is not prohibited, but to the contrary essential for our societies.[1258]

Overall, a too politicised judicial activism (e.g. by means of an ICJ verdict in favour of endangered states [1259]) would likely face severe criticism, as the judiciary has not been democratically elected.[1260] It might therefore be naïve to expect from international law in general or international case law in particular to solve problems as complex as climate change without the respective political support.[1261] This applies especially with regard to a concrete liability: According to which approach should liability shares be determined?[1262] Which state would

---

1250 *Tomuschat* in: Hestermeyer et al., 3 (28 et seq.).

1251 See *Sands*, p. 701.

1252 See *Sands*, p. 701; *Beyerlin*, OYIL 2007, 425 (427); *Handl*, 37 Envtl Pol'y & L. 2007, 116 (121).

1253 See *Spier* in: Faure/Peeters, 47 (48).

1254 See *Nanda* in: WJU 2010, 42 (45); similar: *Kunig*, Jura 1998, 160 (163).

1255 See *Handl*, OYIL 2007, 531 (544).

1256 See *von Glahn/Taulbee*, p. 528 et seq.

1257 *Tomuschat* in: Hestermeyer et al., 3 (23 et seqq.) summarises the work of the ILC in the last two decades.

1258 See *Tomuschat* in: Hestermeyer et al., 3 (15 et seq., 23).

1259 Procedural aspects will be addressed in more detail further below, see § 4. F.

1260 See *Haritz*, p. 85.

1261 See *Birnie et al.*, p. 1.

1262 *Tomuschat* in: Hestermeyer et al., 3 (8 et seqq.) portrays the difficulties to determine liability shares based on international law and scientific level of knowledge only.

have to provide an endangered state with a new state territory? These most relevant questions cannot be answered satisfactorily based on customary international law only.

cc. Sea Level Rise Fund

Another answer to the complexity and uncertainties of liabilities for sea level rise is the proposal to implement a sea level rise fund.[1263] In this way, escalating costs of single states could be avoided.[1264] It is *inter alia* being referred to a resolution of the General Assembly from 1989 which "calls upon the international community, in particular the developed countries, to consider contributing generously to the Trust Fund" that had been established by the IPCC.[1265] According to authors holding this viewpoint, the implementation of a fund would adequately consider the interests of all parties involved.[1266]

dd. Political Dimension of the Problem

International law arises from political relationships and behaviour.[1267] The interaction between politics and (already established) international law affects the development of new norms.[1268] Any practical solution of the situation of endangered states therefore must not ignore the political impact on the international decision process.

It is almost impossible to outline the complexity of contradicting political interests comprehensively or even to summarise them appropriately. This begins with conflicting long-term and short-term interests of any state.

Regarding a hypothetical claim for endangered states to a new state territory, the required land and the costs for relocation would probably not overstrain the international community. Less than 850.000 citizens of endangered states would have to be relocated (not all at the same time) when Tuvalu, Nauru, Kiribati, the Bahamas and the Maldives become inundated.[1269] That is merely about 0.3% of

---

1263 See *Kehrer*, p. 340 et seq.

1264 See *Kehrer*, p. 343.

1265 See U.N. Doc. A/RES/44/207, No. 8 et seq.

1266 See *Kehrer*, p. 344. The same view has been taken e.g. by *Faure/Peeters* in: id., 255 (258).

1267 See *Ipsen* in: id., para. 3, marginal no. 2 et seq.

1268 See *Ipsen* in: id., para. 3, marginal no. 4.

1269 According to the CIA World Factbook, these 5 states have the following (rounded) amounts of citizens: 11,000 (Tuvalu), 9,000 (Nauru), 104,000 (Kiribati), 322,000 (The Bahamas), 394,000 (The Maldives), see https://www.cia.gov/library/publications/the-world-factbook/, last accessed 29 April 2014.

the climate refugees expected by the end of this century.[1270] The international community – especially its more affluent members – would most likely pay considerable shares of the respective costs either way (in the form of humanitarian aid, due to an emergency plan, an international treaty etc.). This applies regardless of whether these are costs of an immigration scenario or whether they are based on a claim leading to a relocation. Endangered states will (like other states) most likely be dependent on funds and resources provided by other wealthier states.

Why then should these other states be reluctant to accept a claim based on which endangered states could relocate and continue their community elsewhere? From the perspective of wealthier states, a first disadvantage of this approach could be the 'publicity factor': Humanitarian aid has the sound of charity, where stronger members of a community use their power to help their weaker fellows. A binding claim to a new state territory has the opposite effect: Because the stronger members do not sufficiently care about their weaker fellows' fates, they can only be domesticated by international law. This is evidently a less attractive way to spend money.

But this is probably not the highest hurdle: The threat of escalating costs might be the tacit key counterargument for a claim-based relocation. If endangered states were provided with a new state territory, e.g. Bangladesh could raise the question why SIDS are compensated comprehensively and other states with vast climate change damage are not, although their costs might be many times higher. This could ultimately lead to a domino effect of climate change liability.

If a threat for a general climate change liability impends, the wealthier (and more powerful) states will likely do anything to counteract this threat. If this damage indeed amounts to 5-20% of the global GDP annually[1271], the implications for the global economy would be disastrous. It is – especially from the legal perspective – impossible to predict what would happen then. However, history and common sense rather support the conclusion that emitting states will try to defend their wealth, thus try to avoid vast cost risks.

Any call for a claim of endangered states derived from customary law therefore has to point out the uniqueness of their situation, which justifies to provide them with a claim whereas other states that are adversely affected by climate change might not benefit from a comparable treatment.

1270 This percentage is based on the prediction of 250 million climate change refugees by the end of this century, see *Human Tide*, p. 6.

1271 As predicted in the *Stern Review*, Summary of Conclusions, p. vi.

ee. Statement

Endangered states do have a claim to a state territory.

The no harm rule is the appropriate cause of action for climate change damage. In the context of climate change, this principle alone yet cannot determine the degree of due diligence applicable in interstate relations. A general liability for climate change damage cannot be established, given the importance of state practice in this field of law as well as the political unwillingness to risk excessive costs.[1272]

The scenario of endangered states differs from this general finding. The prospect of a total land loss, threatening the existence of whole nations, affects more principles in environmental and general international law, which have to be used as interpretational guidelines for 'due diligence' in the present case. In short, the examination of these principles leads to the following conclusions: A claim for endangered states mirrors the responsibility structure for climate change and it is a sustainable approach. It reflects the ideology on which post-war international law is based, responds adequately to new challenges and fairly balances contradicting interests. It respects the values of the international community while treating endangered states as equally sovereign. Also, it corresponds to the development of international law to become more obligatory and to focus more intensively on the interests of the individual. A considerable majority of the relevant principles in international law argues that states did not act with due diligence. They therefore must right the wrong committed.[1273] According to the ICJ, "reparation must, as far as possible, wipe out al1 the consequences of the illegal act and reestablish the situation which would, in al1 probability, have existed if that act had not been committed."[1274] The granting of a new state territory is the most appropriate legal consequence to establish not the *status quo ante*, but the closest scenario to that status.

To better judge these summarised findings, it is important to consider the only other option. If in the SIDS' case, a sufficient degree of due diligence could be assessed, this would necessarily entail a global immigration scenario. This would most likely signify the end of UN member states due to the permanent lack of a state territory. It would refuse the endangered states' citizens right to determine themselves and counteract human rights provisions aiming at ensuring the protection of social and/or cultural aspects of life. On balance, this would not

---

1272 For a discussion regarding liability based on the no harm rule alone see above § 4. B. 4.

1273 See *Millar et al.* in: Gerrard/Wannier, 433 (440).

1274 *Chorzow Factory Case*, 5 (47).

correspond to various legal principles, as examined within this thesis, but would predominantly serve to avoid costs.

Beyond the affirmation of such a claim, its implementation has to be determined.

The implementation of a fund[1275] cannot solve the problem. First, if it is not restricted to the scenario of state threatening inundation, the problem of escalating costs would not be solved: Voluntary contribution would not suffice to compensate the damage[1276]. Obligatory contributions would likewise not be accepted by potential contributors. Second, endangered states do not need money to keep their statehood, but they need a new state territory. A fund could not provide this kind of compensation.

Almost all authors who oppose a (direct) climate change liability are considering a general liability for *any* damage caused by global warming, while this thesis only considers one aspect of potential endangered states' claims. This aspect differs in two crucial regards from a general liability for climate change damage: First, only assessable costs impend. Second, a possible state extinction affects a far broader field of international law, as demonstrated within this thesis.

A claim of endangered states to a new state territory would hence not necessarily entail a general climate change liability. The situation of endangered states is unique: They are in danger to cease their existence as legal entity 'state.' The qualification 'state' is the most essential attribute for a participation in the international community as a sovereign and equal member. This exceptional threat as well as the comprehensively elaborated peculiarities of the situation of endangered states support the conclusion that it is possible (and justifiable) to assess a lack of 'due diligence' in the case of endangered states despite the finding that there is no general liability for any climate change damage of any state[1277].

Concluding, a balance of interest clearly argues for a lack of due diligence and thus for a claim of endangered states. Many of the discussed principles are based on a balance of conflicting interests, e.g. the no harm rule (respectively Principle 21)[1278], the principle of shared natural resources[1279], the principle of sustainable development[1280] or the concept of international emergency law[1281].

1275 See above § 4. C. 4. b. cc.

1276 See *Millar et al.* in: Gerrard/Wannier, 433 (464).

1277 See above § 4. B. 5.

1278 See *Wolfrum*, DVBl. 1984,. 493 (494 et seq.).

1279 See *Handl*, 26 Nat. Resources J. 1986, 405 (412).

1280 See *Birnie et al.*, p. 115.

1281 See *Partsch* in: Strupp/Schlochauer, Vol. III, p. 258 et seq.

How, in this context, could a balance of different states' interests possibly lead to the acceptance of one party's extinction – especially with regard to the respective degree of responsibility for the present situation?

Beyond, it must be stressed that this claim already has to exist before the respective state gets uninhabitable. In this context, the precautionary principle[1282] enables endangered states to request relief even in the absence of scientific certainty due to the irreversible nature of this environmental damage.[1283] As the example of The Republic of the Marshall Islands shows, such a country clearly cannot wait until the anticipated harm occurs before seeking a remedy because by then it will cease to exist.[1284] There is no convincing reason why the judicial protection of endangered states should be narrowed down to a scenario where they have already lost their state territory. A potential trial could take years in which the status of the respective citizens would be unclear. Also, it would be uncertain whether the respective state (or former state) would still qualify as a proper plaintiff at the ICJ.[1285] For lack of equally substantial counter-arguments, the claim of endangered states therefore has to exist as soon as their future uninhabitability can be proven as a fact based on the usual standard of proof, potentially alleviated by the precautionary principle[1286].

5. Legal and Political Scopes of a State Relocation

A potential state relocation comprises both political and legal aspects, while international law can only concern itself with the latter.

The ICJ or other institutions of international jurisdiction are hardly in the position to comprehensively decide upon key issues of international law, which the international community has been addressing for decades in conference after conference without satisfactory results. The answer to the question 'who pays what?' is traditionally left to the states' discretion. International courts therefore have been cautious regarding general principles as a source of law in those

---

1282 This principle has been examined further above in the context of causation, see § 4. B. 4. d. aa. (2).

1283 See *Larson*, 21 Mich. J. Int'l L. 1999-2000, 495 (513).

1284 See *Larson*, 21 Mich. J. Int'l L. 1999-2000, 495 (513).

1285 This question will be addressed and affirmed further below, see § 5. B. This opinion, however, would most likely be challenged, which would lead to a further weakening of the position of endangered states.

1286 This principle has been examined further above in the context of causation, see § 4. B. 4. d. aa. (2).

cases where this would result in judicial lawmaking independent of the will of states.[1287]

Despite the existence of a claim, it is thus unrealistic that international law will be able to e.g. satisfactorily determine liability shares amongst the international community. Which state has to pay which amount? To which extent should historical responsibilities affect the respective liability share? These highly political questions cannot be decided by international law. The cobweb of individual acts by states cannot be disentangled without an international authority vested with decision-making powers.[1288]

An answer to this dilemma could be provided by the *Gabčikovo-Nagymaros Case*. In this decision, summarised above[1289], the ICJ required the parties to "look afresh at the effects on the environment" for which they "must find a satisfactory solution"[1290]. First and foremost, this is an example of a binding legal consequence that emerged from customary environmental law. But "[i]t is not for the Court to determine what shall be the final result of these negotiations to be conducted by the Parties. It is for the Parties themselves to find an agreed solution."[1291] The ICJ thereby affirmed a binding commitment comprising a duty to negotiate and to come to a mutual agreement, while leaving the details to the states' discretion. "Such an approach enables international courts to further the objective of sustainable development […] while relieving them of the impossible task of deciding what is and what is not sustainable."[1292] The *Gabčikovo-Nagymaros Case* ended in a judgement requiring the parties to negotiate a solution – an outcome that is unsurprising in a multilateral case that involves fundamental issues of social, economic and political choice.[1293] This ruling allows room for flexible solutions, which are not necessarily dictated by international law, but which accommodate the interests of all parties, to the extent this is possible.[1294]

Similarly, the ICJ in its *Advisory Opinion on Kosovo* made clear

> "*that the fact that a question has political aspects does not suffice to deprive it of its character as a legal question […]. Whatever its political aspects, the Court cannot refuse to*

1287 See *Birnie et al.*, p. 220.
1288 See *Tomuschat* in: Hestermeyer et al., 3 (10).
1289 See above § 4. C. 2. c. bb.
1290 *Gabčikovo-Nagymaros Case*, p. 78 para. 140.
1291 *Gabčikovo-Nagymaros Case*, p. 78 para. 141.
1292 *Birnie et al.*, p. 127.
1293 See *Birnie et al.*, p. 213.
1294 See *Birnie et al.*, p. 213.

respond to the legal elements of a question which invites it to discharge an essentially judicial task [...]."[1295]

This approach can be transferred to the current question: The existence of a claim of endangered states to a new state territory has been affirmed. Yet, from the legal perspective, it is an impossible task to decide upon precise liability shares. Moreover, it is impossible to determine where exactly an endangered state should be relocated. The *Gabčikovo-Nagymaros Case* and the ICJ *Advisory Opinion on Kosovo* show that this is not necessary. A state relocation has both legal and political aspects. International law can only provide answers to legal uncertainties, in our case the existence of a claim to a state territory. The states themselves have to negotiate and to decide upon political issues – i.e. where to relocate the state to, how to determine compensation for the donor state and how to finance the costs. In certain parts, this approach corresponds to the *liability ex delicto*[1296] approach according to which answers to these questions cannot be derived from international law (e.g. the ARS), but can only be solved by mutual agreement.[1297]

International case law rarely leads to remedies which amount to specific performance.[1298] Thus, "[a] climate litigant that was successful in establishing a breach of the source state's primary obligation may find that the court was unwilling to do more than order the disputants to return to the negotiating table."[1299]

These remarks require further illustration. In practice, this legal conclusion could, for example, lead to the following scenario: Based for example on a judicial ruling which requires the opposing parties in a claim to negotiate an option for a specific state relocation, a certain state may consent to give up a certain part of its territory (either an island or a part of its mainland) in order to enable an endangered state to relocate. Of course, this 'donor state' would have to be compensated by the international community (respectively all debtors). Both the purchase price as well as the liability shares would be the result of a political

1295 *ICJ Advisory Opinion on Kosovo*, 403 (415) para. 27; see also *Bavishi*, Raj/*Barakat*, Subhi: "Procedural Issues related to the ICJ's advisory jurisdiction," briefing paper no. BP41E of the Legal Response Initiative, p. 7 et seq., available at http://legalresponseinitiative.org/wp-content/uploads/2013/09/BP41E-Briefing-Paper-The-ICJ-Advisory-Opinion-Procedure-11-June-2012.pdf, last accessed 29 April 2014.

1296 See above § 4. B. 4. e. bb.

1297 See *Tomuschat* in: Hestermeyer et al., 3 (10).

1298 See *Werksman* in: Gerrard/Wannier, 409 (423).

1299 *Werksman* in: Gerrard/Wannier, 409 (423).

negotiation. For example, they could stipulate a certain mode of liability[1300] or release single states from the group of debtors. In the course of this, the 'donor state' could, for example, consolidate its budget and also benefit from a political advantage as a 'white knight' – two facts which could make the partial sacrifice of territorial sovereignty more attractive. These thoughts do not intend to suggest a relocation e.g. of Tuvalu to a Mediterranean Greek island. Of course, cultural, geological, climatic and other implications need to be considered when choosing a suitable destination for relocation.

But this is only one example. It would also be possible, for example, to (partially) finance a state relocation by licensing the exploitation of exterritorial resources, for instance the Polar Regions, the high sea and/or the (former) state territory of the respective endangered state. As set out above, in the end it is left to the states' discretion *how* they answer the claim of endangered states, while international law is the basis for the existence of the claim itself. By accepting this existing claim – e.g. due to an international judgement[1301] – the international community can effectively be encouraged to address the situation of endangered states more intensively and to solve the problem adequately without curtailing their creativity how best to answer this claim in detail.

D. Claim Opponents

Assigning responsibility regarding legal remedy for accelerated sea level rise is a fundamental difficulty.[1302] The entire global community is responsible, as everybody produces GHG.[1303] The difficulties however are more of a practical and procedural nature, because from a perspective of substantive law, there are only two conceivable options to determine liability more precisely: Either the international community is liable as a whole or the single states share a collective liability.

A working paper for the Commission on Human Rights touches on the question of a claim to replacement of a lost inundated territory with a view to SIDS.[1304] The author therein presumes that any claim would be against the international community as a whole, rather than against a particular state.[1305]

1300 In the context of liability for damages resulting from sea level rise, *Kehrer* examines the so-called pollution share liability (p. 320 et seqq.) as well as the so-called probability liability (p. 327 et seqq.).

1301 More detailed elaborations will be made further below, see § 4. F.

1302 See *Larson*, 21 Mich. J. Int'l L. 1999-2000, 495 (503).

1303 See *Larson*, 21 Mich. J. Int'l L. 1999-2000, 495 (503).

1304 See U.N. Doc. E/CN.4/Sub.2/AC.4/2004/CRP.1, p. 4 para. 10.

1305 See U.N. Doc. E/CN.4/Sub.2/AC.4/2004/CRP.1, p. 4 para. 10.

The other option is a liability of all states. This could either be a joint and several debt, or a sum of individual debts. In either case, all states would be potential opponents. In other words, either any defendant is liable to the plaintiff for the whole damage (and has the right to obtain partial reimbursement internally within the circle of debtors) or instead any defendant is only liable for the respective fractional part of the damage.[1306]

It is important to remind oneself of the content of the claim of endangered states: A new state territory, whereby all states have to find mechanisms to negotiate at least three questions: Which state will place a part of its territory at their disposal? What would constitute adequate compensation for this state? How will such compensation be financed?

The possibility of finding the entire international community liable seems little convincing as it is not responsible for national GHG emissions. As discussed, the basic right to emit GHG originates from a state's territorial sovereignty.[1307] This makes the no harm rule a concept that further develops the principle of good neighbourliness[1308]. This principle applies in the interstate relations, not in the relation between one state and the superordinate international community. Also, the international community does not possess any territory of its own which could be the object of compensation for land loss.

There might be a potential responsibility of the international community as author having contributed to climate change.[1309] However, the only way in which one could construct an intellectual link would be based on its failure to act as the conscience of humankind.[1310] One needs to bear in mind that the international community is not organised as an integrated whole.[1311] Every state has different interests – it is possible that some states would strongly encourage the claim of endangered states to a new state territory and others would like to object.

It is therefore not necessary to decide upon the international community's status as recognised subject of international law.[1312] Only the liability of states can be applicable. This liability has to be joint and several: The debtors are liable for providing a new state territory and they will have to negotiate the details. Due to the fact that the individual share of liability cannot be determined by a court, but

---

1306 See *Wright*, 21 U.C. Davis L. Rev. 1987-1988, 1141 (1141).

1307 See above § 4. B. 4. e. bb.

1308 See *Sands*, p. 197.

1309 See *Tomuschat* in: Hestermeyer et al., 3 (12).

1310 See *Tomuschat* in: Hestermeyer et al., 3 (12).

1311 See *Tomuschat* in: Hestermeyer et al., 3 (12).

1312 *Paulus* elaborates on this question in detail.

rather will need to be negotiated by the debtors[1313], liability for a fractional part of the injury would make no sense.

There remains, however, a crucial issue to this mode of liability: It is unclear whether joint and several liability is part of customary international law.[1314] This question has been examined based on international and national case law in the similar case of (general) liability for sea level rise damage.[1315] In this context, indivisibility is a necessary prerequisite for joint and several liability.[1316] This requirement is satisfied in the present case: Neither the new state territory endangered states can claim, nor the negotiations required to determine the details, can be divided. However, concerns regarding the effectiveness of internal reimbursement amongst debtors, in particular, lead to the conclusion that joint and several debt cannot be considered as an established part of international law.[1317]

The present case yet differs significantly: Given a hypothetical successful lawsuit, for example one brought by Kiribati against the United States, this would not impose the duty on the losing party to provide the plaintiff with a new state territory. It would merely be a declaratory judgement obliging the defendant to negotiate with fellow states in order to identify and finance a territory to which the plaintiff could relocate. This means that, in the endangered states' cases, these reasonable concerns[1318] do not apply.

All states are thus jointly and severally liable to provide threatened endangered states with a new state territory, whereby the details of this claim (e.g. liability shares, selection of appropriate new state territory) need to be negotiated amongst the debtors.

E. Limits of Liability

As already indicated, a fair balance of interests is a prerequisite both legally and practically for a successful deliniation of a relocation claim.

The respective citizens, represented by their state institutions, predominantly shape the interests of endangered states. Their interests have to be taken into account, especially while negotiating where the respective endangered state could be relocated. The example of the state Israel shows that an allocation of a state

1313 See above § 4. C. 5.

1314 See *Kehrer*, p. 314 et seqq.

1315 See *Kehrer*, p. 314 et seqq.

1316 See *Kehrer*, p. 317 et seq.

1317 See *Kehrer*, p. 317.

1318 See the statement of *Kehrer*, p. 318 et seq.

territory to a certain people can lead to lengthy conflicts. Of course, the history and conflicting interests in the case of Israel differ in many regards – it is however the most prominent allocation of a state territory to a people.

In the case of endangered states, the international community should preferably look for states nearby to relocate. A relocation to a more or less familiar region with similar climate, vegetation and if possible even the same neighbouring states etc. would considerably diminish the negative effects of a state relocation for the affected citizens and better enable them to successfully establish the infrastructure of their state on a new territory. For example, a relocation of Tuvaluan citizens (though not of the state Tuvalu itself) to the Fijian Island 'Kioa' was already considered almost a decade ago.[1319] In 2012, Kiribati announced a similar plan to relocate its more than 100.000 citizens: It began to buy land in Fiji – on the second largest island Vanua Levu – to enable Kiribati citizens to migrate step by step.[1320] A comparable solution to relocate a state not too far away from its origin would best mirror the interests of endangered states' citizens.

However, a fair balance of interest means that the interests of the claim opponents also have to be taken into account. This is a wide subject as there is a great number of potential opponents – and thus numerous diverse interests. At the very least, the interest of a potential 'donor state' which (yet voluntarily) surrenders a part of its territory – and thus a part of its territorial sovereignty – has to be considered and pondered. Most of the different parties' interests though will have to be addressed in the course of the negotiations. Hence the establishment of a detailed balance of interest is predominantly a political task, not a legal one.

F. Procedural Options

1. Introduction

No substantive claim is relevant unless it can be effectively enforced.[1321] Access to justice is an indispensable prerequisite to ensure effective enforcement and

1319 See The Age (Australia): "Tuvalu's Tides Divide Scientists," (25 August 2004), available at http://www.theage.com.au/articles/2004/08/24/1093246516150.html, last accessed 29 April 2014.

1320 See Paul Chapman, "Entire Nation of Kiribati to Be Relocated Over Rising Sea Level Threat," The Telegraph, 7 March 2012, available at http://www.telegraph.co.uk/news/worldnews/australiaandthepacific/kiribati/9127576/Entire-nation-of-Kiribati-to-be-relocated-over-rising-sea level-threat.html, last accessed 29 April 2014.

1321 See *Birnie* et al., p. 211.

compliance with environmental law that has already been adopted.[1322] However, "the greatest challenge to proceeding with climate change litigation [...] is finding a venue with jurisdiction."[1323]

Improved tools to enforce international environmental law have only developed slowly in the last few decades.[1324] Currently, there is no central institution for the enforcement of international environmental law.[1325]

Various forms of dispute settlement machinery are listed in Art. 33 UN-Charter:

> "*negotiation, enquiry, mediation, conciliation, arbitration, judicial settlement, resort to regional agencies or arrangements, or other peaceful means of their own choice.*"

Of course, an endangered state aiming to enforce its claim to a new state territory would in all likelihood first try to negotiate in order to find a solution, rather than file a lawsuit without any prior attempt to negotiate a bilateral or multilateral solution. This subchapter, however, focuses on the question, of the options endangered states have if no consent with its counterparts can be achieved.

Authors who considered a *general* climate change liability mention different disadvantages to enforceing international law if it involves the obligatory resort to judicial institutions.[1326] The relationship between the states concerned could suffer, international litigation is often long, expensive and complex, furthermore there is the risk of difficulties relating to evidence, apart from which the character of some law is rather unsettled.[1327] However, in light of the consequences that a rise of sea level could have for these island states, legal proceedings could become their last resort. There might be no other basis for enforcing customary law.[1328] This is especially true with regard to the poor outcome of international climate change negotiations thus far.

In the following, this subchapter shall outline the advantages and disadvantages of different approaches how the claim of endangered states to a new state territory could be enforced.

1322 See *Pring/Pring* in: FS Nanda, 482 (483).
1323 *Werksman* in: Gerrard/Wannier, 409 (428).
1324 See *Bothe* in: FS Steinberger, 83 (84 et seqq.).
1325 See *Hobe*, p. 530.
1326 See *Birnie* et al., p. 211.
1327 See *Birnie* et al., p. 211.
1328 See *Birnie* et al., p. 237.

2. International Court of Justice

According to Art. 1 ICJ Statute, the International Court of Justice is the principle judicial organ of the United Nations. Invoking the ICJ would thus be the most obvious way to enforce an international claim. According to Art. 34(1) ICJ Statute, only states can be parties in cases before the court. As claimant and opponents are states, this condition is met.[1329]

There are basically two options for a legal proceeding of an endangered state at this judicial organ: It could either sue one or more opponents, Art. 40(1) ICJ Statute. Or it could alternatively ask the UN General Assembly or the Security Council to request an Advisory Opinion from the ICJ, Art. 65(1) ICJ Statute, Art. 96 UN-Charter.[1330]

a. Institute Proceedings

Few environmental claims between two states thus far have been brought to the ICJ.[1331] Even the Chernobyl accident in 1986 did not motivate any state to bring a claim against the Soviet Union.[1332] This does however not preclude such claims for the future.

Various considerable hurdles yet complicate this option. First of all, as the claim would not be based on a treaty but on customary international law, the consent of the defendant would be required.[1333] This prerequisite is a consequence of the respective state's sovereignty.[1334] As there would be little motivation for potential defendants to submit themselves voluntarily to the jurisdiction of the ICJ,[1335] this fact is a substantial obstacle that makes this option little promising. Consent of a sued state cannot be expected.

1329 However, this prerequisite could not be fulfilled if a state has lost its territory with the consequence of losing statehood. This question will be addressed further below, see § 5. B.

1330 *Jacobs*, 14 Pac. Rim L. & Pol'y J. 2005, 103 (115), lists, *inter alia*, these two options examining a potential lawsuit brought by Tuvalu against the United States; *Nanda* in: WJU 2010, 42 (54).

1331 See *Sands*, p. 771 et seq.

1332 See *Sands*, p. 771.

1333 See *Nanda* in: WJU 2010, 42 (54), who discusses a potential lawsuit brought by Tuvalu against the United States with regard to a *general* climate change liability; *Werksman* in: Gerrard/Wannier, 409 (426).

1334 See *Kehrer*, p. 313.

1335 See *Jacobs*, 14 Pac. Rim L. & Pol'y J. 2005, 103 (115), fn. 85.

Assumed that an endangered state would not file a lawsuit against *all* other states that excessively emitted GHG, the so-called indivisible rule could additionally prompt the ICJ to deny its jurisdiction: This rule has first been established by the ICJ in the *Monetary Gold Removed from Rome Case* from 1954 and has been continuously applied ever since.[1336] Referring to Art. 62 ICJ Statute, the Court made clear that the Statute cannot be regarded as authorising proceedings to be continued in the absence of a third party, given that this party's legal interest "would not only be affected by a decision, but would form *the very subject-matter* of the decision."[1337] If the core of a potential verdict would affect the legal interests of a state not being party of the lawsuit, the ICJ thus could not decide upon this matter.[1338]

The indivisible rule's scope of application remains unclear heretofore.[1339] The applicability of this rule in the context of *general* liability for sea level rise has been examined[1340], a scenario in which likewise all other states would be opponents. The subject-matter of a potential dispute are certain GHG emissions that are qualified as being contrary to international law.[1341] This object of dispute can be decided upon independently of the amount or classification of other states' emissions, which makes the indivisible rule inapplicable in the context of liability for sea level rise as other states would not automatically be affected by the subject-matter of the decision.[1342]

The ICJ itself considered the indivisible rule in a decision from 1992 that had parallels to the object of this study. In the *Certain Phosphate Lands in Nauru Case*, Australia had argued that, based on the ruling in the *Monetary Gold Removed from Rome Case*, it cannot be held liable solely because New Zealand and the United Kingdom were equally responsible.[1343] The ICJ responded that,

> *"[i]n the present case, a finding by the Court regarding the existence or the content of the responsibility attributed to Australia by Nauru might well have implications for the legal situation of the two other States concerned, but no finding in respect of that legal situation will be needed as a basis for the Court's decision on Nauru's claims against Australia. Accordingly, the Court cannot decline to exercise its jurisdiction."*[1344]

1336 See *Kehrer*, p. 313.
1337 *Monetary Gold Removed from Rome Case*, 19 (32), emphasis added.
1338 See *Kehrer*, p. 313.
1339 See *Ohlhoff*, p. 195.
1340 See *Kehrer*, p. 313 et seq.
1341 See *Kehrer*, p. 314.
1342 See *Kehrer*, p. 314.
1343 See *Certain Phosphate Lands in Nauru Case*, 240 (259), para. 49 et seq.
1344 *Certain Phosphate Lands in Nauru Case*, 240 (261 et seq.), para. 55.

These findings also apply to the case of endangered states. This applies especially with a view to the legal nature of a potential verdict: The claim does not immediately aim at affirmative relief in form of a so-called adjucation based on which a certain territory is being transferred into another states' competence[1345]. Such an intervention in a state's sovereignty would require the acknowledgement of the states being parties to a lawsuit.[1346] The claim rather confirms and determines the opponent's duty to negotiate how the claimant will be provided with a new state territory.[1347] This declaratory judgement does not immediately affect the legal interests of another state that might not be party to the legal conflict, even if the basis of decision making in essence is identical as compared with the relationship between this third state and the claimant. One or more state's duty to negotiate can be determined without the compelling consequence that this simultaneously is a decision regarding other states' duty to negotiate.

The indivisible rule would thus not be an obstacle to file a lawsuit at the ICJ. The required opponent's consent however makes this option little promising, whereby a non-predictable development of international politics might amend this latter point of view.[1348]

b. Request an Advisory Opinion

"[T]here may be merit in seeking an ICJ advisory opinion [...] as the consequences of climate change and the current international failure to meet the [UN] FCCC goals are both spectacular failures which the future generations of the SIDS will have to inherit."[1349]

Art. 65(1) ICJ Statute, and Art. 96 UN-Charter establish the opportunity to request an Advisory Opinion. This proceeding is only open to authorised bodies of international law. Thus an endangered state cannot request such an opinion as legal entity 'state' alone, but it can try to exert influence on an entitled international body, for example together with other affected or supporting countries.

1345 See *Zippelius*, p. 86.

1346 See *Nanda* in: WJU 2010, 42 (54), who discusses a potential lawsuit brought by Tuvalu against the United States with regard to a *general* climate change liability.

1347 See above § 4. C. 5.

1348 Additional comments on the relevance of political circumstances and the importance of public opinion will be made further below, see § 4. F. 6.

1349 *Gillespie*, 22 UCLA J. Envtl. L. & Pol'y 2003-2004, 107 (129).

Only five institutions of the United Nations and 16 specialised agencies of the United Nations are entitled to make such a request.[1350] Whereby pursuant to Art. 96 lit. a ICJ Statute the Security Council and the United Nation General Assembly can request that the Court give an Advisory Opinion on any legal question, according to Art. 96 lit. b ICJ Statute other bodies are only entitled to do so regarding legal questions arising from within the scope of their activities. It is doubtful that any other UN organ or one of the specialised agencies would consider a distribution of a state territory to an endangered state (or a negotiation concerning this matter) being "within the scope of their activities."[1351] Therefore, only the Security Council and the United Nation General Assembly can be taken into consideration.

An endangered state seeking for an ICJ Advisory Opinion would hence have to address one or both of these bodies. The Security Council is not very promising in that regard. Out of its 15 members (Art. 23(1) UN-Charter), according to Art. 23(3) UN-Charter nine member states would have to vote in favour of the endangered states' desire – including the five permanent members. Art. 23 (1) UN-Charter determines that these are the Republic of China, France, the Union of Soviet Socialist Republics (legal successor: Russian Federation), the United Kingdom of Great Britain and Northern Ireland, and the United States of America. Albeit not entirely impossible, it is leastwise highly unlikely that all these five veto powers would support an advance of endangered states to request an Advisory Opinion.[1352] This opinion seems to be shared by various SIDS' UN Permanent Representatives who consider the Security Council not to the right venue for dealing with climate change.[1353]

This narrows the options down to the UN General Assembly solely.[1354] Art. 18 UN-Charter determines the majority requirements within this body. According to Art. 18(2) UN-Charter, decisions on important questions shall be made by a two-thirds majority of the members present and voting. Amongst the

---

1350 See "How the Court Works," International Court of Justice, available at http://www.icj-cij.org/court/index.php?p1=1&p2=6#advisory, last accessed 29 April 2014.

1351 Similar: *Nanda* in: WJU 2010, 42 (54).

1352 *Nanda* in: WJU 2010, 42 (54) supports the same conclusion regarding a hypothetical attempt on the part of Tuvalu to seek an advisory opinion from the ICJ via the Security Council.

1353 See http://www.innercitypress.com/sc2closedclimate021513.html, last accessed 29 April 2014.

1354 *Werksman* in: Gerrard/Wannier, 409 (428) also proposes a request for an Advisory Opinion by the UN General Assembly.

(non-conclusive) examples provided to further shape 'important questions,' this provision *inter alia* mentions recommendations with respect to the maintenance of international peace and security, the suspension of the rights and privileges of membership and the expulsion of members. For other questions, according to Art. 18(2) UN-Charter a majority of the members present and voting is sufficient.

A decision about a request for an Advisory Opinion would in the present case likely count as 'important question' as this ultimately leads to the decision whether the respective endangered state has a claim to a new state territory and with that a perspective to further exist; a question with even more severe consequences for the affected state than an expulsion from the United Nations. It is difficult to imagine that such an unprecedented issue would be considered a non-important question. This means that, based on the contemporary 193 United Nations member states, an endangered state would need 129 to vote in favour of its approach, provided that all member states participate in the vote and no member state abstained from voting. A request for an Advisory Opinion would hence require "broad political support from both developed and developing countries."[1355] This is a very considerable, but not insurmountable procedural hurdle. By all means, it is probably easier to find 129 supporting states on this isolated question than to hope for consent of basically all states in the course of climate change negotiations of the COP.

The applicability of the indivisible rule would not come into question in the context of an Advisory Opinion: Art. 66(1) ICJ Statute determines that all states entitled to appear before the court will be given notice of the request for an Advisory Opinion. Due to this procedural rule, every state that is affected by the very subject-matter of a potential court decision can participate in the court proceeding further specified in Artt. 66 et seqq. ICJ Statute.

The objective of an Advisory Opinion generally is purely advisory.[1356] However, the lack of binding force is unlikely to considerably diminish the efficacy of this procedure as compared with a potential lawsuit leading to a verdict between claimant and opponent. This is the case for several reasons:

First, the findings of an Advisory Opinion, containing the World's Court's view on important issues of international law, carry great legal weight and moral authority and contribute to the development of international law.[1357] As this

1355 *Werksman* in: Gerrard/Wannier, 409 (429).

1356 See *Ago*, 85 Am. J. Int'l L. 1991, 439 (439).

1357 See *Bavishi*, Raj/*Barakat*, Subhi: "Procedural Issues related to the ICJ's advisory jurisdiction," briefing paper no. BP41E by the Legal Response Initiative,

procedure is aimed at stating the law, it can be considered a judicial function in a broad sense.[1358]

Second, it has already been pointed out that international courts have been cautious regarding general principles as a source of law in cases where this would result in judicial lawmaking independent of the will of states[1359]. A request by the UN General Assembly to give an Advisory Opinion would give the ICJ that necessary legitimisation to decide upon an issue, which would traditionally be more likely to be considered a state concern. The legitimisation of the ICJ would particularly be enhanced considering the required two-thirds majority within the UN General Assembly to make such a request.

This would additionally imply a strong new argument for a claim of endangered states: Opposing state practice is being considered as one of the main hurdles to affirm a claim to compensation for damage resulting from climate change.[1360] This is particularly relevant, since the judiciary has not been democratically elected.[1361] These counter-arguments would be weakened if a two-thirds majority of the world's leaders were to call upon the ICJ in this matter and hence forgo to find a satisfying answer to this question by themselves in the traditional way of political negotiations.

This line of reasoning leads to the remarkable conclusion that a procedural course of action can (and in this case should) have implications on the substantial question that is being decided upon. It additionally strengthens the position taken above regarding the existence of a claim of endangered states[1362] as most substantial counter-arguments (contradicting state practice and the advice not to make jurisdiction independent of the will of states) would be significantly weakened. This would leave none of the substantial arguments against a claim of endangered states to a new state territory.[1363]

---

p. 2, available at http://legalresponseinitiative.org/wp-content/uploads/2013/09/BP41E-Briefing-Paper-The-ICJ-Advisory-Opinion-Procedure-11-June-2012.pdf, last accessed 29 April 2014.

1358 See *Conforti*, p. 275.

1359 See *Birnie et al.*, p. 220; *Spier* in: Faure/Peeters, 47 (48).

1360 See *Tomuschat* in: Hestermeyer et al., 3 (27 et seqq.); similar (not regarding climate change, but the necessity not to overstretch international law): *Kunig*, Jura 1998, 160 (163).

1361 See *Haritz*, p. 85.

1362 See above § 4. C. 4. b. ee.

1363 For a summary of counter-arguments see above § 4. C. 4. b. bb.

3. International Environmental Court

For decades, authors have advocated the necessity to implement an International Environmental Court: As far back as 1990, the establishment of such an institution was described as "urgently needed."[1364] This call was reasoned with the rising relevance the environment has and will have as a cause of conflict.[1365] An International Court for the Environment therefore has to be established soon, not only to force repair of ecological damage, but also in order to make individuals and states respect prevention rules.[1366] Furthermore, there is a need to give states as well as individuals better access to legal protection of their respective rights, granted by experts in international environmental law.[1367]

Over the last decade, hundreds of environmental courts or tribunals have been established around the world.[1368] In early 2012, about 465 environmental courts or tribunals were known to exist or to have been authorised in a total of 46 countries, with over 70 percent of these forums having been created since 2005.[1369] Authors predict that these kinds of forums will be the dominant dispute resolution model for environmental risks and crises in the decades to come.[1370]

The ICJ responded to the increasing importance of environmental disputes by establishing an Environmental Chamber in 1993.[1371] However, not a single case had come before this chamber in the following 13 years.[1372] Thus, it was abolished.[1373] This might be explained by the rare occasions in which environmental issues arise in isolation in international law.[1374] Even significant environmental cases like the *Gabčikovo-Nagymaros Case* or the *Pulp Mills Case* were largely about the law of treaties, international waterways, state responsibility and

---

1364 See e.g. *Postiglione*, 20 Envtl. L. 1990, 321 (323).
1365 See *Postiglione*, 20 Envtl. L. 1990, 321 (323).
1366 See *Postiglione*, 20 Envtl. L. 1990, 321 (325).
1367 See *Hey*, p. 3.
1368 See *Pring/Pring* in: FS Nanda, 482 (482).
1369 See *Pring/Pring* in: FS Nanda, 482 (484). The definition of "environmental court or tribunal" however is quite broad, e.g. comprising "individual judges within generalist courts who have training and expertise in environmental law and to whom environmental cases are assigned formally or informally," see *id.*, p. 483.
1370 See *Pring/Pring* in: FS Nanda, 482 (482).
1371 See *Hey*, p. 2.
1372 See *Birnie* et al., p. 255.
1373 See *Birnie* et al., p. 255.
1374 See *Birnie* et al., p. 255.

state succession.[1375] A broad variety of international judicial bodies have decided upon environmental cases[1376], so that the establishment of a specialised court might not be necessary.

Nevertheless, the discussion about an International Court for the Environment does not abate: For example, an NGO called the 'International Court for the Environment Coalition' promotes institutional reform to hold both states and non-state actors on account.[1377]

In order to effectively address the threats, which climate change imposes on the international community, the development of a suitably institutional framework is important indeed.[1378] To date, no judicial body such as an international environmental court exists. If such a body were to be set up, it might act as an additional tribunal to decide upon the claims of endangered states. Furthermore, the considerable amount of recently created environmental courts indicates the rising relevance of environmental disputes as well as the increased legal protection in the field of environmental law worldwide. As long as an international environmental court does not exist, however, endangered states would have to assert their claim by one of the traditional ways.

4. International Tribunal for the Law of the Sea

Apart from the two judicial bodies mentioned (of which one does not yet exist), the ITLOS could be considered in terms of a potential lawsuit – as it is one of the bodies at the global level that has already handed down decisions in relevant environmental cases[1379].

Art. 21 of the Statute of the International Tribunal for the Law of the Sea[1380], Art. 293 No. 1 UNCLOS determine that the jurisdiction of the tribunal basically comprises the application of UNCLOS and other rules of international law not incompatible with the UNCLOS. According to Art. 20 No. 1 ITLOS Statute, the tribunal is furthermore open to states as parties.

The UNCLOS includes provisions that can also be relevant in the present case, e.g. Art. 194(2) UNCLOS regarding the duty of all states to take all measures necessary to ensure that activities under their jurisdiction do not cause damage

---

1375 See *Birnie* et al., p. 255.

1376 See *Hey*, p. 1 et seqq.

1377 See ICE Coalition at http://icecoalition.com/, last accessed 29 April 2014.

1378 See *Yamin/Depledge*, p. 570.

1379 See *Hey*, p. 1.

1380 Hereinafter, the Statute of the International Tribunal for the Law of the Sea will be referred to as ITLOS Statute.

by pollution to other states and their environment. Also, most of the discussed principles will most likely be compatible with the UNCLOS, hence can be applied by the ITLOS.

Despite possible advantages for endangered states at this tribunal as compared with the ICJ (especially from the procedural point of view) it is however quite obvious that the ITLOS would not be the appropriate institution where endangered states would file a lawsuit aimed at legal confirmation of its claim to a new state territory. The ITLOS is established for disputes concerning the UNCLOS, whereby the claim of endangered states clearly would not have its focus on the law of the Sea. A claim aiming at a new state territory based at the UNCLOS and other international law compatible with this convention would appear to be too artificially construed to justify jurisdiction of the ITLOS.

5. Judicial Efforts of Endangered States so far

Why has there been so little effort by endangered states to enforce their interests judicially thus far?

Small island nations are predominantly still hoping for effective mitigation strategies rather than considering adaption to the previously unimaginable scenario of a land loss so intense that a state relocation (or emmigration) might become necessary. It is a considerable psychological hurdle to accept the increasing probability of this becoming necessary – and also to communicate this change of paradigm on the domestic front. It would require the realisation that mitigation efforts to sufficiently prevent sea level rise (i.e. global warming) have failed.

Focussing on adaption or loss and damage might in this context give the inadvertent impression that endangered states and other SIDS are giving up the attempt to try to protect their homeland from sea level rise. This impression likewise might arise on both the domestic as well as the international front. This could lead to consequences that were originally not intended, e.g. a further negative impact on the attempt to reduce GHG emissions by international negotiations.

Notwithstanding this, there are some scattered cases of judicial efforts. For example in the year 2002, Tuvalu tried to institute proceedings before the ICJ against the United States in response to their refusal to ratify the Kyoto Protocol.[1381] This consideration caused excitement within the community of international lawyers

1381 See *Jacobs*, 14 Pac. Rim L. & Pol'y J. 2005, 103 (103).

focussing on international environmental law.[1382] Yet within the last decade no progress has been made in that regard.

More recently, Palau has taken legal steps. In September 2011, *President Johnson Toribiong* in his statement at the General Debate announced that

> *"Palau and the Republic of the Marshall Islands will call upon this General Assembly to seek, on an urgent basis, pursuant to Article 96 of the UN Charter, an advisory opinion from the International Court of Justice on the responsibilities of States under international law to ensure that activities carried out under their jurisdiction or control that emit greenhouse gases do not damage other States."*[1383]

According to the summary of a press conference released by the UN Department of Public Information in February 2012, *President Johnson Toribiong* added that this request "would complement and not conflict with efforts to create a negotiated international climate regime."[1384]

The aim "to ensure that activities carried out under [a state's] jurisdiction or control that emit[s] greenhouse gases do not damage other states"[1385] is an approach that (in contrast to this thesis' key claim) focuses on mitigation rather than adaption or loss and damage. This proceeding aims at both raising awareness of the reality after 20 years of climate change negotiation as well as providing judicial "guidance to the negotiation track."[1386]

It was commented that – from a strategic point of view – Palau's request for an Advisory Opinion would contradict diplomatic climate change negotiations.[1387] However, with an eye towards the failure to advance efforts for negotiations at the recent Rio+20 Earth Summit, this approach might perhaps be "their best

---

1382 See e.g. *Nanda* in: WJU 2010, 42 (54); *Jacobs*, 14 Pac. Rim L. & Pol'y J. 2005, 103 (103 et seqq.); *Weinbaum*, 20 Pac. Rim L. & Pol'y J. 2011, 429 (429 et seqq.).

1383 Statement by the Honorable Johnson Toribiong, President of the Republic of Palau, to the 66th Regular Session of the United Nations General Assembly, 22 September 2011, p. 4, available at http://gadebate.un.org/sites/default/files/gastatements/66/PW_en.pdf, last accessed 29 April 2014.

1384 U.N. Press release from 3 February 2012, available at http://www.un.org/News/briefings/docs/2012/120203_ICJ.doc.htm, last accessed 29 April 2014.

1385 U.N. Press release from 3 February 2012, available at http://www.un.org/News/briefings/docs/2012/120203_ICJ.doc.htm, last accessed 29 April 2014.

1386 U.N. Press release from 3 February 2012, available at http://www.un.org/News/briefings/docs/2012/120203_ICJ.doc.htm, last accessed 29 April 2014.

1387 See *Robert Esposito* in "Ask the experts: Climate change and international law," interview dated 10 August 2012, available at http://www.pbs.org/wnet/need-to-know/uncategorized/ask-the-experts/14420/, last accessed 29 April 2014.

strategy."[1388] Moreover, as an Advisory Opinion will lead to "a non-binding result,"[1389] it would not pillory emitting states as much as a lawsuit would do – a chance to avoid or to minimise "international strife."[1390] Also, it could serve as an "important legal precedent" that supports other strategies endangered states could consider to strengthen their position.[1391]

Palau's attempt to urgently strive for an Advisory Opinion does not seem to have made any noteworthy progress yet. Overall, the legal efforts of endangered states and other SIDS to mitigate climate change or to claim compensation for the adverse effects of climate change have not been particularly ambitious. This supports the conclusion that within the international community, substantial oppositions have to be overcome to effectively enforce legal proceedings in favour of endangered states.

6. Strategic Implications

The aforementioned procedural options for endangered states to assert their claims appear to pose a considerable threshold. Especially the need to convince two-thirds of all states to vote in favour of an Advisory Opinion is quite demanding. Consequently, endangered states and other SIDS undertook only minor efforts to enforce their legal protection in court. The following thoughts aim to illustrate that the success of legal protection depends to a significant extent on the respective circumstances as well as on the strategy endangered states choose to pursue their claim.

The weak position of endangered states, which gives them the moral high ground, might be used as a promising trump card. The uniqueness of a potential claim before, or Advisory Opinion of an international judicial body concerning the claim of a small and vulnerable island state to a new state territory, would

---

1388 *Robert Esposito* in "Ask the experts: Climate change and international law," interview dated 10 August 2012, available at http://www.pbs.org/wnet/need-to-know/uncategorized/ask-the-experts/14420/, last accessed 29 April 2014.

1389 *Robert Esposito* in "Ask the experts: Climate change and international law," interview dated 10 August 2012, available at http://www.pbs.org/wnet/need-to-know/uncategorized/ask-the-experts/14420/, last accessed: 29 April 2014.

1390 *Robert Esposito* in "Ask the experts: Climate change and international law," interview dated 10 August 2012, available at http://www.pbs.org/wnet/need-to-know/uncategorized/ask-the-experts/14420/, last accessed 29 April 2014.

1391 *David Hunter* in "Ask the experts: Climate change and international law," interview dated 10 August 2012, available at http://www.pbs.org/wnet/need-to-know/uncategorized/ask-the-experts/14420/, last accessed 29 April 2014.

generate considerable international attention. The fairly recent declaration of *President Johnson Toribiong* of Palau is one of the many examples for the potential to effectively catch the attention in the media: "We're engaged in an epic battle to save planet Earth,"[1392] he proclaimed. Others stress that "[t]he story of an entire nation's destruction has the potential to awaken the world to the real dangers of climate change."[1393]

Depending on the respective situation of international politics and the reporting of the media concerning this matter, there might be a scenario where the pressure on governments is high not only within the international community, but also on the domestic front of wealthier states to accept a responsibility towards endangered states. Media bring the climate change issue to the attention of the public and can place pressure on politicians to act, as they did at the forefront of the Kyoto Protocol.[1394]

Public opinion can play a vital role in politics. This was already the case at *President Lincoln's* time who declared in 1858 that "[o]ur government rests in public opinion. Whoever can change public opinion can change the government practically just so much."[1395] And this was still the case in 2013, when *President Obama*, invoking his predecessor, agreed by saying "I always read a lot of Lincoln, and I'm reminded of his adage that, with public opinion, there's nothing you can't accomplish; without it, you're not going to get very far."[1396]

The internet might intensify this effect: 'Wikileaks,' (German) 'Guttenplag' or 'Anonymous' and last but not least the Arab Spring are some examples for the increasing importance and power of public opinion (or decentrally organised interest groups).

NGOs at the international level, e.g. Islands First,[1397] and many others especially in the environmental field furthermore enforce the influence of non-state actors on international politics and law. Art. 66 No. 2 ICJ Statute even establishes

---

1392 U.N. Press release from 3 February 2012, available at http://www.un.org/News/briefings/docs/2012/120203_ICJ.doc.htm, last accessed 29 April 2014.

1393 *Larson*, 21 Mich. J. Int'l L. 1999-2000, 495 (522).

1394 See *Yamin/Depledge*, p. 59.

1395 *Lincoln* in: Lapsley, 283 (284 et seq.) (Fragment of a Speech at a Republican Banquet in in Chicago, 10 December 1858).

1396 Franklin Foer and Chris Hughes, "Interview: Barack Obama Is Not Pleased: The President on His Enemies, the Media, and the Futures of Football," New Republic, 27 January 2013, available at http://www.newrepublic.com/article/112190/obama-interview-2013-sit-down-president, last accessed 29 April 2014.

1397 See www.islandsfirst.org.

the procedural opportunity in the course of an Advisory Opinion to call to appear before the court such organisations considered as likely to be able to furnish information on the question.

From the current *status quo*, the odds might be long that states sued at the ICJ, e.g. the USA or China, would provide the required consent to conduct a lawsuit. Also, it might be rather unlikely that these states would support requesting an ICJ Advisory Opinion. But this might change in the future, possibly based on the pressure of public opinion – a strategy that might especially be successful in the Western world where the media impact is particularly powerful. "The combination of public exposure, diplomatic pressure, and international legal obligations may be enough to turn the tide."[1398]

7. Statement

So far, the SIDS' diplomacy has been characterised by pragmatism and reasonableness, preferring consensus building to obstruction and confrontation.[1399] This strategy however did not protect them from the existence-threatening future some of them are facing today. It might therefore be advisable to broaden the strategic perspective. In the course of this, recourse to the ICJ is a legitimate part of a "multi-prong effort" to continuously built political support.[1400]

The ICJ currently is the only jurisdictional body in international law, which endangered states could reasonably use to pursue their claim. The breadth of its missions affords the court the opportunity to combine evolving elements of international law.[1401] Specialised tribunals do not possess this broad spectrum of jurisdiction.[1402] The variety of fields of law affected by the factual and legal future of endangered states (environmental principles, general principles, human rights, right to self-determination, state responsibility, the core essence of the UN legal framework, the historical context, the development of international law as well as socio-economic implications) suggest a broad positioned legal forum. Existing environmental forums on the international level are hampered not only by lack of binding international law, but also by limited jurisdiction,

1398 *Larson*, 21 Mich. J. Int'l L. 1999-2000, 495 (522).

1399 See *Slade*, 17 Temp. Int'l & Comp. L.J. 2003, 531 (534).

1400 *David Hunter* in "Ask the Experts: Climate Change and International Law," 10 August 2012, available at http://www.pbs.org/wnet/need-to-know/uncategorized/ask-the-experts/14420/last accessed 29 April 2014.

1401 See *Gordon* in: FS Nanda, 74 (89).

1402 See *Gordon* in: FS Nanda, 74 (89).

unwillingness of states to bring issues to an international arbiter and last but not least by limited enforcement powers.[1403] The ICJ shares some of these problems, but certainly overall to a lesser extent. Also, the ICJ is the principal judicial organ of the United Nations (Art. 1 ICJ Statute) which strengthens its authority as compared with specialised international tribunals. The paramount uniqueness of a sinking states' claim to ultimately defend its existence makes the ICJ the only conceivable court for this kind of claim.

SIDS thus far predominantly "take comfort in some of the pronouncements of the World Court" rather than this body actually helping them to enforce their legal interests.[1404] The increasing number of cases filed at the ICJ can be explained more by a desire to obtain diplomatic cover for practical solutions, which the parties are willing to accept anyway, than interpreting this development as indicating increased confidence in this legal forum.[1405]

Despite valid criticisms about the potential of an international court judging a diverse, complex and discordant community of sovereign states, there also are many examples of effective and groundbreaking ICJ decisions. In spite of such traditional dispute settlement techniques having undeniable disadvantages in the field of environmental law, at least they provide a way to hold a fellow state to account.[1406] Moreover, the ICJ is the major forum of the international adjudicative, thus, ultimately, endangered states do not have any other significant option if they seek an alternative to the hitherto rather ineffectual international environmental negotiations.

The evolution of international environmental law as well as the increasing possibilities and effectiveness of its legal enforcement suggest that within the next few decades the chances of success are likely to improve in both the substantial as well as the procedural field of law. The relevance of international environmental litigation might increase sooner rather than later.[1407] It might therefore be advisable for endangered states to wait before taking legal action. At this moment in time an ICJ Advisory Opinion is the only possible measure to enforce their claim to a new state territory.

1403 See *Pring/Pring* in: FS Nanda, 482 (487).

1404 *Slade*, 17 Temp. Int'l & Comp. L.J. 2003, 531 (538).

1405 See *Gordon* in: FS Nanda, 74 (89).

1406 See *Yamin/Depledge*, p. 382.

1407 See *Yamin/Depledge*, p. 17, who focuses, however, on litigation based on mutual environmental agreements rather than based on environmental principles.

§ 5. Consequences for the Statehood of Endangered States

A. Introduction

Endangered states "must be prepared to deal with the virtually unprecedented situation of physically losing their [...] territory."[1408] Based on their claim to a new state territory as discussed in the previous chapter, it is advisable for endangered states to start pursuing their interests early enough in order to facilitate a relocation before their current territories are inundated. Firstly, however, what happens to the statehood of endangered states' when they lose their state territory due to inundation without already having relocated to another place has to be clarified.

Some of this thesis' findings can be restated at this juncture. The examination of the endangered states' claim in § 4 was motivated by the realisation that there are currently only two conceivable consequences if a state permanently loses its (present) state territory due to inundation. Based on current international law and the contemporary concept of states, the most obvious result of the loss of a state's constitutive element would be its alteration in its status as a legal entity ('state') to a *sui generis* subject of international law.[1409] Its population would have to migrate to another or several other states.[1410] The second alternative, a state relocation while preserving the respective statehood,[1411] is only possible on two conditions: First, the non-territorial status must not be permanent. Second, a state relocation (and thus its continuation as an identical legal entity at another location) must be possible according to international law.

The first condition of the second alternative is met: As outlined in the previous chapter, endangered states have a claim to a new state territory.[1412] The limits of international law in not suppling precise details for such a claim[1413] as well as the limits and difficulties regarding its legal enforcement[1414] do not change this fact. The non-territorial status is not (necessarily) permanent as long as such a

---

1408 *Markovich/Annandale*, 5 Asia Pac. J. Envtl. L. 2000, 135 (146).

1409 See *Grote Stoutenburg* in: Gerrard/Wannier, 57 (58).

1410 See *Jarvis*, 9 Seattle J. Soc. Just. 4477 2010-2011, 447 (449).

1411 See *Jarvis*, 9 Seattle J. Soc. Just. 4477 2010-2011, 447 (449).

1412 See above § 4. C. 4. b. ee.

1413 See above § 4. C. 5.; § 4. E.

1414 See above § 4. F.

claim exists (or its existence is at least unclear) *and* the respective state is willing to pursue such a claim.

However, a preservation of statehood despite the (non-permanent) loss of the respective state's territory must also be compatible with international law. There is no precedence for this scenario.[1415] International law thus far has failed to adequately address this issue.[1416] The following sections will examine statehood in a scenario of permanent indundation, based on both the findings of the previous chapters as well as the approaches of the international community in other cases of temporary non-compliance with the three basic state criteria.[1417]

B. Maintaining or Losing Statehood?

Does international law allow states to continue to exist despite the loss of their current state territory? First of all, other examples of incomplete states and state practices in comparable cases shall be considered (see under 1.). As the current legal world order has been shaped by the impressions of the collapse caused by World War II,[1418] these considerations shall predominantly – but not solely – focus on state practice since 1945. Subsequently, additional arguments and counter-arguments for the preservation of endangered states' statehood will be considered (see under 2. and 3.). In addition, the approach to implement what is called a "Nation Ex-Situ"[1419] will be outlined (see under 4.), before an answer to this chapter's line of enquiry is put forward.

1. Governments in Exile, Failed States, and other Examples in State Practice

The following selection of examples illustrates the inconsistency in state practice regarding requirements of statehood criteria. Other examples that are pertinent to the legal analysis of the present question will also be provided.

Governments in exile are an obvious example of state practice not following principles.[1420] With regard to SIDS' citizens, it begs the question of whether

1415 See U.N. Doc. A/HRC/10/61 (2009), p. 14 et seq., para. 41.

1416 See *Jarvis*, 9 Seattle J. Soc. Just. 4477 2010-2011, 447 (449).

1417 The criteria are a people, sovereignty, and a state territory, see above § 3. B. 1.-3.

1418 See *Grewe/Khan* in Simma, 2nd ed., Drafting History, marginal no. 1.

1419 See *Burkett* in: Gerrard/Wannier, 89 et seqq.

1420 Similar: *Burkett* in: Gerrard/Wannier, 89 (98).

they too are entitled to some form of government in exile in case of a state extinction.[1421]

There are various forms of governments in exile, which partially differ in their legal classification.[1422] The traditional use of the term 'government in exile' describes an authority that, based in exile, claims to be the government of a state that is under the effective control of another authority.[1423] This other authority can be a colonial power, a belligerent occupant, its "local puppet," or could have achieved power via a revolution or a *coup d'état*.[1424] Examples for governments in exile include Cambodia, Haiti, Kuwait, and – depending on the respective legal (and/or political) point of view, Tibet.[1425]

Recognised governments in exile share most of the rights to which a common government is entitled – e.g. immunity from the jurisdiction of other states' courts.[1426] The ILC made it clear in its comments on its "Draft Articles on Jurisdictional Immunities of States and Their Property" that the term 'state' not only refers to a government, but that, in addition, state practice has long recognised that a suit against a foreign government is identical with a proceeding against the state.[1427] Moreover, governments in exile usually benefit from the inviolability of their respective seat.[1428] Overall, governments in exile basically have the same representative and jurisdictional competence (with the exception of a legislative authority inside national territory) and enjoy the same privileges and immunities in foreign states, as if they were recognised *in situ* governments located in their state's territory.[1429]

This shows, overall, a rather flexible understanding of a government that exerts the sovereign rights of its respective state. This practice therefore implies a "principle of effectiveness."[1430] An inverse relationship can be identified between effectiveness and legitimacy of governments in exile.[1431] A lower degree

---

1421 See U.N. Doc. E/CN.4/Sub.2/AC.4/2004/CRP.1, p. 34 para. 10.

1422 For a detailed examination of the different forms of governments in exile, see *Koberg*.

1423 See *Talmon*, p. 8.

1424 See *Talmon*, p. 8.

1425 See *Talmon*, p. 8 et seq.

1426 See *Talmon*, p. 253.

1427 See Commentary on ILC Draft Articles 1991, Art. 2.1(b)(i), p. 15 para. 9 with examples for this state practice.

1428 See *Talmon*, p. 256 et seq.

1429 See *Talmon*, p. 272.

1430 *Conforti*, p. 54.

1431 See *Koberg*, p. 3.

of effectiveness is often compensated by a higher degree of legitimacy.[1432] In comparison with endangered states, governments in exile are not an example for the entire absence of one of the basic state criteria. It is, however, proof of a non-static interpretation in state practice of what is sufficient to bridge a shortcoming of a state criterion. Furthermore, the treatment of governments in exile offers proof of a pragmatic rather than principled approach in international law. This broadens the scope for potential solutions in the case of endangered states.

There is one further noteworthy parallel. Traditionally, a government in exile has to have both a factual option as well as a serious endeavour to regain its territory.[1433] Similarly, the question of whether an inundated endangered state could maintain its statehood can only be discussed seriously if the respective endangered state has both the (potentially uncertain) factual option as well as the serious will to relocate the state to another place. In other words, as already mentioned above, the non-territorial status must not be permanent – there must at least be a concrete perspective to regain the criterion 'state territory.'

Even more similar to the possible future of endangered states is the example of what is called 'failed states.'[1434] A failed state presupposes two conditions: First, a classification as a state, and second, the respective entity must have once conformed to the requirements of statehood but no longer does so.[1435] This latter condition is, generally speaking, met by entities that have collapsed, i.e. do not have an effective government anymore.[1436] A failed state is a state which still has a legal capacity despite its inability to act.[1437] Hence a loss of sovereignty (which is one of the constitutive state criteria) marks the point in time when a state collapses and becomes a failed state. This definition is very similar to the one outlined previously in this thesis to define at what point an inundated state territory cannot be considered such anymore.[1438]

For instance, Somalia, the Congo, Liberia, Bosnia-Herzegovina, and Rwanda have been considered to be failed states.[1439] The reasons for the failure of these states have their historical roots in (de)colonisation and the conclusion of the

1432 See *Koberg*, p. 3.
1433 See *Koberg*, p. 323.
1434 Similar: *Burkett* in: Gerrard/Wannier, 89 (97), arguing for a so-called Nation Ex-Situ.
1435 See *Ferreira*, 41 Comp. & Int'l L.J. S. Afr. 2008, 428 (431).
1436 See *Ferreira*, 41 Comp. & Int'l L.J. S. Afr. 2008, 428 (433).
1437 See *Thürer* in: Thürer et al., 9 (13).
1438 See above § 3. B. 3. b. bb.
1439 See *Crawford*, p. 701; *Thürer* in: Thürer et al., 9 (11).

Cold War.[1440] This suggests a certain responsibility of other states for the collapse of the states – another parallel that can be drawn to the situation of endangered states threatened by anthropogenic rises in sea level. In both cases, the respective state collapse is (partially) caused by powers outside the affected state.

Failed states are usually considered to be a risk for global security – and for the international system as a whole.[1441] The usual course of action following state failure is to allow them to further function as legal entities at an international level through, *inter alia*, membership of international organisations.[1442] Thus, an extended period of anarchy within a state does not lead to its extinction.[1443] It has been stated that ineffective statehood cannot and must not be mirrored in international law.[1444] However, particular circumstances may justify partial elimination of statehood criteria.[1445] As early as 1950, it was remarked that this state practice is proof of the fact that it is not the government (or sovereignty), but the people, which is the determining factor of what constitutes a state in international law.[1446]

Several issues that arise from failed states involve basic principles of international law, including the principle of sovereign equality, the right to self-determination, the peacekeeping function of the international framework, and human rights.[1447] These aspects of international law (complemented by a tort law approach) are also key issues on which this thesis focuses. Overall, the parallels between failed states and endangered states are striking. "[I]n view of the fact that even so-called failed States continue to exist as States, the same would likely apply to a disordered island State, especially because its governmental collapse would not (only) be caused by internal factors but be precipitated by externally imposed climate change."[1448]

One pre-World War II example for case law containing pertinent remarks for transitional lack of territorial sovereignty is the *Advisory Opinion on the Aaland Island* dated 1920 that had been provided by the International Committee of Jurists.[1449] The Council of the League of Nations had mandated this committee to

---

1440 See *Thürer* in: Thürer et al., 9 (11).
1441 See *Leidenmühler*, summarising issues with regard to global security policy (p. 29 et seqq.) and with regard to the international system as a whole (p. 34 et seqq.).
1442 See *Ferreira*, 41 Comp. & Int'l L.J. S. Afr. 2008, 428 (436).
1443 See *Crawford*, p. 722.
1444 See *von Engelhardt*, 45-2 VRÜ 2012, 222 (222).
1445 See *Kreijen*, p. 33.
1446 See *Verdross* in: FS Klang, 18 (19).
1447 See *Thürer* in: Thürer et al., 9 (14).
1448 *Grote Stoutenburg* in: Gerrard/Wannier, 57 (68).
1449 See LNOJ Suppl. no. 3, 1920.

judge the legal aspects of the Aaland Island case.[1450] Citizens of the island were willing to determine by plebiscite whether to remain under Finnish sovereignty or to be incorporated into the Kingdom of Sweden.[1451] The jurists stated in their Advisory Opinion that if the essential basis of territorial sovereignty is lacking, "either because the State is not yet fully formed or because it is undergoing transformation or dissolution, the situation is obscure and uncertain from a legal point of view, and will not become clear until the period of development is completed and a definite new situation, which is normal in respect to territorial sovereignty, has been established".[1452]

These remarks are considered proof of "the link between territorial sovereignty and statehood becom[ing] manifest".[1453] At first sight, this remark seems to argue for a strict application of statehood criteria, especially with regard to the necessity of a territory. This would be an argument against maintaining statehood in the case of endangered states. The author however, takes account of the general relevance of territory in international law, which indeed has increased during the development of states.[1454] For endangered states, which expect temporary land loss the remarks made in this Advisory Opinion point instead to the unclarity of a transitional status, stressing the necessity to await the completion of the development until legal certainty is restored. This argues in favour of a preservation of the *status quo* until the ambiguity is resolved.

Other examples of an inconsistent and rather flexible interpretation of statehood have already been elaborated on: The handling of recognition,[1455] the political approach in the course of accepting new member states to the UN,[1456] the ongoing discussion about statehood criteria,[1457] as well as the historical development of the concept of the 'state' itself.[1458]

2. Arguments for Preservation of Statehood

Numerous findings made in this thesis argue for a preservation of statehood when endangered states will be inundated.

1450 See LNOJ Suppl. no. 3, 1920, p. 3.
1451 See LNOJ Suppl. no. 3, 1920, p. 3.
1452 LNOJ Suppl. no. 3, 1920, p. 6.
1453 *Shaw*, NYIL 13, 61 (75).
1454 See above § 3. D.
1455 See above § 3. C. 1.
1456 See above § 3. D. 4.
1457 See above § 3. C.
1458 See above § 3. D.

When an endangered state becomes uninhabitable and thus loses its state territory, this status is only temporary: The claim to a new state territory[1459] creates the option for endangered states to be provided with a new state territory in the long term. This option makes a preservation of the respective statehood reasonable, as evidenced in the aforementioned arguments.

As just outlined, state practice has proven to be flexible.[1460] While the parties involved – states and international organisations – predominantly abide by international law,[1461] there are some cases in which political interests supersede international principles.[1462] When opportune, states have been seen to be pragmatic rather than principled[1463].

Attempts to agree upon a binding definition of the term 'state,' e.g. at the San Francisco Conference, foundered on diverging understandings of an appropriate concept of states.[1464] The MCRDS, described as the most widely accepted source for a definition of statehood,[1465] was signed by the representatives of 19 Pan-American states, out of which only five have ratified it.[1466] Not only does this indicate international disagreement, but it could also be indicative of the aim to remain flexible in that regard.

Some of the findings with relation to statehood made in § 3 also argue for a broader interpretation of statehood in times of climate change. Despite the (non-binding) definition provided in Art. 1 of the MCRDS, the definition of 'state' is negotiable,[1467] as the historical use of the term as well as the ongoing discussion about its criteria prove.[1468] The "dilemma" of the concept of statehood is the flexibility of its reference object.[1469] The use of the term 'state' is historically

---

1459 See above § 4. C. 4. b. ee.

1460 See also: *Burkett* in: Gerrard/Wannier, 89 (91).

1461 See *Verdross/Simma,* § 385.

1462 See *Kriele*, § 18, p. 82; *Verdross/Simma,* § 385.

1463 See *Birnie et al.*, p. 213.

1464 See *Darsow*, p. 112.

1465 See *Grant*, 37 Colum. J. Transnat'l L. 1998-1999, 403 (403).

1466 See *Grant*, 37 Colum. J. Transnat'l L. 1998-1999, 403 (456). The signing states were Argentina, Brazil, Chile, Columbia, Cuba, Dominican Republic, Ecuador, El Salvador, Guatemala, Haiti, Honduras, Mexico, Nicaragua, Panama, Paraguay, Peru, United States, Uruguay, Venezuela.

1467 See *Kreijen*, p. 33.

1468 See above § 3. D. (history); § 3. C. (discussion about statehood criteria).

1469 See *Isensee* in: HStR, para. 15 No. 46.

contingent, as its criteria vary over time.[1470] There is no immutable definition of what a state is.[1471] Factual and legal statehood criteria are shifting crucially.[1472]

The prevailing opinion regarding the legal relationship between a state and its territory has likewise been subject to reinterpretation.[1473] It is evolving and changing. Every new generation provides it with a new shape amending or overruling the established understanding.[1474] History has shown the different approaches to statehood, with the current focus on territorial sovereignty rather than on personal affiliation being the result of a slow and long development.[1475]

In 1625, for example, it was made clear that "the rights of a people" (here the author was referring to what today would be considered as state) do not depend on the state territory, but on the respective people only.[1476] If a people migrates, it thus remains the same legal subject.[1477] The change of its sovereign, e.g. the implementation of a king, thus does not amend any debts or contracts agreed upon beforehand.[1478] Until today (according to an essay published in 1950), maintaining international liability is the key reason for the ascription of importance to a people when speaking of state identity in international law.[1479] Thus, according to constant state practice, neither a revolution nor a *coup d'état* can suspend the identity of a state according to international law.[1480] Other authors similarly argue that whereas a disappearance of governments is not unusual, the extinction of a state has so far been a rare occurence.[1481]

It is also being argued that – even if a given endangered state does not have the prospect of a new territory to which to relocate – "other States have a moral and perhaps even legal duty to continue recognizing island States that have lost their effective statehood."[1482] International law related to statehood, according to this viewpoint, is based on the two competing principles of effectiveness and

1470 See *Grant*, 37 Colum. J. Transnat'l L. 1998-1999, 403 (408, 457).
1471 See *Müller*, p. 16.; *Crawford*, p. 667.
1472 See *Shaw*, p. 197.
1473 See above § 3. B. 3. b. aa.
1474 See *Müller*, p. 16.
1475 See above § 3. B. 3. b. aa. with further references.
1476 See *Grotius*, Book 2, Chapter 9, § 3.
1477 See *Grotius*, Book 2, Chapter 9, § 7.
1478 See *Grotius*, Book 2, Chapter 9, § 8, No. 3.
1479 See *Verdross* in: FS Klang, 18 (19).
1480 See *Verdross* in: FS Klang, 18 (19).
1481 See *Shaw*, p. 208.
1482 *Grote Stoutenburg* in: Gerrard/Wannier, 57 (58).

legality.[1483] The latter principle concerns fundamental norms, i.e. *jus cogens* in the sense of Art. 41(2) ARS.[1484] In the case of endangered states, their extinction due to anthropogenic climate change "affects fundamental norms of international law, such as the right to self-determination and permanent sovereignty over natural resources."[1485] As a breach of these norms in the technical sense cannot be assessed, states are at least morally obliged to further recognise deterritorialised endangered states.[1486] Based on reasons of international justice and solidarity, statehood would likely be preserved in the sense of a legal fiction even if a state does no longer fulfil traditional statehood criteria.[1487] This recommended approach is being viewed as "the greatest structural transformation international law has seen since the establishment of the so-called Westphalian order."[1488]

In contrast to the present thesis, this viewpoint does not examine a claim to a new state territory and thus considers a permanent deterritorialised scenario. Nevertheless, it pleads to further equip endangered states with all rights (and duties) arising from statehood. Thus, from this point of view, endangered states should *a fortiori* maintain their statehood as their deterritorialised status is only transitional and they can relocate based on the claim to a new state territory.[1489]

The singularity of losing a state territory due to permanent inundation also calls for an amended interpretation of the concept of state in the present case. The unique situation in which the endangered states find themselves especially applies regarding the moment when state criteria are considered: International law so far focused on the genesis of states.[1490] In order to become a state, the criteria have to be met. The present thesis, however, considers the unprecedented case of the loss of one criterion and of the absence of a legal successor state. This is a crucial distinction that justifies a different treatment. In this context, the conserving character of international law needs to be mentioned: Even if a state loses significant characteristics, it usually does not lose its legal status.[1491] An only temporary loss of constitutive statehood criteria thus does not lead to the extinction of the state as a legal subject in international law.[1492] A state thus can

---

1483 See *Grote Stoutenburg* in: Gerrard/Wannier, 57 (58).
1484 See *Grote Stoutenburg* in: Gerrard/Wannier, 57 (58, 75).
1485 *Grote Stoutenburg* in: Gerrard/Wannier, 57 (59).
1486 See *Grote Stoutenburg* in: Gerrard/Wannier, 57 (59).
1487 See *Grote Stoutenburg* in: Gerrard/Wannier, 57 (66).
1488 *Grote Stoutenburg* in: Gerrard/Wannier, 57 (87).
1489 See above § 4. C. 4. B. ee.
1490 See above § 3. E.
1491 See *Kunig*, Jura 1986, 344 (346).
1492 See *Aden*, ZvglRWiss 2007, 490 (493).

exist as legal subject in international law despite a lack of its legal capacity – as long as this status is not permanent.[1493]

Similar remarks are made which promote the continuance of a state: The requirement of territory is described to be rather a constituent of government and independence than a distinct criterion of its own.[1494] This leads to the continuity of states also when changes in governments, constitutions, territories, and populations occur.[1495] Even if these changes are drastic, the same state can be said to continue to exist.[1496] After a state has once been firmly established, there is hence a strong presumption of its continued existence.[1497]

The preservation of the statehood of endangered states would furthermore avoid legal uncertainties. A scenario of the loss of statehood would raise a considerable amount of follow-up questions many of which have been elaborated in the context of human rights implications for indigenous peoples in states threatened with extinction for environmental reasons[1498]:

- Will the termination of the legal entity 'state' happen by itself or is some kind of recognition of non-existence required, e.g. on the part of the United Nations?
- Does a disappearance of a state automatically lead to concurrent legal consequences in all international organisations of which the state in question is member?
- Who, if anyone at all, will then be responsible for national debts?
- Will the expiration of statehood have consequences for the status of internal or territorial waters or an exclusive economic zone?
- Which status will the respective citizens and legal persons registered or incorporated in such territories have?
- What happens to the diplomatic status of the respective states' representatives?

Apart from these examples, countless other questions would arise, e.g. the question of what the consequences for the membership and voting rights of such an entity at the United Nations would be – according to Artt. 3, 4 UN-Charter, only states qualify as members. The (former) states could thus likely lose their membership and their voting rights (Art. 18 UN-Charter). In the overall context, this

1493 See *Aden*, ZvglRWiss 2007, 490 (493).
1494 See *Crawford*, p. 52.
1495 See *Crawford*, p. 667.
1496 See *Crawford*, p. 667 et seq.
1497 See *Crawford*, p. 715.
1498 For the listed examples of legal uncertainty, see U.N. Doc. E/CN.4/Sub.2/AC.4/2004/CRP.1, p. 3 et seq. para. 8.

consequence would be serious for the affected state and difficult to communicate domestically as well as internationally.

Especially the rights of citizens deserve closer attention in this context: It appears to be the necessary consequence that the termination of statehood would cause the end of citizenship. Being a citizen of a state that does not exist anymore seems irrational. The legal consequence of losing citizenship however would likely infringe the respective citizens' right to self-determination[1499] as well as their human right to nationality codified in Art. 15 UNDHR.[1500] Also, the citizens of a state that used to be endangered and is now extinct will not become refugees in the sense of the 1951 Convention on the Status of Refugees.[1501] This treaty does not recognise as refugees persons who have to leave their (former) state for reasons relating to the environment.[1502]

Legal questions and difficulties such as the ones outlined above, all of which constitute fuel for grueling political conflicts, can be avoided or at least considerably diminished with a single step: By maintaining statehood.

Also, problematic aspects of equity and fairness arise when, for example, the procedural possibilities of taking legal steps could be restricted by revoking statehood: Art. 34(1) ICJ Statute determines that only states can be parties in cases before the court. Also, if an endangered state were to stop being a member of the UN General Assembly – which with regard to Artt. 3, 4 UN-Charter is logically consistent with the loss of statehood – its possibilities to promote a request for an ICJ Advisory Opinion would be significantly curtailed if not revoked. Ultimately, endangered states could lose their legal protection – an outcome that would be inconsistent with the principle of sovereign equality, one of the very core principles in international law,[1503] codified in Art. 2 No. 1 UN-Charter.

Regardless of the particular scenario of endangered states, various authors commented on the necessity of a state territory for speaking of statehood. These comments furthermore support the preservation of statehood even in the absence of a state territory. It has been stated, for example, that a state territory is not essential to a state's existence.[1504] A non-territorial society is a true state

1499 See above § 4. C. 3. c.

1500 Regarding human rights, see above § 4. C. 3. b.

1501 See U.N. Doc. E/CN.4/Sub.2/2005/28, p. 3 para. 8.

1502 See U.N. Doc. E/CN.4/Sub.2/2005/28, p. 3 para. 8.

1503 See *Jacobs*, 14 Pac. Rim L. & Pol'y J. 2005, 103 (120). This principle has been elaborated in the context of a SIDS' claim to a new state territory, see above § 4. C. 3. e. bb.

1504 See *Salmond*, p. 99.

when organised in such a way that the fulfilment of the essential functions of government are ensured.[1505] A state without a fixed territory hence is, according to this view, perfectly possible.[1506]

The following two major functions are ascribed to a state territory: The shelter function ensuring security and the possibility of acting as a springboard for citizens' opportunities.[1507] The ultimate pursuit is to render 'the good life' possible.[1508] The territory thus has been brought into existence for the sake of the people.[1509] The concept of territorial sovereignty "is one of self-preservation, but also one of preserving the community's way of life, the right to self-government, freedom and whatever opportunity a free people is entitled to."[1510]

This approach has its supporters: "Territorial sovereignty is the answer provided by international law as regards the needs for security, stability and identity felt by a group within a certain area."[1511] In this context, the *Separate Opinion by Judge Alvarez* in the *Corfu Channel Case* is revealing.[1512] Referring to the evolution of state sovereignty, *Alvarez* points out the growing importance of social independence and the dominance of general interest over state interest to then conclude that sovereignty has become "an *institution*, an *international social function* of a psychological character."[1513]

These functions of territory, territorial sovereignty, as well as the relevance of sovereignty (whose scope would be at least considerably diminished if the legal entity 'state' ceases to exist) can be viewed as arguments for a preservation of statehood in the case of inundation. Individual and collective interests such as security, identity, scope of opportunities, as well as stability are better protected by the preservation of statehood than it would be the case in the insecure and unclear scenario of a *sui generis* subject of international law.

As early as 1975, the growing insignificance of territory in international law has been pointed out.[1514] New technological developments, for example, have reduced the relevance of the territorial factor.[1515] The failure of international law

1505 See *Salmond*, p. 99.
1506 See *Salmond*, p. 99.
1507 See *Gottmann*, p. 14.
1508 See *Gottmann*, p. 14.
1509 See *Gottmann*, p. 14.
1510 *Gottmann*, p. 15.
1511 *Shaw*, NYIL 13, 61 (79) invokes the following separate opinion.
1512 See *Corfu Channel Case*, ICJ Reports, 1949, p. 4 et seqq.
1513 *Corfu Channel Case*, ICJ Reports, 1949, p. 4 (43).
1514 See *Dembinski*, ASDI 1975, 121 (121 et seqq.).
1515 See *Dembinski*, ASDI 1975, 121 (145).

to adapt to problems of contemporary international relations, according to this viewpoint, lies in its concentration upon territory as the fundamental concept of international law.[1516] Both international politicians and lawyers would thus far have not sufficiently appreciated the changes that have occurred which affect the theory of the supremacy of territorial states.[1517] This lack of adaption is considered to be the source of many restraints for international mechanisms,[1518] which makes the search for solutions an urgent and grave problem mankind is confronted with.[1519]

These remarks likewise support a point of view that focuses on the interests of the affected individuals rather than to interpret the current concept of statehood as being self-serving. It can be deemed as certain that preserving statehood despite a temporary non-territorial status would be in the respective citizens' interest.

Finally, there are considerable political reasons to preserve statehood, some of which have already been mentioned. Despite their sometimes artificial results, they are noteworthy as international law often depends on the will of the actors.[1520] The question of state continuity can be one of international politics as well as one of law, i.e. a considerable inconsistency and lack of clarity can be observed in this context.[1521]

Exceedingly noteworthy in that context is a reasoning considering failed states. It explains the respective state practice, which is being referred to as "apparent illogical practice,"[1522] with the following political interests[1523]:

- Legal and political uncertainties shall be avoided, wherefore rich and powerful countries preserve the legal fiction of statehood rather than to accept responsibility for these territories;
- A worsening of the internal conditions is being feared, wherefore the international community tries to keep up the pretence of statehood hoping that soon a functioning government can be installed;

1516 See *Dembinski*, ASDI 1975, 121 (121).
1517 See *Dembinski*, ASDI 1975, 121 (123).
1518 See *Dembinski*, ASDI 1975, 121 (152).
1519 See *Dembinski*, ASDI 1975, 121 (152).
1520 See *Crawford*, p. 668.
1521 See *Mälksoo*, 69 Nordic J. Int'l L. 2000, 289 (306).
1522 *Ferreira*, 41 Comp. & Int'l L.J. S. Afr. 2008, 428 (436).
1523 For all the following enumerated examples, see *Ferreira*, 41 Comp. & Int'l L.J. S. Afr. 2008, 428 (437).

- As the concept of statehood is by no means clear-cut, disagreement in particular situations could lead to severe conflicts, therefore the international legal system rather seeks to maintain the *status quo*;
- The respective legal entity can be better held accountable regarding duties arising from international treaties, but also regarding obligations towards its inhabitants, e.g. the protection of human rights.

Without exception, these arguments likewise apply to the scenario of a temporary non-territorial status with unclear prospects. In the history of international law, failed states are (from a legal point of view) probably the most similar example to the likely future scenario of endangered states. In both cases, one of the three (traditional) state elements is missing, the future development is unclear, legal uncertainties and conflicts impend, and the interests of fellow states comprise stability and accountability. Failed states are an insightful example for state practice being driven by political interests. With the basic requirements being applied rather strictly in the formative stages of the respective state, this handling has proven to get more loose once a state's continuity is at stake.[1524]

3. Arguments for '*sui generis*' Subject of International Law

Based on this thesis' assumption that the claim to a new state territory *does* exist, only few counter-arguments are left that argue against preserving the statehood of inundated states.

The most obvious argument is of course the non-compliance with traditional statehood criteria. Despite the development of the concept of states in the last centuries, despite inconsistent state practice, and despite the ongoing discussion about statehood criteria, it can be deemed as general contemporary consensus (despite few dissenting opinions) that the existence of a state presupposes a respective state territory.[1525] Territorial sovereignty, for which a state territory is an indispensable prerequisite, is being considered as essential before a state can be considered as such.[1526] Therefore, according to one view, a state without a state territory is not possible.[1527]

1524 See *Kreijen*, p. 34.

1525 See e.g. *Shaw*, p. 198 (referring to the Montevideo Convention); *Hobe*, p. 68 (referring to the doctrine of three elements by *Jellinek*); *Craven* in: Evans, 203 (220) (referring to the Montevideo Convention); *Epping* in: Ipsen, para. 5, marginal no. 2 (referring to the doctrine of three elements by *Jellinek*).

1526 See *Shaw*, NYIL 13, 61 (73).

1527 See *Oppenheim*, § 169, p. 451.

E.g., *Kehrer* examines the legal status of endangered states after the loss of their respective state territory.[1528] She considers three possible reasons for softening the doctrine of three elements in this case: The people, the mere necessity to further exist, and a potential recognition.[1529] Finally, she concludes that an inundated state loses its statehood and potentially devolves into an unclear subject of international law with legal uncertainties, which, due to the lack of binding international rules for this scenario, would have to be negotiated and elaborated by the international community.[1530] She refers to the unprecedented subject of international law that has lost its statehood as "inundated entity."[1531]

In the context of examining failed states, the consequences of losing one statehood criterion were assessed.[1532] Regarding the loss of a state territory, this formerly merely theoretical thought becomes real due to sea level rise in endangered states like e.g. Tuvalu.[1533] International law does not provide any norms for this scenario.[1534] From the perspective of conventional international law, this implies the demise of a state.[1535]

Beyond this, only political considerations might support the conclusion that states could try to shape international law (e.g. by depriving the respective legal entity of its statehood) to proclaim the termination of an inundated state's statehood.

Unsurprisingly, state practice has proven to focus on domestic rather than on international interests. It could be expedient for certain states – especially for major GHG emitters as well as those who delayed progress in climate change negotiations for their benefit – to work towards a legal understanding that inundated endangered states cannot count as states anymore. If these states would succeed with that approach, they could incidentally deprive endangered states of their legal protection. This could be an attractive strategy for opponents to a potential claim to avoid potential compensation duties. The most obvious way would be

---

1528 See *Kehrer*, p. 62 et seqq.

1529 See *Kehrer*, p. 62 et seq., 63 et seq., 64 et seqq.

1530 See *Kehrer*, p. 69.

1531 *Kehrer*, p. 69, using the German term "Überflutungsgebilde".

1532 See *Leidenmühler*, p. 259.

1533 See *Leidenmühler*, p. 259 et seq., footnote 1347.

1534 See *Leidenmühler*, p. 264.

1535 See *Leidenmühler*, p. 259 with further references. However, *Leidenmühler* subsequently points out that state practice does not follow such a purely juridical approach (p. 278 et seqq.).

to challenge the idea of an endangered states' claim to a new state territory.[1536] The successful invalidation of this theory would be a valuable argumentative aid: If there is no claim to a territory, the non-territorial status is permanent with no perspective to re-establish statehood criteria. Thus, a continuation of statehood makes no sense. Facing the risk of excessive costs,[1537] more powerful states could come to the conclusion that making use of their influence by promoting this outcome would be in their best interest.

4. Nation Ex-Situ

Recently, an approach has been made to treat deterritorialised SIDS as so-called 'Nations Ex-Situ.'[1538] With regard to endangered states, this "landless [...] State is an inevitable evolution of contemporary [...] statehood."[1539] A Nation Ex-Situ would thus be a new form of state, i.e. a development of the traditional territorial state based on the doctrine of three elements. This would mark a fundamental shift from the Westphalian organization of the global community.[1540]

The reasoning of this approach is based on many aspects and principles which also have been examined in the context of the present thesis: The flexible nature of the notion 'state'[1541] (especially regarding failed states and governments in exile)[1542], the necessity to adapt international law to a changed world,[1543] human rights,[1544] as well as the purpose of international law to maintain global peace and security.[1545] Based on these considerations, "[t]o the extent that it was ever a strict condition, international law can abandon territory as a requirement of statehood."[1546]

The crucial difference to the present thesis' approach is permanence: As the author did not have a claim to a new state territory in mind, the deterritorialised status of the legal subject has no prospect of change. This reduces the legal scope for solutions for what happens to the statehood of endangered states when they

---

1536 See above § 4. C. 4. b. ee.
1537 See *Sands*, p. 701.
1538 See *Burkett* in: Gerrard/Wannier, 89 et seqq.
1539 *Burkett* in: Gerrard/Wannier, 89 (91).
1540 See *Burkett* in: Gerrard/Wannier, 89 (92).
1541 See *Burkett* in: Gerrard/Wannier, 89 (94).
1542 See *Burkett* in: Gerrard/Wannier, 89 (97).
1543 See *Burkett* in: Gerrard/Wannier, 89 (95).
1544 See *Burkett* in: Gerrard/Wannier, 89 (103).
1545 See *Burkett* in: Gerrard/Wannier, 89 (106).
1546 *Burkett* in: Gerrard/Wannier, 89 (102).

lose their state territory. If the Nation Ex-Situ approach is complemented by a (prospective) claim to a new state territory, this would, based on the same reasoning, simply lead to the preservation of an endangered state's statehood despite the temporary absence of a state territory.

Arguments for a Nation Ex-Situ thus likewise apply for maintaining statehood in the scenario this thesis examines.[1547] Both approaches consider a transitional and non-permanent deterritorialised status of a certain endangered state.

5. Statement

If endangered states have a claim to a new state territory when facing a future of inundation, as suggested in this thesis,[1548] it is clear that a temporary non-territorial status should not lead to the loss of statehood. Not only has state practice proven to be flexible when it comes to interpreting the notion 'state', especially in the similar case of failed states. Also, the legal uncertainties that would arise if statehood were denied would not be in the interest of the parties involved, including opponents to potential claims.

But also if one doubts the existence of such a claim, there is much to be said for the preservation of statehood. This at least applies as long as the question regarding such a claim has not been answered bindingly *and* the respective state (still) strives for the clarification of this legal issue. If these conditions are met, the arguments which prevailingly support the preservation of statehood would likewise apply.

As long as there is an opportunity – no matter how small – for endangered states to relocate and proceed as a state, they have to be enabled to further enforce their interest. This possibility would be endangered when they would not further qualify as a state but, for example, would become, as suggested, a *sui generis* subject of international law whose citizens are stateless – a scenario that has been deemed to be even worse than being refugees.[1549]

Not only legal aspects (such as the principle of sovereign equality and the structure of responsibility for the loss of the endangered states' territory) argue for the preservation of their statehood. Political considerations support this finding, as well. The legal uncertainties and the potential for conflict as well as the advantage of having clear rules for negotiations with authorities that can be held accountable for an entities' treaty obligations and other obligations make it far

1547 See above § 5. B. 2.

1548 See above § 4. C. 4. b. ee.

1549 See *Markovich/Annandale*, 5 Asia Pac. J. Envtl. L. 2000, 135 (147).

more appealing also for opponents to potential claims to agree upon a continuation of statehood.

State practice is further evidence for the likeliness of this outcome. This applies especially with an eye towards the handling of failed states. *Leidenmühler* (subsequent to assessing that, from a purely legal perspective, a loss of a state criterion leads to the respective state's demise)[1550] examines state practice[1551] and concludes that state failure does not lead to the loss of statehood.[1552] This even applies in cases of permanent state failure, whereby due to juridical difficulties this can legally only be explained with a fiction of statehood.[1553] State practice regarding failed states clearly shows that it is possible to accept statehood in cases, which do not correspond to traditional perceptions of international law. As compared with states having failed due to decolonisation or the end of the Cold War, other states carry an even more obvious responsibility for the threat posed to the statehood of endangered states.

Furthermore, the substitution of the territory is no hindrance to the preservation of the same state. Of course, the state would have changed. But this does not imperatively lead to a different legal entity for following reasons: First, the current (and persuasive) understanding of the relationship between a state territory (the objectivist theory, or competence theory)[1554] states that territorial sovereignty describes nothing but the range of a state's regional competence.[1555] Former theories, according to which a territory was considered similar to a human body,[1556] were criticised especially because it was considered as untenable to regard an amendment of a state territory as an amendment of the state itself.[1557]

Second, the people are the determining element, which the other elements – state sovereignty and state territory – are meant to serve.[1558] If a given people collectively moves elsewhere while retaining its current sovereignty structures, there is little need to complicate this step by construing a need for a new state as legal successor of the former state.

1550 See *Leidenmühler*, p. 259 et seqq.
1551 See *Leidenmühler*, p. 273 et seqq.
1552 See *Leidenmühler*, p. 335.
1553 See *Leidenmühler*, p. 335.
1554 See above § 3. B. 3. b. aa. (5).
1555 See *Radnitzky*, 20 AöR 1906, 313 (340).
1556 See above § 3. B. 3. b. aa. (3) (object theory, or property theory); § 3. B. 3. b. aa. (4) (space theory, or quality theory).
1557 See *Schade* in: Kraus, p. 5; *Radnitzky*, 20 AöR 1906, 313 (315).
1558 See *Isensee* in: HStR, para. 15, marginal no. 54.

Third, from a practical point of view, it avoids legal uncertainties to preserve the same state. The same (relocated) state would of course be bound by the same international treaties, including potential debts. The question which claims and duties a potential successor state would have as compared with its predecessor could be avoided.

Starting point of the elaboration of the statehood of inundated endangered states was the realisation that its continuance is only possible if the respective endangered state has a new state territory in prospect and that a state relocation needs to be possible according to international law.[1559] This chapter and the previous one reasoned that both conditions are met.

Also, the arguments for a relocation strategy and those for an immigration strategy have been outlined and discussed. The balance of interest distinctly points in one direction: To the preservation of the statehood of endangered states by relocation.

1559 See above § 4. A. 1.

§ 6. Summary and Conclusions

As mentioned at the outset, endangered states find themselves amid a myriad of challenges posed by global warming. Their ability to exert influence on the international level, furthermore, is limited. Most other states do not share the interest in developing concepts for the future of these states that stand to lose their territory. The reason is that accepting any liability for climate change risks opening a "Pandora's box": Once such liability is conceded, a hardly controllable domino effect could be triggered that could lead to immeasurable financial risks, especially for industrialised states.

While this thesis has aimed to assess from a legal perspective the situation that endangered states face, it also had to take into account the political scope for at least three reasons. First, state practice is based to a considerable degree on political interests. Second, political interests – especially of more powerful states – limit, to a certain extent, the potential for the medium term development of international law. Third, as in almost any case in international law, there is more than one opinion on how to interpret a certain norm, treaty, principle, or the like, meaning that states will always tend to assent to a view serving their respective interest. Their countries' short-term interests will in this context often be of greater importance for political leaders than a long-term interest exceeding a time span in which they themselves can reap the fruits of their labours.

This thesis has aimed to outline a solution for the future of endangered states that corresponds best to international law and, additionally, is practicable within the constraints imposed by political considerations of the stakeholders.

For Tuvalu, Nauru, Kiribati, the Maldives, and the Bahamas, the current scientific level of knowledge outlined in § 2 suggests a significant threat to their respective existence within this century. The efforts of these and other countries to mitigate climate change have failed and continue to fail for the most part. Their measures to adapt to changes expected in the not-too-far future predominantly comprise the search for new living spaces for their citizens. The idea addressed by this thesis, the legal justification of a claim to a new state territory has not yet been communicated publicly by any of these states.

However, even if this idea may seem far-fetched at first glance, there is much to be said for such a claim. As examined in §§ 4 and 5, key principles of both general as well as environmental international law can be called upon to argue for such a claim. As there is compelling evidence for causation between GHG emissions and sea level rise, the question of liability (based on the no harm rule) narrows down to the question of what degree of due diligence is binding between fellow states who have not reached contractual agreement. Considering tort law only, much can be said for such a treaty being the necessary pre-requisite in order to trigger liability. The opposing point of view would lead to general liability for any damage arising from global warming – an outcome that might be considered as fair and just but has two crucial counter-arguments. First, regarding the impending consequences of global warming (and the resulting costs) as well as the current power structure in the world, it must be deemed highly unlikely that general liability will be implemented in practice. Second, the degree of obligation in international law is not too high. Limited capabilities in terms of litigation or law enforcement exemplify this circumstance. Liability must be derived from customary international law with caution as it quickly conflicts with at least one other determining principle in international law: The principle of state sovereignty.

In the case of an inundation of entire state territories, the legal implications differ from the above, more general finding in crucial aspects – especially with regard to the balancing of the sovereignty of different states, codified in the principle of sovereign equality. Overall, considerable and significant arguments of both general and environmental international law, aiming to protect either the states themselves or their respective citizens, strongly argue for a compensation of endangered states for the future loss of their state territories.

International law needs to provide answers to a rapidly changing reality.[1560] *Scharf* speaks of "Grotian Moments," a term that aims to describe "a paradigm-shifting development in which new rules and doctrines of customary international law emerge with unusual rapidity and acceptance."[1561] *Sterio* defines this term as a moment that causes shifts and changes in the legal theory of statehood.[1562] These changes in international law, according to her, are driven by the effects of globalisation and argue for amending the concept of the traditional notion of statehood.[1563]

The same argument has to be made in the context of climate change. Within this century, vast changes are to be expected due to this man-made natural phenomenon. This will inevitably lead to legal changes as well, one of which has been examined within this thesis, resulting in the proposal to relocate entire states. It is conceivable that this strategy indeed might at first appear bizarre. However, it would correspond to the principles of international law. Moreover, it

1560 See *Leidenmühler*, p. 37.
1561 *Scharf*, 43 Cornell Int'l L. J. 2010, 430 (440).
1562 See *Sterio*, 39 Denv. J. Unt'l L. & Pol'y 2010, 209 (236).
1563 See *Sterio*, 39 Denv. J. Unt'l L. & Pol'y 2010, 209 (236 et seq.).

is a concept that is practical especially regarding political impediments. This is particularly true with an eye towards the other alternative, i.e. a migration scenario for the citizens of endangered states. Not only would such a scenario cause grief and misery, it would also not be preferable from the perspective of potential 'donor-states.' They would most likely bear the costs anyway, and the reputation of the international system as a whole could be damaged if the international community abandons its most vulnerable members.

Endangered states do have a claim to a state territory against those fellow states that failed to exercise proper care in terms of their GHG emissions. An ICJ Advisory Opinion is currently the only procedural option to enforce such a claim. This claim mirrors most fundamental principles in international law and additionally provides an outcome that fairly balances contradicting interests. International law, however, cannot provide endangered states with the details of their claim, e.g. where to relocate, how to compensate a 'donor-state,' or how to apportion the costs of this relocation. These political questions have to be solved in negotiations.

The preservation of statehood during a potential (non-permanent) period without a state territory is the logical and necessary perpetuation of this legal assessment. Endangered states thus will remain states even while they will have lost their state territory.

Bibliography

Addo, Michael K.: The Legal Nature of International Human Rights, Leiden/Boston 2010.

Aden, Menno: ‚Internationale Notzuständigkeit' in: 106 Zeitschrift für vergleichende Rechtswissenschaft 2007, p. 490 et seqq.

Ago, Roberto: "Binding' Advisory Opinions of the International Court of Justice' in: 85 American Journal of International Law 1991, p. 439 et seqq.

Aminzadeh, Sara C.: 'A Moral Imperative: The Human Rights Implications of Climate Change' in: 30 Hastings International and Comparative Law Review 2007, p. 231 et seqq.

Ashe, John William: 'Small island developing states and global climate change: overcoming the constraints' in: 23 Natural Recources Forum 1999, p. 187 et seqq.

Barnett, Jon: 'Human rights and vulnerability to climate change' in: Human Rights and Climate Chance (ed.: Humphreys, Stephen), Cambridge 2010, p. 257 et seqq.

Berber, Friedrich: Lehrbuch des Völkerrechts, Vol. I, 2nd ed., München 1975.

Beyerlin, Ulrich: 'Different Types of Norms in International Environmental Law' in: The Oxford Yearbook of International Environmental Law (eds.: Bodansky, Daniel/Brunée, Jutta/Hey, Ellen), Oxford 2007.

Beyerlin, Ulrich: ‚Grenzüberschreitender Umweltschutz und allgemeines Völkerrecht' in: Staat und Völkerrechtsordnung, Festschrift für Karl Doehring (eds.: Hailbronner, Kay/Ress, Georg/Stein, Torsten), Berlin et al. 1989, p. 37 et seqq.

Birnie, Patricia/*Boyle*, Alan/*Redgwell*, Catherine: International Law and the Environment, 3rd ed., Oxford et al. 2009.

Blay, Samuel Kwaw Nyameke: 'Self-Determination Versus Territorial Integrity in Decolonization' in: 18 New York University Journal of International Law and Politics 1985-1986, p. 441 et seqq.

Blomquist, Robert F.: 'Comparative Climate Change Torts' in: 46 Valparaiso University Law Review 2011-2012, p. 1053 et seqq.

Bodansky, Daniel: 'The United Nations Framework Convention on Climate Change: A Commentary' in: 18 Yale Journal of International Law 1993, p. 451 et seqq.

Bothe, Michael: ‚Vollzugsdefizit im Völkerrecht – Überlegungen zu 30 Jahren Umweltrecht' in: Cremer, Hans-Joachim et al. (eds.); Tradition und Weltoffenheit des Rechts, Festschrift für Helmut Steinberger, Berlin et al. 2002, p. 83 et seqq.

Brownlie, Ian: Principles of Public International Law, 7th ed., Oxford 2008.

Brunnée, Jutta/*Goldberg*, Silke/*Lord*, Richard/*Rajamani*, Lavanja: 'Overview of legal issues relevant to climate change' in: Climate Change Liability (eds.: id.), Cambridge et al. 2012, p. 23 et seqq.

Brunnée, Jutta/*Goldberg*, Silke/*Lord*, Richard/*Rajamani*, Lavanja: 'Policy Considerations' in: Climate Change Liability (eds.: id.), Cambridge et al. 2012, p. 50 et seqq.

Burkett, Maxine A.: 'The Nation Ex-Situ' in: Gerrard, Michael B./Wannier, Gregory E. (eds.); Threatened Island Nations – Legal Implications of Rising Seas and a Changing Climate, Cambridge 2013, p. 89 et seqq.

Castellanos-Jankiewicz, Léon: 'Causation and International State Responsibility', ACIL Research Paper No 2012-07 (Shares Series) 2012.

Chinkin, Christine M.: 'The Challenge of Soft Law: Development and Change in International Law' in: 38 International and Comparative Law Quarterly 1989, p. 850 et seqq.

Clarkson, Stephen/*Wood*, Stepan: A Perilous Imbalance: The Globalization of Canadian Law and Governance, Vancouver 2010.

Conforti, Benedetto: The Law and Practice of the United Nations, 3rd ed., Leiden/Boston 2005.

Cooper, Jessica B.: 'Environmental Refugees: Meeting the Requirements of the Refugee Definition' in: 6 New York University Environmental Law Journal 1998, p. 480 et seqq.

Crawford, James: The creation of states in international law, 2nd ed., Oxford 2006

Culley, Denis: 'Global Warming, Sea Level Rise and Tort' in: Ocean and Coastal Law Journal 2002, p. 91 et seq.

Dembinski, Ludwik: 'Le Territoire et le Developpement du Droit International' in: Annuaire suisse de droit international, 1975, p. 121 et seqq.

Darsow, Thomas: Zum Wandel des Staatsbegriffes, Frankfurt a. M. 1984.

Doehring, Karl: Völkerrecht, 2nd ed., Heidelberg 2004.

Dubats, Elizabeth: 'An Inconvenient Lie: Big Tobacco Was Put on Trial for Denying the Effects of Smoking; Is Climate Change Denial Off-Limits?' in: 7 Northwestern Journal of Law & Social Policy 2012, p. 511 et seqq.

Dupuy, Pierre-Marie: 'The place and role of unilateralism in contemporary international law' in: European Journal of International Law, 2000, p. 19 et seqq.

Dworkin, Ronald: Taking Rights Seriously, Harvard 1978.

Eckstein, Gabriel E.: 'Commentary on the U.N. International Law Commission's Draft Articles on the Law of Transboundary Aquifers' in: 18 Colorado Journal of International Environmental Law and Policy 2007, p. 537 et seqq.

Engelhardt, Marie von: ‚Die Völkerrechtswissenschaft und der Umgang mit Failed States – Zwischen Empirie, Dogmatik und postkolonialer Theorie' in: 45-2 Verfassung in Recht und Übersee 2012, p. 222 et seqq.

Epiney, Astrid: „Das ‚Verbot erheblicher grenzüberschreitender Umweltbeeinträchtigungen': Relikt oder konkretisierungsfähige Grundnorm?" in: Archiv des Völkerrechts 1995, p. 309 et seqq.
Epiney, Astrid/*Scheyli*, Martin: Strukturprinzipien des Umweltvölkerrechts, Baden-Baden 1998.
Evans, Malcolm D.: International Law, 3rd ed., Oxford 2010.
Fagan, David N.: 'Achieving Restitution: The Potential Unjust Enrichment Claims of Indigenous Peoples against Multinational Corporations' in: 76 New York University Law Review 2001, p. 626 et seqq.
Faure, Michael/*Peeters*, Marjan: 'Concluding remarks' in: Faure, Michael/Peeters, Marjan (eds.); Climate Change Liability, Cheltenham (UK)/Northampton, MA, USA 2011, p. 255 et seqq.
Feng, Lin/*Buhi*, Jason: 'The Copenhagen Accord and the Silent Incorporation of the Polluter Pays Principle in International Climate Law: An Analysis of Sino-American Diplomacy at Copenhagen and Beyond' in: 18 Buffalo Environmental Law Journal 2010-2011, p. 1 et seqq.
Ferreira, Gerrit M.: 'Good Governance and the Failed State' in: Comparative and International Law Journal of Southern Africa 2008 Vol. 41, Issue 3, p. 428 et seqq.
Fricker, Karl Victor: ‚Vom Staatsgebiet' in: Tübinger Universitäts-Schriften 1867–1868.
Friedmann, Wolfgang: 'The Uses of 'General Principles' in the Development of International Law' in: 57 American Journal of International Law 1963, p. 279 et seqq.
Funtowicz, Silvio O./*Ravetz*, Jerome R.: 'Uncertainty, Complexity and Post-Normal Science' in: 13 Environmental Toxicology and Chemistry 1994, p. 1881 et seqq.
Geiger, Rudolf: Grundgesetz und Völkerrecht, 5th ed., München 2010.
Gerber, Karl Friedrich Wilhelm von: Grundzüge des deutschen Staatsrechts, Aalen 1969, Reprint of the 3rd ed. (Leipzig 1880)
Gillespie, Alexander: 'Small Island States in the Face of Climatic Change: The End of the Line in International Environmental Responsibility' in: 22 UCLA Journal of Environmental Law & Policy 2003-2004, p. 107 et seqq.
Gitay, Habiba/*Bettencourt*, Sofia/*Kull*, Daniel/*Reid*, Robert/*McCall*, Kevin/*Simpson*, Alanna/*Krausing*, Jarl/*Ebinger*, Jane/*Ghesquiere*, Francis/*Fay*, Marianne; Executive Summary: 'Buildingresilience: integrating climate and disaster risk into development – the World Bank Group experience', Vol. 2, World Bank, Washington DC 2013.
Glahn, Gerhard von/*Taulbee*, James Larry: Law Amongst Nations – An Introduction to Public International Law, 10th ed., Boston et al. 2013.
Gordon, Edward: 'The ICJ: On Its Own' in: Nanda, Anjali/Mundt, Alissa (eds.); Perspectives on International Law in an Era of Change: Festschrift in Honor of Professor Ved P. Nanda; Lincoln NE 2012, p. 74 et seqq.

Gordon, Ruth: 'Climate Change and the Poorest Nations: Further Reflections on Global Inequality' in: 78 University of Colorado Law Review 2007, p. 1159 et seqq.

Gottmann, Jean: The Significance of Territory, Charlottesville, Virginia 1973.

Grant, Thomas D.: 'Defining Statehood: The Montevideo Convention and its Discontents', in: 37 Columbia Journal of Transnational Law 403, 1998-1999.

Grote Stoutenburg, Jenny: 'When do States Disappear? Thresholds of Effective Statehood and the Continued Recognition of 'Deterritorialized' Island States' in: Gerrard, Michael B./Wannier, Gregory E. (eds.); Threatened Island Nations – Legal Implication of Rising Seas and a Changing Climate, Cambridge 2013, p. 57 et seqq.

Grotius, Hugo: De jure belli ac pacis, 1st ed., Paris 1625.

Hampson, Francoise J.: ‚Staatsbürgerschaft, Ethnizität und Nationalität – Haben Nationen ein Recht auf Staatenbildung?' in: H.-J. Heintze (ed.), Selbstbestimmungsrecht der Völker, 1997, p. 60 et seqq.

Handl, Günther: 'Natural Uses of Transboundary Air Resources: The International Entitlement Issue Reconsidered' in: 26 Natural Resources Journal 1986, p. 405 et seqq.

Handl, Günther: 'Transboundary Impacts' in: Bodansky, Daniel/Brunée, Jutta/Hey, Ellen (eds.); The Oxford Yearbook of International Environmental Law, Oxford 2007.

Handl, Günther: 'International Accountability for Transboundary Environment Harm Revisited: What Role for 'State Liability'?' in: 37 Environmental Policy and Law 2007, p. 116 et seqq.

Haritz, Miriam: Inconvenient Deliberation: The Precautionary Principle's Contribution to the Uncertainties Surrounding Climate Change Liability, Alphen aan de Rijn 2011.

Hartmann, Ulrike: Die Entwicklung im internationalen Umwelthaftungsrecht unter besonderer Berücksichtigung von erga omnes-Normen, Frankfurt a.M. 2000.

Häußler, Ulf: ‚Räume im Völkerrecht: Luft-, See- und Weltraumrecht im Überblick' in: Juristische Arbeitsblätter 2002, p. 816 et seqq.

Hey, Ellen: Reflections on an International Environmental Court, The Hague 2002.

Herweijer, Celine/*Muir-Wood*, Robert: 'Liability for Climate Change and the Emerging Role of Probabilistic Risk Attribution Science' in: World Jurist Association (ed.); Addressing Climate Change – a Survey of National and International Law from around the World, Bathesda, MD, 2010, p. 224 et seqq.

Hinds, Caroline: Umweltrechtliche Einschränkungen der Souveränität – Völkerrechtliche Präventionspflichten zur Verhinderung von Umweltschäden, Frankfurt a.M., 1997.

Hobbes, Thomas: Leviathan, London 1651.

Hobe, Stephan: Einführung in das Völkerrecht, 9th ed., Tübingen 2008.

Hoffmaister, Juan P./*Stabinsky*, Doreen: ‚Loss and damage: Some key issues and considerations for SIDS expert meeting', Briefing Paper on Loss and Damage, SIDS Expert Meeting, 9-11 October 2012, Bridgetown, Barbados.

Humphreys, Stephen: 'Introduction: Human Rights and Climate Change' in: Human Rights and Climate Chance (ed.: id.), Cambridge 2010, p. 1 et seqq.

Ipsen, Knut: Völkerrecht, 5th ed., München 2004.

Isensee, Josef/*Kirchhof*, Paul (eds.), Handbuch des Staatsrechts der Bundesrepublik Deutschland, 3rd ed., Heidelberg 2004.

Jacobs, Rebecca Elizabeth: 'Treading Deep Waters: Substantive Law Issues in Tuvalu's Threat to Sue the United States in the International Court of Justice' in: 14 Pacific Rim Law & Policy Journal 2005, p. 103 et seqq.

Jarvis, Ryan: 'Sinking Nations and Climate Change Adaption Strategies' in: 9 Seattle Journal of Social Justice 2010-2011, p. 447 et seqq.

Jellinek, Georg, Allgemeine Staatslehre, 3rd ed., Berlin 1922 (reprint)

Kaczorowska, Alina: Public International Law, 4th ed., London/New York 2010.

Kehrer, Franziska: Staatenverantwortlichkeit und Meeresspiegelanstieg, Frankfurt am Main 2009.

Klüber, Johann Ludwig: Oeffentliches Recht des teutschen Bundes und der Bundesstaaten, Frankfurt am Main 1817.

Knox, John H.: 'Linking Human Rights and Climate Change at the United Nations' in: 33 Harvard Environmental Law Review 2009, p. 477 et seqq.

Koberg, Alexander: Die Exilregierung im Völkerrecht, Frankfurt a.M. 2005.

Kreijen, Gerard: State Failure, Sovereignty and Effectiveness: Legal Lessons from the Decolonization of Sub-Saharan Africa, Leiden 2003.

Kriele, Martin: Einführung in die Staatslehre, 3rd ed., Opladen 1988.

Krüger, Herbert: Allgemeine Staatslehre, Stuttgart 1964.

Kunig, Philip: ‚Das völkerrechtliche Delikt' in: Jura 1986, p. 344 et seqq.

Kunig, Philip: ‚Staatenehre im Völkerrecht' in: Jura 1998, p. 160 et seqq.

Larson, J. Chris: 'Racing the Rising Tide: Legal Options for the Marshall Islands' in: 21 Michigan Journal of International Law 1999-2000, p. 495 et seqq.

Lapsley, Arthur Brooks (ed.): The Writings of Abraham Lincoln, Volume 2, 1843-1858, New York 1905.

Lauterpacht, Hersch: 'Recognition of States in International Law' in: 53 The Yale Law Journal 1943-1944, p. 385 et seqq.

Lefeber, René: Transboundary Environmental Interference and the Origin of State Liability, The Hague 1996.

Leidenmühler, Franz: Kollabierter Staat und Völkerrechtsordnung, Wien/Graz 2011.

Leiserowitz, Anthony/*Maibach*, Edward/*Roser-Renouf*, Connie/*Hmielowski*, Jay D.: Politics & Global Warming: Democrats, Republicans, Independents and the Tea Party; Yale University and George Mason University, New Haven, CT 2011.

Liszt, Franz von: Völkerrecht, 12th ed., Berlin 1925.

Lowe, Vaughan: 'Sustainable Development and Unsustainable Arguments' in: Boyle, Alan/Freestone, David (eds.); International Law and Sustainable Development: Past Achievements and Future Challenges, Oxford et al. 1999, p. 19 et seqq.

Machiavelli, Nicollò: Il Principe, 1513.

Mälksoo, Lauri: 'Professor Uluots, the Estonia Government in Exile and the Continuity of the Republic of Estonia in International Law' in: 69 Nordic Journa lof International Law, Issue 3, 2000, p. 289 et seqq.

Markard, Nora/*Emmert*, Simone/*Trjanowski*, Alexandra/*Löhr*, *Tillmann*/*Walter*, Anne: ‚Flüchtling oder Migrant – Braucht Europa ein neues Migrationsrecht?' in: ZAR 2009, p. 27 et seqq.

Markovich, Vivial/*Annandale*, David: 'Sinking Without a Life Jacket? Sea Level Rise and the Position of Small Island States in International Law' in: 5 Asia Pacific Journal of Environmental Law 2000, p. 135 et seqq.

Mayer, Paul: Die rechtliche Bedeutung des Staatsgebiets für den Staatsbegriff, Greifswald 1915.

McIntyre, Stephen/*McKitrick*, Ross: 'Corrections to the Mann et al. (1998) Proxy Data Base and Northern Hemispheric Average Temperature Series', in: 14 Energy & Environment, 2003, p. 751 et seqq.

Millar, Ilona/*Gascoigne*, Catherine/*Caldwell*, Elizabeth: 'Making Good the Loss – An Assessment of the Loss and Damage Mechanism under the UNFCCC Process' in: Gerrard, Michael B./Wannier, Gregory E. (eds.); Threatened Island Nations – Legal Implications of Rising Seas and a Changing Climate, Cambridge 2013, p. 433 et seqq.

Müller, Adam: Die Elemente der Staatskunst, Sechsunddreißig Vorlesungen (1808/09), reprint from 1936, Meersburg.

Münchener Kommentar zum BGB (eds.: Säcker, Franz Jürgen et al.), 6th ed., Vol. 2, Munich 2012.

Nanda, Ved P.: 'Climate Change, Developing Countries, and Human Rights: An International Law Perspective' in: World Jurist Association (ed.); Addressing Climate Change: A Survey of National and International Law from around the World, Bethesda, Maryland, 2010, p. 44 et seqq.

Ohlhoff, Stefan: Methoden der Konfliktbewältigung bei grenzüberschreitenden Umweltproblemen im Wandel, Berlin et al. 2003.

Oppenheim, Lassa: International Law – A Treatise; London et al. 1955.

Oschmann, Volker/*Rostankowski*, Anke: ‚Das Internationale Klimaschutzrecht nach Kopenhagen' in: Zeitschrift für Umweltrecht 2010, Vol 2, p. 59 et seqq.

Paulus, Andreas L.: Die internationale Gemeinschaft im Völkerrecht, München 2001.

Peel, Jacqueline: Science and Risk Regulation in International Law, Cambrigde 2010.

Peel, Jacqueline: 'Environmental Protection in the Twenty-first Century: The Role of International Law' in: Axelrod, Regina S./VanDeveer, Stacy D./ Downie, David Leonard (eds.); Global Environment: Institutions, Law and Policy, 3rd ed., Washington D.C. 2011, p. 48 et seqq.

Peters, Glen P./*Andrew*, Robbie M./*Boden*, Tom/*Canadell*, Josep G./*Ciais*, Philippe/*Le Quéré*, Corinne/*Marland*, Gregg/*Raupach*, Michael R./*Wilson*, Charlie: 'The challenge to keep global warming below 2 °C' in: Nature Climate Change 2013, Vol. 3, p. 4 et seqq.

Postiglione, Amedeo: 'A More Efficient International Law on the Environment and Setting up an International Court for the Environment Within the United Nations' in: 20 Environmental Law 1990, p. 321 et seqq

Powers, Ann/*Stucko*, Christopher: 'Introducing the Law of the Sea and the Legal Implications of Rising Sea Levels' in: Gerrard, Michael B./Wannier, Gregory E. (eds.); Threatened Island Nations - Legal Implications of Rising Seas and a Changing Climate, Cambridge 2013, p. 123 et seqq.

Pring, George/*Pring*, Catherine: 'The Future of Environmental Dispute Resolution' in: Nanda, Anjali/Mundt, Alissa (eds.); Perspectives on International Law in an Era of Change: Festschrift in Honor of Professor Ved P. Nanda; Lincoln NE 2012, p. 482 et seqq.

Radnitzky, Ernst: ‚Die rechtliche Natur des Staatsgebietes' in: 20 Archiv für öffentliches Recht 1906, p. 313 et seqq.

Redgwell, Catherine: 'Intergenerational Equity and Global Warming' in: Churchill, Robin/Freestone, David (eds.); International Law and Global Climate Change, London 1991, p. 41 et seqq.

Rensmann, Thilo: „Die Humanisierung des Völkerrechts durch das ius in bello – Von der Martens'schen Klausel zur 'Responsibility to Protect'" in: ZaöRV 2008, p. 111 et seqq.

Robinson, Alexander/*Calvoy*, Reinhard/*Ganopolski*, Andrey: 'Multistability and critical thresholds of the Greenland ice sheet' in: 2 Nature Climate Change 2012, p. 429 et seqq.

Roeben, Volker: 'Responsibility in International Law' in: Bogdandy, Armin von/ Wolfrum, Rüdiger (eds.), Max Planck Yearbook of United Nations Law, Vol. 16, Leiden/Boston 2012, p. 99 et seqq.

Salmond, John W.: Jurisprudence or the Theory of the Law, 2nd ed., London.

Sands, Philippe: Principles of International Environmental Law, 3rd ed., Cambridge 2012.

Schachter, Oscar: 'The Charter's Origins in Today's Perspective' in: 89 American Society of International Law Proceedings 1995, p. 45 et seqq.

Schade, Wolfgang: Wesen und Umfang des Staatsgebietes in: Internationalrechtliche Abhandlungen (ed.: Kraus, Herbert), Berlin 1934.

Scharf, Michael P.: 'Seizing the 'Grotian Moment': Accelerated Formation of Customary International Law in Times of Fundamental Change' in: 43 Cornell International Law Journal 2010, p. 439 et seqq.

Schröder, Meinhard: ‚Waldschäden als Problem des internationalen und des europäischen Rechts' in: Deutsches Verwaltungsblatt 1986, Vol. 23, p. 1173 et seqq.

Schweisfurth, Theodor: Völkerrecht, Tübingen 2006.

Shaw, Malcolm Nathan: 'Territory in International Law' in: Netherlands Yearbook of International Law, Vol. 13 (1982), p. 61 et seqq.

Shaw, Malcolm Nathan: International Law, 6th ed., Cambridge 2008.

Simma, Bruno (ed.): Charter der Vereinten Nationen, 1st ed., München 1991.

Simma, Bruno (ed.): The Charter of the United Nations, 2nd ed., Oxford 2002.

Simma, Bruno/*Pulkowski*, Dirk: 'Of Planets and the Universe: Self-contained Regimes in International Law' in: The European Journal of International Law, Vol. 17 No. 3, 2006.

Slade, Tuiloma Neron: 'The Making of International Law: The Role of Small Island States' in: 17 Temple International and Comparative Law Journal 2003, p. 531 et seqq.

Smend, Rudolf: Staatsrechtliche Abhandlungen und andere Aufsätze, 2nd ed., Berlin 1968.

Spier, Jaap: 'High Noon: Prevention of Climate Damage as the Primary Goal of Liability?' in: Faure, Michael/Peeters, Marjan (eds.); Climate Change Liability, Cheltenham (UK)/Northampton, MA, USA 2011, p. 47 et seqq.

Shearer, Ivan A.: Starke's International Law, 11th ed., London et al. 1994.

Stehr, Nico/*von Storch*, Hans: ‚Anpassung und Vermeidung oder von der Illusion der Differenz' in: GAIA – Ökologische Perspektiven für Wissenschaft und Gesellschaft 3/2008, p. 270 et seqq.

Sterio, Milena: 'A Grotian Moment: Changes in the Legal Theory of Statehood', in: 39 Denver Journal of International Law and Policy, 2010-2011, p. 209 et seqq.

Strupp, Karl/*Schlochauer*, Hans-Jürgen: Wörterbuch des Völkerrechts, Vol. I-III, 2nd ed., Berlin 1960 (Vol. I), 1961 (Vol. II.), 1962 (Vol. III)

Sunstein, Cass R.: 'Beyond the Precautionary Principle', University of Chicago Law & Economics, Olin Working Paper No. 1 49 (January 2003); available at http://ssrn.com/abstract=307098

Talmon, Stefan: Recognition of Governments in International Law: With Particular Reference to Governments in Exile; Oxford 1998.

Tanaka, Yoshifumi: 'Regulation of Land-Based Marine Pollution in International Law: A Comparative Analysis Between Global and Regional Legal Frameworks' in: Zeitschrift für ausländisches öffentliches Recht und Völkerrecht 2006, p. 535 et seqq.

Thürer, Daniel: ‚Das Selbstbestimmungrecht der Völker' in: Archiv für öffentliches Recht 1984, p. 113 et seqq.

Thürer, Daniel: ‚Der Wegfall effektiver Staatsgewalt: ‚The failed State" in: Thürer, Daniel/Herdegen, Matthias/Hohloch, Gerhard (eds.); Wegfall effektiver Staatsgewalt: The Failed State, Heidelberg 1995, p. 9 et seqq.

Tomuschat, Christian: 'Global Warming and State Responsibility in: Hestermeyer, Holger/Matz-Lück, Nele/Seibert-Fohr, Anja/Vöney, Silja (eds.), Law of the Sea in Dialogue, Sonderdruck aus Beiträge zum ausländischen öffentlichen Recht und Völkerrecht 221, Heidelberg 2011, p. 3 et seqq.

Vanderheiden, Steve: Atmospheric Justice – A Political Theory of Climate Change, Oxford 2008.

Verdross, Albrecht: ‚Die völkerrechtliche Identität von Staaten' in: Braun, Rudolf et al. (eds.), Festschrift für Heinrich Klang zum 75. Geburtstag, Wien 1950, p. 18 et seqq.

Verdross, Albrecht/*Simma*, Bruno: Universelles Völkerrecht, Theorie und Praxis, 3rd ed., Berlin 1984.

Verheyen, Roda: ‚Der Beitrag des Völkerrechts zum Klimaschutz – Globale Aufgabe, globale Antworten?' in: Koch, Hans-Joachim/Caspar, Johannes (eds.) Klimaschutz im Recht,Baden-Baden 1997, p. 20 et seqq.

Verheyen, Roda: Climate Change Damage and International Law – Prevention Duties and State Responsibility, Leiden 2005.

Voigt, Christina: 'State Responsibility for Climate Change Damages' in: 77 Nordic Journal of International Law 2008, p. 1 et seqq.

Warner, Koko/*van der Geest*, Kees/*Kreft*, Sönke/*Huq*, Saleemul/*Harmeling*, Sven/*Koen* Kusters/*de Sherbinin*, Alex: Evidence from the frontlines of climate change: Loss and damage to communities despite coping and adaptation. Loss and Damage in Vulnerable Countries Initiative. Policy Report. Report No. 9. Bonn: United Nations University Institute for Environment and Human Security (UNU-EHS), 2012.

Weinacht, Paul-Ludwig: Staat – Studien zur Bedeutungsgeschichte des Wortes von den Anfängen bis ins 19. Jahrhundert, Berlin 1968.

Weinbaum, Aura: ‚Unjust Enrichment: An Alternative to Tort Law and Human Rights in the Climate Change Context?' in: 20 Pacific Rim Law & Policy Journal 2011, p. 429 et seqq.

Weiss, Edith Brown: 'The Emerging Structure of International Environmental Law' in: Vig, Norman J./Axelrod, Regina S. (eds.); Global Environment: Institutions, Law and Policy, Washington D.C. 1999, p. 98 et seqq.

Wenger, Kaimipono David: 'Causation and Attenuation in the Slavery Reparations Debate' in: 40 University of San Francisco Law Review 2006, p. 279 et seqq.

Werksman, Jacob David: 'Could a Small Island Successfully Sue a Big Emitter?' in: Gerrard, Michael B./Wannier, Gregory E. (eds.); Threatened Island Nations - Legal Implications of Rising Seas and a Changing Climate, Cambridge 2013, p. 409 et seqq.

Wold, Chris/*Hunter*, David/*Powers*, Melissa: Climate Change and the Law, Newark/San Francisco 2009.
Wolfrum, Rüdiger: 'Die grenzüberschreitende Luftverschmutzung im Schnittpunkt von nationalem Recht und Völkerrecht' in: Deutsches Verwaltungsblatt 1984, Vol. 11, p. 493 et seqq.
Wright, Richard W.: 'Allocating Liability Among Multiple Responsible Causes: A Principled Defense of Joint and Several Liability for Actual Harm and Risk Exposure' in: 21 U.C. Davis Law Review, 1987-1988, p. 1141 et seqq.
Würtenberger, Thomas D.: ‚Der Klimawandel in den Umweltprüfungen' in: Zeitschrift für Umweltrecht 2009, p. 171 et seqq.
Yamin, Farhana/*Depledge*, Joanna: The International Climate Change Regime – A Guide to Rules, Institutions and Procedures, Cambridge 2004.
Zander, Joakim: The Application of the Precautionary Principle in Practice: Comparative Dimensions, Cambridge et al. 2010.
Zerger, Frithjof: ‚Klima- und umweltbedingte Migration' in: ZAR 2009, p. 85 et seqq.
Zippelius, Reinhold, Allgemeine Staatslehre, 8th ed., München 1982.

Please note: UN-Documents are cited by their respective document signature. This signature enables to access the full text e.g. at http://www.un.org/en/documents/index.shtml.